Action, Ethics, and Responsibility

Action, Ethics, and Responsibility

edited by Joseph Keim Campbell, Michael O'Rourke, and
Harry S. Silverstein

A Bradford Book
The MIT Press
Cambridge, Massachusetts
London, England

MIT Press books may be purchased at special quantity discounts for business or sales promotional use. For information, please email special_sales@mitpress.mit.edu or write to Special Sales Department, The MIT Press, 55 Hayward Street, Cambridge, MA 02142.

This book was set in Stone Sans and Stone Serif by Toppan Best-set Premedia Limited. Printed and bound in the United States of America.

Library of Congress Cataloging-in-Publication Data

Action, ethics, and responsibility / edited by Joseph Keim Campbell, Michael O'Rourke, and Harry S. Silverstein.
    p.   cm.—(Topics in contemporary philosophy)
"A Bradford book."
Includes bibliographical references and index.
"The essays in this volume derive from presentations given at the ninth annual Inland Northwest Philosophy Conference (INPC), held March 31–April 2, 2006 in Pullman, Washington and Moscow, Idaho"—Acknowledgments.
ISBN 978-0-262-01473-1 (hardcover: alk. paper)—ISBN 978-0-262-51484-2 (pbk.: alk. paper)
1. Responsibility—Congresses. I. Campbell, Joseph Keim, 1958–. II. O'Rourke, Michael, 1963–. III. Silverstein, Harry, 1942–. IV. Inland Northwest Philosophy Conference (9th: 2006: Moscow, Idaho, and Pullman, Wash.).
BJ1451.A28   2010
170—dc22

2010006928

10 9 8 7 6 5 4 3 2 1

Contents

Acknowledgments

The essays in this volume derive from presentations given at the ninth annual Inland Northwest Philosophy Conference (INPC), held March 31–April 2, 2006, in Pullman, Washington, and Moscow, Idaho. The conference received considerable administrative and financial support from a number of individuals and institutions. We would like to thank the philosophy departments at Washington State University (David Shier, Chair) and the University of Idaho (Douglas Lind, Chair), the College of Liberal Arts at Washington State University (Erich Lear, Dean), the Provost's Office and the College of Letters, Arts & Social Sciences at the University of Idaho (Joe Zeller, Dean), the research offices at both universities, and the departmental administrative managers, Dee Dee Torgeson and Diane Ellison. We also thank the Idaho Humanities Council, a state-based affiliate of the National Endowment for the Humanities, for a grant that made it possible to hold the Public Forum on Environmental Problems, Responsibility, and Action.

Those who presented papers at INPC 2006 were encouraged to submit their work for possible inclusion in this volume and, after a process of peer evaluation, only a few were selected. We had to pass on a large number of quality essays, many of which will appear elsewhere, and that is our loss. For help with the selection process and other matters, we are grateful to John Davenport, Julia Driver, Eric Gampel, Ish Haji, Gilbert Harman, Pamela Hieronymi, David Hunt, Todd Long, Michael McKenna, Eddy Nahmias, Michael Nelson, Shaun Nichols, Cara Nine, Nikolaj Nottelmann, L. A. Paul, Tim Schroeder, Judi Smetana, Holly Smith, Manuel Vargas, David Velleman, Khadri Vihvelin, Russell Wahl, Kit Wellman, and Michael Zimmerman.

Finally, Delphine Keim Campbell, Rebecca O'Rourke, and Lorinda Knight continue to stick with us and support us in delivering the INPC and these volumes—"Thanks" doesn't go nearly far enough.

1   Action, Ethics, and Responsibility: A Framework

Joseph Keim Campbell, Michael O'Rourke, and Harry S. Silverstein

The essays in this volume concern a wide variety of topics, all of which are significantly related to the issue of responsibility, including metaphysics, action theory, ethics and moral theory, and the philosophy of law. The first section of this introductory chapter will consider metaphysics; the second will focus on the remaining topics.

1   The Metaphysics of Moral Responsibility

As a provisional definition, let's suppose that a person is *morally responsible* for performing an action if and only if he is an appropriate subject of moral praise or blame (Fischer and Ravizza 1998, 6). Given this understanding, what conditions are necessary in order for a person to be praiseworthy or blameworthy for what he does? Historically, philosophers have noted at least two kinds of conditions: a freedom-relevant condition and an epistemic condition (Fischer and Ravizza 1998, 13; cf. Aristotle 1985). We will consider each of these, beginning with the former.[1]

There is no generally accepted view of the freedom-relevant condition for moral responsibility. Nonetheless, a few uncontroversial tenets may be stated. First, philosophers generally agree that a person is morally responsible for his action only if he has free will (cf. van Inwagen 2008). Second, they acknowledge that 'free will' is an expression of art, and that saying that someone has free will is not intended to entail that he has a *will* with the property of being *free* (van Inwagen 1983, 8). Third, most contemporary philosophers agree that free will is connected with free action. Thus, a person has (or had) free will if and only if some of his actions are (or were) free. Some contend that free will is a property of *choices* or *intentions* rather than *actions*, but this distinction is illusory, for choices may be regarded as internal actions.

The *free will thesis*, then, is the claim that some persons have free will, where that claim is understood in accordance with the above tenets. But beyond those few tenets there is much disagreement. Traditionally, philosophers have assumed that an action is free only if the person *could have done otherwise* or, more formally, the person had *alternative possibilities of action*. Call this the *alternatives view* of free will. This view was accepted by nearly all philosophers until Harry Frankfurt (1969) offered prima facie counterexamples to the following thesis:

The Principle of Alternative Possibilities (PAP)   A person is morally responsible for what he has done only if he could have done otherwise.

Given that moral responsibility requires free will, those who reject PAP require a different view of free will. According to the *source view*, an action is free only if the agent is the source of the action. Versions of this view range from those requiring that the agent be the ultimate source or cause of his action (Strawson 1986; Pereboom 2001; Smilansky, this volume) to those requiring that he be merely an adequate source or cause, where by 'adequate' we mean merely that one is a source but not an ultimate source of his actions (McKenna 2001; Fischer and Ravizza 1993; Fischer 1994; Fischer, this volume).

For centuries, the central issue in debates about free will was the problem of free will and determinism, and views on the subject were defined in terms of this problem—and this issue, including its offshoots, remains central to many current philosophical discussions. According to *compatibilism*, the free will thesis is compatible with determinism, whereas *incompatibilism* is the denial of compatibilism. *Libertarianism* is the conjunction of incompatibilism and the free will thesis; *hard determinism* is the conjunction of incompatibilism and determinism; and *soft determinism* is the conjunction of determinism, compatibilism, and the free will thesis.[2]

Developments in physics, specifically in quantum mechanics, have led many philosophers to reject the thesis of determinism. Thus, many contemporary writers don't fit into the tripartite categories of libertarianism, soft determinism, and hard determinism (Campbell, O'Rourke, and Shier 2004b, 3-7). In fact, the latter two categories are rarely if ever used. A better classification of contemporary views would be libertarianism (Ginet 1990; Kane 1996; O'Connor 2000; Clarke 2003; Coffman and Smith, this volume), compatibilism (Frankfurt 1988; Fischer and Ravizza 1993; Fischer 1994; Watson 2004; Wolfe, Russell, and Fischer, this volume), and free will skepticism (Strawson 1986; Honderich 1988 and 2002; Smilansky 2000;

Pereboom 2001; Smilansky, this volume). According to *free will skepticism*, the free will thesis is false. Thus, free will skepticism is a *metaphysical* view, not an epistemological view. Most free will skeptics do not endorse the thesis of determinism, so they are not hard determinists.[3] Of course, some of the views noted above may be mixed and matched with others to formulate new views. Thus, we may distinguish between *alternatives compatibilism* and *source compatibilism* as well as *alternatives incompatibilism* and *source incompatibilism*.

It might be helpful to cover some of the main arguments given in support of the theses noted above. First, there is the *consequence argument* for incompatibilism:

If determinism is true, then our acts are the consequences of the laws of nature and events in the remote past. But it is not up to us what went on before we were born, and neither is it up to us what the laws of nature are. Therefore, the consequences of these things are not up to us. (van Inwagen 1983, 16)

Peter van Inwagen (1983, ch. 3) offers three formal versions of this argument, but Carl Ginet (1966) is credited with the first contemporary formal version.

Another important argument for the incompatibilism between determinism and the claim that some persons are morally responsible for their actions is the *manipulation argument*. The manipulation argument contrasts *manipulation cases*—where agents are manipulated and presumed not to be morally responsible for their actions—with *determinism cases*—where the agent's actions are embedded in a deterministic world. The *no-difference claim* states that there is no substantive difference between these kinds of examples. Therefore, the lack of moral responsibility in manipulation cases extends to determinism cases, and incompatibilism is true (McKenna 2008). Two noteworthy versions of the argument are Derk Pereboom's *four-case argument* (2001, ch. 4) and Al Mele's *zygote argument* (2006, 188–195).

Soft-line replies to the manipulation argument reject the no-difference claim and contend that manipulation cases are distinct from determinism cases. Fischer claims that a morally responsible action has to have the right *history*. An agent has guidance control just in case his behavior (action, choice, omission, etc.) issues from a moderately reasons-responsive mechanism that is the agent's own. Since this account requires mechanism ownership, and since, on his view, mechanism ownership obtains in (some) determinism cases but not in manipulation cases, Fischer is a *soft compatibilist*.

Michael McKenna (2008) has persuasively argued that soft compatibilism is doomed to failure, since better manipulation cases—ones that
appear to be indistinguishable from determinism cases—are always forthcoming. *Hard-line* replies bite the bullet and accept the no-difference claim
of the manipulation argument. However, they deny that all manipulation
cases are incompatible with morally responsible action. Compatibilists
who adopt the hard-line reply to the manipulation argument endorse *hard
compatibilism* (McKenna 2008; Russell, this volume).

Another argument worth noting is the *Mind* argument, named by van
Inwagen for its prevalence in the philosophical journal of the same name
(van Inwagen 1983, 16; Coffman and Smith, this volume). Initially, the
Mind argument is described by van Inwagen as one of three arguments for
compatibilism (1983, ch. 4). The *Mind* argument "occurs in three forms"
or "three closely related strands," each of which has "a common beginning" (126). Later van Inwagen adds that the third strand of the *Mind*
argument "is, strictly speaking, an argument for the *incompatibility* of free
will and *indeterminism*" (148), and he seems to regard subsequent versions
of the argument as being identical with the third strand (van Inwagen
1998, 2000, 2004, 2008). Given this understanding, the *Mind* argument
attempts to get from indeterminism to free will skepticism by exploiting
the connection between indeterminism and luck. Van Inwagen writes:

does postulating or asserting that the laws of nature are indeterministic provide any
comfort to those who would like to believe in metaphysical freedom?[4] If the laws
are indeterministic, then more than one future is indeed consistent with those laws
and the actual past and present—but how can anyone have any choice about which
of these becomes actual? Isn't it a matter of chance which becomes actual? If God
were to "return" an indeterministic world to precisely its state at some time in the
past, and then let the world go forward again, things might indeed happen differently the "second" time. But then, if the world is indeterministic, isn't it just a
matter of chance how things *did* happen in the one, actual course of events? And
if what we do is just a matter of chance—well, who would want to call that freedom?
(van Inwagen 1998, 370; cf. van Inwagen 2000, 14)

This argument is compelling, but it is not clear how it could lend support
to the *incompatibility* of free will and indeterminism.

Suppose that indeterminism is true but that the only instances of causal
indeterminism occur in faraway regions of space-time. How do van Inwagen's observations about indeterministic luck show that agents lack free
will in this scenario? They don't. Van Inwagen knows this and writes:

Incompatibilists maintain that free will requires indeterminism. But it should be
clear even to them that not just any sort of indeterminism will do. Suppose, for

example, that there is exactly one undetermined particle of matter somewhere in the universe, and that it is far from any rational agent, the rest of the universe being governed entirely by strict, deterministic laws. In that case, determinism is, strictly speaking, false. But, clearly, if determinism is incompatible with free will, so is the thesis that everything except one distant particle of matter is determined. (van Inwagen 1983, 126)

According to determinism, every act is determined by prior causes. Indeterminists make no commitments about the causal structure of the world leading up to any particular human action. Thus, indeterminism cannot entail that every act is undetermined let alone that every act is a matter of luck. Perhaps this is why van Inwagen also offers a version of the *Mind* argument in support of restrictivism, the view that "one has precious little free will, that rarely, if ever, is anyone able to do otherwise than he in fact does" (van Inwagen 1989, 405). Nonetheless, it is hard to see how indeterminism is going to help the incompatibilist unless the indeterminism is located in close proximity to human actions. The *Mind* argument suggests that such indeterminism is problematic.

Turning to the epistemic condition for moral responsibility, suppose that Ryan sits down in a chair while attending a philosophy lecture, a chair that is rigged to a bomb that causes the destruction of another building on campus. Ryan, however, is ignorant of the fact that his act of sitting would eventually lead to the building's destruction. Is Ryan morally responsible for the destruction? It seems not.

The epistemic condition for moral responsibility is commonly formulated in terms of *knowledge*, but it should be clear that something less than knowledge is sufficient (Ginet 2000). For instance, if Ryan believed that the chair was rigged to a bomb and his belief turned out to be true, that might be enough to render him morally responsible for the building's destruction. Yet this alone would not entail that Ryan *knew* that the building would explode. Also, Michael Zimmerman has persuasively argued that the epistemic condition is best phrased as a *tracing* principle. He writes: "one is culpable for behaving ignorantly only if one is culpable for being ignorant" (Zimmerman 1997, 423). Putting together the points noted above, a first approximation of the epistemic condition of moral responsibility might be formulated as follows: one is morally responsible for an action (or its consequences) only if one has relevant true beliefs about the nature of that action (or its consequences), or one is negligent in failing to have those beliefs. But the issues here are complicated, as George Sher's contribution to this volume illustrates.

2   Responsibility in Action Theory, Ethics, and the Philosophy of Law

The relation between causal and moral responsibility is associated with an important set of issues relevant to both action theory and ethics. A common initial thought is that one is morally responsible for an event—a harmful event, let's suppose—if and only if one is causally responsible for that event (i.e., roughly, if and only if one's actions constituted or caused that event). But neither half of this biconditional seems to hold up. Omission cases are commonly presented as cases involving moral responsibility without causal responsibility. Suppose that John is the manager of a jewelry store who is obligated to lock the store every night when he leaves, but that one night he forgets, and as a result several valuable items are stolen. A common view is that John is not causally responsible for the thefts, on the ground that omissions are not causes, but that he nonetheless bears at least some of the moral responsibility for them.

Conversely, the Ryan case discussed above constitutes an example of a case involving causal responsibility without moral responsibility. Assuming that Ryan was nonculpably ignorant of the fact that his sitting in that particular chair would blow up a building, then he was not morally responsible for that result; but his sitting in the chair was, or was at least part of, its cause. Moreover, it is at least arguable that there can be cases where one is causally but not morally responsible even where one is fully aware of all relevant facts. Bernard Williams's famous example of "Jim and the Indians" can plausibly, if controversially, be regarded as such a case (Williams 1973, 98–99):

Jim finds himself in the central square of a small South American town. Tied up against the wall are a row of twenty Indians . . . in front of them several armed men in uniform. . . . [The] captain in charge . . . explains that the Indians are a random group of the inhabitants who, after recent acts of protest against the government, are just about to be killed to remind other possible protesters of the advantages of not protesting. However, since Jim is an honoured visitor from another land, the captain is happy to offer him a guest's privilege of killing one of the Indians himself. If Jim accepts, then as a special mark of the occasion, the other Indians will be let off. Of course, if Jim refuses, then there is no special occasion, and [all the Indians will be killed]. Jim, with some desperate recollection of schoolboy fiction, wonders whether if he got hold of a gun, he could hold the captain . . . and the rest of the soldiers to threat, but it is quite clear from the set-up that nothing of that kind is going to work. . . .

If Jim accepts the offer, and thus kills one of the twenty Indians, then it is plausible to say that he is not morally responsible for that Indian's death, since that Indian, along with his nineteen comrades, would have died at the same time and in the same way in any event. But since he's the one who killed that Indian, he would standardly be regarded as causally responsible.[5]

A common initial conception of both causal and moral responsibility that is relevant to Jim's case is the "avoidability" conception, according to which one is causally or morally responsible for a result if and only if one had an alternative that would have avoided that result (compare the discussion of the "alternatives view" in the previous section). But this conception, if it is salvageable at all, requires considerable qualification (and since causal and moral responsibility, as noted above, do not match up precisely, the required qualifications will be somewhat different in the two cases). On one side, there are countless cases in which one could have avoided a certain result and yet one would not be held responsible for it. For example, many people could have prevented the horrors of the Nazi regime by assassinating Hitler before he took power; but we would hardly regard those people as responsible for those horrors.[6]

Conversely, there are many cases where we hold people responsible for results they could not have avoided. Standard examples used here are cases of overdetermination. If Dan and Don simultaneously, and independently, shoot Bill in the head with the intention of killing him, where either shot would have been sufficient to cause Bill's death, then a straightforward application of the "avoidability" conception would absolve both Dan and Don of responsibility, since neither (we may suppose) had an alternative that would have avoided Bill's death; yet this result seems clearly unacceptable.

Comparing this case to Jim's case is instructive. Though Jim's case is not a simple case of overdetermination, it is similar in a crucial respect: just as Dan had no alternative that would have avoided Bill's death (since Bill would have died from Don's shot in any event), so Jim had no alternative that would have avoided the Indian's death (since that Indian, along with the nineteen others, would have been killed by the soldiers if Jim had refused the offered "privilege"). Yet our inclination is to hold Dan, but not Jim, morally responsible for the relevant death. And at least part of the rationale for this distinction, it seems clear, lies in the difference between their goals. Dan's goal was to cause the death of Bill—hence, he would have shot Bill in the head whether Don were involved or not. By contrast, Jim's goal was to save the lives of as many Indians as possible; he accepted the offer only because the Indian he killed would have been killed in any event, and accepting the offer was the only way to save the other nineteen.

But of course these differences in the agents' goals are not relevant to causal responsibility; hence, we have no, or at least fewer, qualms about saying that Jim, like Dan, is causally responsible for the relevant death.

The standard conception of causality used in the law is the "but for" conception;[7] a product's defect, for example, would be deemed to be the cause of a harm if and only if the harm would have not have occurred "but for" that defect. As should be clear, this conception is essentially the "avoidability" conception, differently described; and the law imposes qualifications to this conception analogous to those discussed above. But the connection between legal responsibility and the legal conception of causation is stronger than that between moral responsibility and our ordinary conception of causation; for claims of legal responsibility are legally required to be *based* on causation claims. And the unsurprising result of this requirement is that legal causality judgments are often fundamentally normative. That is, though judgments of legal responsibility are supposed to be based on antecedent, and independent, causality judgments, in fact causality judgments are often based, at least implicitly, on antecedent views as to where legal responsibility should be placed.[8]

There are, of course, other respects in which ethics and the law diverge. For example, judgments of legal wrongdoing vary with the actual results of behavior in a way that judgments of moral wrongdoing do not. Genuinely attempting to murder a person is commonly regarded as morally blameworthy to the same degree as succeeding in murdering a person; but though attempted murder is a legal crime, the punishment for it is significantly less than that for an actual murder. Relatedly, ethics and the law do not standardly deal with "tracing"[9] in the same way. If Jones drives drunk and kills a blameless pedestrian as a result, he would standardly be viewed as both morally and legally culpable on the ground that his getting drunk was voluntary in the requisite sense even if the subsequent drunken act that caused the death was not; but whereas moralists would typically say that it was the original act of getting drunk that was morally culpable and not the nonvoluntary death-causing act that followed, the standard legal judgment would be that the death-causing act was itself legally culpable *in virtue of* its connection with the prior voluntary act.[10] This topic, as it relates to cases of an interesting and unusual sort, is discussed in Robert Schopp's contribution to this volume.

There are, of course, countless issues in philosophical ethics that relate, in a wide variety of ways, to moral responsibility. We conclude with a brief discussion of three such issues, each of which is discussed by contributors to this volume, namely, omissions, the Doctrine of Double Effect, and collective responsibility. First, let us return to omissions. We noted above that omissions are commonly used as examples of cases in which an agent has moral responsibility without, allegedly, causal responsibility. But there is a more fundamental, and much debated, question regarding omissions, namely, whether a morally wrong action (such as killing a person) is morally worse, other things equal, than a comparable morally wrong omission (such as letting a person die). Warren Quinn is one of many philosophers who answer this question in the affirmative; he provided what is now the common label for this view, the "Doctrine of Doing and Allowing" (Quinn 1989). Others, such as Michael Tooley (Tooley 1994) and James Rachels (Rachels 1994), answer this question in the negative. They typically argue that, though killing, for example, is indeed normally worse than letting die, the reason for this derives not from the difference between acts and omissions as such, but from external differences that commonly accompany the act–omission distinction—differences in intention or motivation (e.g., one who kills a person typically desires to see that person dead; one who lets a person die typically does not), in the sacrifice required (e.g., saving a person's life typically requires considerable sacrifice in time, energy, money, etc.; refraining from killing a person typically does not), and so on. Where those external differences are eliminated, such philosophers claim, there is no morally relevant difference between killing and letting die. The contributions to this volume by Helen Frowe and David Chan both focus on this issue.

Another much discussed distinction, a distinction sometimes discussed in conjunction with the act–omission distinction, is the distinction between a harm produced as a means to a good end and a harm produced merely as a side effect of an action aimed at a good end—a distinction that is central to the Doctrine of Double Effect.[11] Alison McIntyre summarizes this doctrine as follows (McIntyre 2001, 219):

Proponents of the Doctrine of Double Effect make two claims: (1) it is sometimes permissible to bring about a harm as a merely foreseen side effect of an action aimed at some good end, even though it would have been impermissible to bring about the same harm as a means to that end, and (2) this is so because of the moral significance of the distinction between intending and foreseeing a harmful consequence of one's own agency.

This doctrine seems at least initially plausible, as the much-discussed cases of "terror bombing" vs. "strategic (or tactical) bombing" (see, e.g., Bratman 1987, ch. 10) bring out: *ceteris paribus*, bombing civilians as a *means* to induce the enemy to surrender seems worse than killing civilians merely as a side effect of bombing aimed at military targets. But what if the strategic bombing required to get the enemy to surrender would result in the "side effect" deaths of 10,000 civilians, whereas terror bombing could achieve the same result by killing *as a means* less than half of the people in that same group? The strategic bombing alternative seems rather hard to defend in such a case. Frances Kamm's contribution to this volume illustrates the complexity of the issues here by considering various atypical forms of terror bombing.

Finally, consider the thorny issue of collective responsibility. On the one hand, many of us are strongly inclined to hold collectives of various sorts responsible for a variety of harms—for example, we may take Germany as a nation (or, alternatively, the German people taken collectively) to be responsible for the Holocaust, various corporations to be responsible for various sorts of environmental pollution, and so on. But on the other hand, collectives as such do not seem to be conscious agents, and thus do not seem to be the sorts of entities to which the ascription of responsibility is even intelligible. This crucial underlying issue—the issue of whether, and in what sense, collectives can legitimately be regarded as agents—is the focus of Todd Jones's contribution to this volume.

3   The Essays in This Volume

As this brief introduction has illustrated—and as seems obvious in any event—moral responsibility is connected with a wide variety of issues. A number of these issues are significantly illuminated by the essays in this volume.

In "A Reappraisal of the Doctrine of Doing and Allowing," David Chan criticizes attempts by deontologists to use this "doctrine" (DDA) and its rationale—that "negative rights and the duty not to cause harm by intervention" take precedence over "positive rights and the duty to provide aid"—to defend the view that killing is worse than letting die. Focusing on the views of Warren Quinn, Chan argues that Quinn's attempt to match this defense to our intuitions in the relevant cases requires ad hoc distortions of Quinn's distinction between negative and positive agency—distortions that undermine the appeal of DDA and vitiate the alleged defense (defending our intuitions by appealing to this distinction becomes circular if this distinction is itself modified to conform to our intuitions). Moreover, Chan contends, Quinn fails to give adequate consideration to other features, such as "the likelihood of harm and the presence of prior commitments," which underlie our intuitions in the relevant cases. Chan concludes by using virtue ethics to sketch a defense of a "middle position" between the deontological view that killing is always worse than letting die and the consequentialist view that there is no morally relevant difference between the two—a "middle position" that allows us to say, for example, that it may be preferable to let y people die than to kill x people if y is somewhat larger than x but not if y is very much larger than x. Chan reaches this result by arguing that, though both a disposition "to avoid killing" and a disposition "to save others from death" are virtues, a person who has the former virtue but not the latter is better than a person who has latter virtue but not the former, and, hence, that the former disposition will be stronger in a virtuous person than the latter.

In "Killing John to Save Mary: A Defense of the Moral Distinction between Killing and Letting Die," Helen Frowe defends the indicated distinction against Michael Tooley and his Moral Symmetry Principle—the principle, roughly, that, other things equal, "there is no moral difference" between initiating a causal process that has a certain outcome and failing to stop a causal process that has that outcome. To avoid apparent counterexamples, Tooley "clarifies" the principle by claiming that, though it asserts "that it is as wrong intentionally to refrain from interfering with a causal process . . . as it is to initiate the process," it nonetheless "does *not* assert that it is as wrong to refrain from *preventing someone else* from initiating a causal process as it is to initiate it oneself." Frowe begins her attack on the Moral Symmetry Principle by focusing on this clarification. She presents cases to show that it is just as implausible to claim that preventing someone else from *continuing* a causal process is morally equivalent to initiating the process oneself as it is to claim that preventing someone else from *initiating* a causal process is morally equivalent to initiating the process oneself—a point that Tooley's "clarification" does not address. Furthermore, she argues, there is no plausible way to fix this problem without eliminating the rationale for adopting the principle in the first place. She then turns to Tooley's claim—a claim also made by James Rachels—"that those who defend the killing–letting die distinction have confused the wrongness of external factors, like motivation, with the comparative wrongness of killing and letting die themselves." We can undermine this claim, she argues, by distinguishing "between being able to avoid *a harm*, and being able to avoid being *at risk* of that harm." Specifically, a killing may be wrong where the comparable letting die is not because the former changes the antecedent risk—for example, it transfers it from one person to another—whereas the latter does not.

In "Making Up One's Mind," Randolph Clarke notes that one can make up one's mind about either of two different kinds of things: about what to *do* and about what to *believe*. Deliberation in the first case involves *practical reasoning* and in the second case involves *theoretical reasoning*. Clarke considers the thesis that these two ways of making up one's mind—*practical deciding* and *cognitive deciding*, respectively—are fundamentally different. He also presents and then responds to recent arguments to the contrary offered by Brian O'Shaughnessy (1980), Gary Watson (2004), and others.

"Conscious Intentions," by Alfred R. Mele, is a sustained piece of conceptual analysis. Mele is concerned with the claim that intentions are essentially conscious, a claim held by some but not all contemporary psychologists: is the claim true, and why do scientists disagree about it? As it turns out, the answer to the first question depends on what kinds of intention one has in mind. Mele distinguishes between *distal* and *proximal intentions*, for instance, where the former are aimed at future actions and the latter are not. It seems that, for example, while I'm driving to the store I (proximally) intend to step on the gas pedal, but I'm rarely if ever consciously aware of this intention. Thus, claims about proximal conscious intentions might be harder, or even impossible, to prove, whereas claims about distal intentions might be more easily supported. Mele then explains how these two different opinions about conscious intentions correspond to two distinct approaches to psychology. This chapter has direct implications for scientific research into the psychological character of intentions.

In "Locke's Compatibilism: Suspension of Desire or Suspension of Determinism?" Charles T. Wolfe investigates John Locke's account of free action. It was Locke who noted that since the will is a power (or set of powers) and freedom is a power, *free will* is strictly speaking a power of a power. Locke found this problematic, and for this reason he was among the first philosophers to shift the attention from free will to *free action*. It is the person who is free, not the will, and the relevant freedom is the freedom to act. Yet despite these contributions, Locke's theory has been judged by many to be incoherent. In this context, Wolfe offers a compelling Lockean, naturalistic view of free action that is an alternative to both libertarian agent causation and reason-based views of action.

E. J. Coffman and Donald Smith's "The Fall of the *Mind* Argument and Some Lessons about Freedom" is a contribution to the debate about the soundness of the *Mind* argument (van Inwagen 1983, 126ff.). As we noted above, the *Mind* argument may be viewed as an argument for the incompatibility of free will and *indeterminism* that is named for its common occurrence in the journal of the same name.[12] According to Coffman and

Smith, the *Mind* argument has an implicit principle, (γ), which holds that an agent has a choice about an event *e* only if there is some event in the causal history of *e* such that he has a choice about it. Reductive libertarians—who claim that agents, not just events, can cause actions—endorse (γ), whereas nonreductive libertarians—who hold that only events can cause actions—reject the principle. Given that (γ) is an implicit premise, if (γ) is false, then the *Mind* argument fails. Furthermore, Coffman and Smith argue that if (γ) is true, then the *Mind* argument also fails. This creates a dilemma that might be instructive to the libertarian. For in choosing one horn over the other he is forced to choose between reductive and nonreductive libertarianism. Coffman and Smith close with their reasons for favoring the latter.

In "Selective Hard Compatibilism," Paul Russell begins with an explication of rational agency theory, which maintains that an agent is free provided that his actions are guided by practical reasoning. One common criticism of this theory is the manipulation argument. Recall that the *no-difference claim* of the argument is that there is no substantive difference between *manipulation cases*, where actions are controlled by external agents, and *determinism cases*. Therefore, the supposed lack of moral responsibility in manipulation cases extends to determinism cases, and determinism is incompatible with moral responsibility. As Russell notes, history matters to the soft compatibilist, for it matters whether or not my action is part of some covert agent's plans. If it is, then I'm not morally responsible for the action.

Russell makes a strong case for rejecting this line of thought in favor of *hard compatibilism*, according to which manipulation alone does not rule out moral responsibility. Hard compatibilists accept the no-difference claim. Given that Russell believes that some persons are morally responsible for their actions, he is left to argue that agents in some manipulation cases are morally responsible for their actions. Using the distinction between the illegitimacy of *holding* an agent morally responsible for his action and the agent's lacking moral responsibility, Russell argues that our judgment that manipulated agents are not morally responsible for their actions might be based on a faulty line of reasoning.

John Martin Fischer's "Manipulation and Guidance Control: A Reply to Long" is a response to a potential counterexample to Fischer's view that was given by Todd Long (2004). Fischer is both a soft compatibilist and a semicompatibilist. He concedes that there is a kind of freedom that is incompatible with determinism—*regulative control*—yet it is not necessary for moral responsibility. Moral responsibility requires only *guidance control*, which is consistent with determinism. Soft compatibilism is prone to new variations of the manipulation argument (McKenna 2008), and Long's strategy follows these same lines. Long offers two contrasting examples involving a man named 'Schmidt'. The first Schmidt example is a determinism case where the agent appears to satisfy Fischer's conditions for moral responsibility. The agent also appears to satisfy these conditions in the second Schmidt example, which is a manipulation case. Otherwise the cases seem indistinguishable. As Fischer notes, even Long is unclear about whether or not Schmidt is morally responsible in the second case. Fischer eventually dismisses Long's challenge and along the way he points to a distinction between soft compatibilism, on the one hand, and both hard compatibilism and theories that claim that *all* manipulation cases threaten moral responsibility, on the other. Fischer seems to regard this distinction as advantageous for soft compatibilism: since soft compatibilists have no sweeping response to those opposing theories, they are forced to consider the details of each case individually and judge it on its own merits.

"Free Will: Some Bad News" adds to Saul Smilansky's complex theory. Smilansky accepts the conclusions of arguments for free will skepticism. He also differs from most free will skeptics, for he endorses two "radical" claims. First, compatibilism has something to offer—Smilansky is a "partial compatibilist" and endorses "compatibilist hard determinism." Second, it is in general better to live under the *illusion* of free will than to embrace free will skepticism. Part of this essay is an update, where Smilansky repeats the case for free will skepticism in light of some contemporary free will theories. In addition, Smilansky addresses recent claims by free will skeptics that life without free will is not so bad. Injustice and pessimism are just some of the consequences of rejecting free will. Unfortunately, the bad news about free will is not just that we don't have it. Smilansky argues that many contemporary philosophers have simply ignored the fundamental problem about our lack of ultimate control over our actions. The only way out is illusion. Van Inwagen (1998), following Chomsky and McGinn, has claimed that we might lack the cognitive capacities needed to solve the free will problem, which would explain its persistence. Smilansky goes further in noting that our difficulty might be not cognitive but emotional.

In "Responsibility and Practical Reason" George Sher focuses on the "knowledge" requirement for responsibility (called above the "epistemic condition")—a requirement that has received much less attention than the "freedom" requirement (the "freedom-relevant condition"). His goal is to "raise some doubts about" a common interpretation of the knowledge requirement, an interpretation he dubs "the searchlight view." According to this view, "how much responsibility any given agent has for what he has done is a direct function of the range of relevant facts of which he was aware." The appeal of this view, Sher believes, derives from the fact that the limits it imposes on an agent's responsibility "are a precise match with what each of us sees as the limits of his own choice situation" when he takes "the deliberative perspective."

Adopting as his "working hypothesis the assumption that the best defense of the searchlight view is likely to involve some premise that makes essential mention of the deliberative perspective," Sher considers one of the two approaches he thinks such a defense might take, an approach that "takes as its point of departure the claim that responsibility itself is a practical rather than a theoretical concept." Focusing on the views of Christine Korsgaard and Hilary Bok, both of whom make this claim, Sher begins by noting that the claim faces an immediate difficulty, namely, that whereas we can deliberate only about our own future actions, "our ordinary concept of responsibility is neither oriented to the future nor restricted to the first person." He then considers the differing ways in which Korsgaard and Bok provide a "more expansive" version of the claim based on a "richer notion of practical reason," a version according to which a concept of responsibility based in practical reason can be applied both to one's own past actions and to the actions of others. And he argues that on neither author's "more expansive" version will it be plausible to restrict such applications to what the relevant agent was aware of at the time of deliberation. In short, we face the following dilemma: on the "least expansive" version of the claim that responsibility is a practical concept, this concept is unacceptably limited to one's own future actions; but on the "more expansive" version, this concept does not conform to the searchlight view. Thus, the suggested defense of the searchlight view fails.

As Todd Jones notes, the much-discussed issue of collective responsibility "remains . . . contentious." In his "The Metaphysics of Collective Agency," he focuses on an essential and, in his view, "comparatively neglected" prior topic, namely, "the precise metaphysical underpinnings of collective agenthood." In particular, he attempts to show "how collective agency might be possible" by outlining a theory of intentionality according to which certain sorts of groups "qualify as having intentional states"—specifically, "representation" and "goal" states. On Jones's theory, what is central to a system's having a goal is that it have "a robust disposition to produce a similar range of end states . . . in a variety of environments"; and "the more ways a system has of producing a certain end state from a variety of initial states, the more comfortable we are of speaking of the system's 'goals.'" Moreover, complicated goal-directed systems typically develop "subsystem" mechanisms for pursuing subgoals and sub-subgoals; and these subgoals are central to Jones's conception of "representation." "I submit," he says, "that we speak of 'representations' when we want to give *further* information about the more *fine-grained* subgoals that a creature has developed by becoming 'tuned' to certain environments in a way that enables it to succeed in its goals and subgoals." Information about the relevant "internal mechanisms" is provided "indirectly *by describing the sort of world* with which the creatures are set up to make appropriate interactions"; and "we call being set up to interact effectively with that kind of world 'having a representation' of that world."

On this theory of intentionality, Jones contends, groups can in principle have both goals and representations, and thus can be intentional systems. Noting that we are likely to resist this characterization because "we already use terms like 'goal' and 'representation' to describe the thinking and behavior of" the groups' members, he acknowledges that the goals of some members of a group may "be the same as the goals that our theory of intentionality would lead us to identify as the group's goals." But the crucial point is that this need not be the case: "on the theory of intentionality given above, it's perfectly possible for a group to have a goal or representation that none of the people in that group has." Jones concludes by conceding that his argument is not sufficient to show that groups can be *moral* agents, and that whether they can be moral agents "is unclear"; but, he contends, "knowing how they can be intentional agents helps give us some promising ways to find that out."

One of the central debates in metaethics is that between internalists and externalists, the former holding (roughly) that there is a *conceptual* connection between believing that one morally ought to do something and intending, or at least having some motivation, to do it, the latter holding that any such connection is merely contingent. Antti Kauppinen contends that "internalists have the upper hand in this debate" despite the fact that they have "difficulty with motivational failures." Thus, in "Moral Judgment and Volitional Incapacity," he attempts to defend internalism in the face of the challenge posed by the most troublesome cases of motivational failure. Typical internalists, such as Gibbard, are noncognitivist internalists—they hold that assent to a judgment such as "I ought to A" consists, in Kauppinen's words, in "a *conative* or *affective* state," a state of, for example, intending to A. But Kauppinen believes that, though "sophisticated" forms of noncognitivist internalism can deal with many cases of motivational failure, including cases of weakness of will, they cannot deal with "the sort of radical motivational failure that Gary Watson has labeled *volitional incapacity*," cases in which "one's self-directed ought-judgment does not result in a corresponding intention." An example is the case of "Incapacitated Michelle," a case in which Michelle fully believes that she ought to deliver an urgent message to her compatriot in the French Resistance, but suffers from such extreme agoraphobia that she cannot get herself even to intend to leave her room—or, thus, to deliver the message.

To retain internalism in the face of such cases, we must, on Kauppinen's view, adopt cognitivist internalism. He concludes his chapter by defending a version of cognitivist internalism based on an "inferentialist" conception of rational capacities, a conception he contrasts with the "coherence" conception adopted by, for example, Michael Smith. In brief, (a) ought-judgments involve inferential commitments rather than practical commitments—this is the "cognitive" component of the view; and yet (b) the inferential commitments involved in ought-judgments themselves rationally require practical commitments—this is the "internalist" component of the view. Hence, we can say both (a) that thinking that one ought to do something while never having any intention of doing it, as in the Incapacitated Michelle case, is possible—thus the view can handle volitional incapacity; and yet (b) that failing to intend to do what one thinks one ought to do is irrational in that it involves failing to fulfill one's inferential commitments—thus the view preserves the central insight of internalism.

The presence of a psychological disorder is normally thought to reduce, and in some cases even to eliminate, a wrongdoer's criminal responsibility. But in "'So Sick He Deserves It': Desert, Dangerousness, and Character in the Context of Capital Sentencing," Robert F. Schopp considers the common view that at least certain types of psychopathology not only fail to mitigate, but actually exacerbate, criminal culpability. The central question he addresses is: "can we identify any circumstances in which psychopathology can legitimately serve as an aggravating factor that increases the level of punishment deserved?" Schopp notes that some court opinions "accept dangerousness as an independent sentencing consideration supporting increased severity of punishment," and that these "appear to conflict" with opinions that "require punishment in proportion to culpability or moral blameworthiness." This raises a second question: "can sentences predicated partially upon judgments of dangerousness, and particularly upon dangerousness associated with psychopathology, conform to a requirement that sentences are proportionate to culpability or desert?"

He answers both questions in the affirmative. The crucial idea is that an agent who engages in criminal conduct may be culpable not merely for that conduct but for developing or retaining the dispositions that led to that conduct. Hence, if those dispositions are pathological dispositions that constitute a greater danger to the public than more ordinary criminal dispositions, it may be justifiable to hold that the agent is more culpable, and thus legitimately subjected to more severe punishment, than an agent who engages in similar conduct on the basis of less dangerous dispositions. Further, even where agents are not responsible for the original generation of the relevant pathological dispositions—for example, where those dispositions resulted from sexual abuse during childhood—they may still be responsible, Schopp contends, for "continuing to engage in an extended pattern of conduct that retains and exacerbates those dispositions." He concludes by arguing that his views are perfectly compatible with "liberal principles of political morality" that "define distinct public and nonpublic domains and limit the state's authority to apply coercive force to the public domain." For he is not claiming that one can legitimately be punished simply for having, or for having culpably developed or retained, objectionable dispositions; rather, he is claiming only that consideration of an agent's dispositions, and thus his or her character, in imposing punishment is permissible when the agent "engages in culpable criminal conduct" and thereby "injects those aspects of his character that generate harm or risk to others into the public domain."

Frances Kamm's "Types of Terror Bombing and Shifting Responsibility" expands on typical discussions of "terror bombing" versus "tactical bombing" by considering "nonstandard forms of terror bombing." Kamm argues that such nonstandard bombing is "also wrong according to criteria that can be used to condemn standard terror bombing," but that "different forms of terror bombing can distribute responsibility for outcomes in different ways and for different things." She rejects the common view that the special wrongness of standard terror bombing (intentionally bombing noncombatants—NCs—to produce terror among NCs to, e.g., induce them to get their government to surrender) lies in the "intentions to harm and to produce terror to civilians," contending rather that the relevant feature is that it is "true of terror bombing but not of collateral damage that, given what an agent does, it is necessary that harm and terror are causal means to achieving his end."

With this as background she considers several nonstandard cases that differ from standard terror bombing in that, though the harm and/or terror are necessary causal means to the relevant end, (a) the objective is straightforwardly "military" (e.g., the blowing up of a military target) rather than "political," and (b) the harm and/or terror produce the desired result purely "mechanically," bypassing "people's judgment and will." She contends that at least some of these cases can be condemned on the same grounds as standard terror bombing, despite the fact that, because these cases have a military objective, "many practitioners of war" would not have regarded them as instances of terror bombing. Turning to the mechanical–nonmechanical distinction, in standard terror bombing cases, unlike her cases, the goal is achieved by altering—that is, (arguably) corrupting through, for example, cowardice—the NCs' "judgment and deliberately willed political behavior"; and this means that part of the responsibility for the ultimate result (e.g., surrender) falls on the NCs themselves. This suggests that Kamm's nonstandard, mechanical cases might be preferable to the standard case because they save the NCs from corrupted judgment and behavior and the responsibility associated therewith. But although "it may be better in some way for the person himself" to be used mechanically rather than to be corrupted, Kamm contends that this is counteracted by the idea that "it is contrary to the *importance of being a person*" to bypass his agency. In brief, though being used mechanically "could be . . . better *for* him, it is more at odds with the importance *of* him."

Notes

1. These two conditions do not exhaust the metaphysical issues relevant to moral responsibility; other issues include, e.g., the relation between moral and causal responsibility, personal identity, and possibly additional cognitive considerations. The relation between moral and causal responsibility, which is a significant issue in action theory and ethics, will be considered briefly in the second section of this chapter.

2. According to the thesis of determinism, "given the past and the laws of nature, there is only one possible future" (van Inwagen 1983, 65). For similar definitions of key theories in the free will debate, see van Inwagen 1983, 13–14. William James (1956) was the first to distinguish between hard and soft determinism.

3. Ted Honderich (1988, 2002) is an exception, in that he is a free will skeptic who endorses the thesis of determinism. But Honderich is not really a hard determinist either, since he rejects incompatibilism along with compatibilism (Honderich 2004). Note that Honderich's usage of these terms is slightly different from ours. Nonetheless, his views defy easy categorization.

4. One may equate *metaphysical freedom* with the *alternatives* view of free will.

5. The view that Jim is causally responsible for that Indian's death can be questioned, on the ground that he had no alternative that would have avoided that result. Conversely, some people's intuitions incline them to the view that Jim is morally as well as causally responsible. But certainly a common, if not consensus, view is that Jim is causally but not morally responsible for the death of the Indian he kills.

6. If, *per impossibile*, one such person had certain foreknowledge of those horrors, we might be inclined to say that that person bore some moral responsibility for them; but we still presumably would not ascribe causal responsibility to that person.

7. "In legal terms, a defendant's behavior is a cause of an event if it wouldn't have occurred 'but for' the defendant's behavior" (Miller 1990, 272).

8. Arthur Miller acknowledges this rather explicitly in the following description of how the law would deal with a case of overdetermination (Miller 1990, 273, italics added):

[a] teen-age girl . . . tries to scent a burning candle by pouring perfume on it. . . . flames spring out, and her blouse and the nearby curtains catch fire. At the same time, her four-year-old brother . . . opens the oven door, stands on it, the range tips over, and the flame from the gas ignites his toys on the floor. Both fires spread and together they destroy the entire house and everyone in the family. The truth is, either of the blazes would have done the same damage.

Both the perfume company and the stove maker will argue that . . . it should not be liable because the defect was not the but-for cause of the damage. *Rather than let these two defendants . . . escape liability on account of the fortuity that their respective products happened to prove defective at the same time*, the law says that the causation requirement is satisfied if either one was a "substantial factor" in bringing about the harm.

9. Cf. the brief discussion of tracing, and the Zimmerman quotation, in the first section above.

10. All of this suggests that the issue of "moral luck," which has been much discussed since the seminal papers by Thomas Nagel (Nagel 1976) and Bernard Williams (Williams 1976), would have special relevance to the law. For an article on this topic, see Eisikovits 2005.

11. Foot (1967) considers both distinctions—and introduces the "trolley" cases, which of course have been much discussed in the literature in connection with these distinctions ever since. There is, in general, a huge literature on these issues; an extremely small, and quite arbitrary, sample of this literature, in addition to items already mentioned, includes Thomson 1976, 1985; Glover 1977; Bratman 1987 (especially ch. 10); Boorse and Sorensen 1988; Fischer 1992; Fischer and Ravizza 1994; and McIntyre 2001.

12. Strictly speaking, the conclusion of the *Mind* argument is the incompatibility between free will and a very limited indeterminism, e.g., indeterminism about events that play a role in human behavior (van Inwagen 1983, 126–127).

References

Aristotle. 1985. *Nicomachean Ethics*. Trans. T. Irwin. Indianapolis: Hackett.

Boorse, C., and R. Sorensen. 1988. Ducking Harm. *Journal of Philosophy* 85:115–134.

Bratman, M. 1987. *Intention, Plans, and Practical Reason*. Cambridge, Mass.: Harvard University Press.

Campbell, J., M. O'Rourke, and D. Shier, eds. 2004a. *Freedom and Determinism*. Cambridge, Mass.: MIT Press.

Campbell, J., M. O'Rourke, and D. Shier. 2004b. Freedom and Determinism: A Framework. In *Freedom and Determinism*, ed. J. Campbell, M. O'Rourke, and D. Shier. Cambridge, Mass.: MIT Press.

Campbell, J., M. O'Rourke, and D. Shier, eds. 2005. *Law and Social Justice*. Cambridge, Mass.: The MIT Press.

Clarke, R. 2003. *Libertarian Accounts of Free Will*. Oxford: Oxford University Press.

Eisikovits, N. 2005. Moral Luck and the Criminal Law. In *Law and Social Justice*, ed. J. Campbell, M. O'Rourke, and D. Shier. Cambridge, Mass.: The MIT Press.

Fischer, J. M. 1992. Thoughts on the Trolley Problem. In J. M. Fischer and M. Ravizza, *Ethics: Problems and Principles*. Fort Worth, Tx.: Harcourt Brace Jovanovich.

Fischer, J. M. 1994. *The Metaphysics of Free Will: An Essay on Control*. Oxford: Blackwell.

Fischer, J. M., and M. Ravizza. 1992. *Ethics: Problems and Principles*. Fort Worth, Tx.: Harcourt Brace Jovanovich.

Fischer, J. M., and M. Ravizza. 1993. Introduction. In *Perspectives on Moral Responsibility*, ed. J. M. Fischer and M. Ravizza. Ithaca, N.Y.: Cornell University Press.

Fischer, J. M., and M. Ravizza. 1994. Ducking Harm and Sacrificing Others. *Journal of Social Philosophy* 25 (3):135–145.

Fischer, J. M., and M. Ravizza. 1998. *Responsibility and Control: A Theory of Moral Responsibility*. Cambridge: Cambridge University Press.

Foot, P. 1967. The Problem of Abortion and the Doctrine of the Double Effect. *Oxford Review* 5:5–15. Reprinted in Foot 1978 and Fischer and Ravizza 1992.

Foot, P. 1978. *Virtues and Vices and Other Essays in Moral Philosophy*. Berkeley, Calif.: University of California Press.

Frankfurt, H. 1969. Alternate Possibilities and Moral Responsibility. *Journal of Philosophy* 66:828–839. Reprinted in Frankfurt 1988.

Frankfurt, H. 1988. *The Importance of What We Care About*. Cambridge: Cambridge University Press.

Ginet, C. 1966. Might We Have No Choice? In *Freedom and Determinism*, ed. K. Lehrer. New York: Random House.

Ginet, C. 1990. *On Action*. Cambridge: Cambridge University Press.

Ginet, C. 2000. The Epistemic Requirements for Moral Responsibility. *Philosophical Perspectives* 14:267–277.

Glover, J. 1977. *Causing Death and Saving Lives*. Middlesex: Penguin Books.

Honderich, T. 1988. *A Theory of Determinism: The Mind, Neuroscience, and Life-Hopes*. Oxford: Clarendon Press. Reprinted in 1990 as the paperbacks: *Mind and Brain* (vol. 1) and *The Consequences of Determinism* (vol. 2).

Honderich, T. 2002. *How Free Are You?* 2nd ed. Oxford, New York: Oxford University Press.

Honderich, T. 2004. After Compatibilism and Incompatibilism. In *Freedom and Determinism*, ed. J. Campbell, M. O'Rourke, and D. Shier. Cambridge, Mass.: MIT Press.

James, W. 1956. The Dilemma of Determinism. In *The Will to Believe and Other Essays*. New York: Dover.

Kane, R. 1996. *The Significance of Free Will*. New York: Oxford University Press.

Kane, R., ed. 2002. *The Oxford Handbook on Free Will*. Oxford: Oxford University Press.

Long, T. 2004. Moderate Reasons-Responsiveness, Moral Responsibility, and Manipulation. In *Freedom and Determinism*, ed. J. Campbell, M. O'Rourke, and D. Shier. Cambridge, Mass.: MIT Press.

McIntyre, A. 2001. Doing Away with Double Effect. *Ethics* 111:219–255.

McKenna, M. 2001. Source Incompatibilism, Ultimacy, and the Transfer of Non-Responsibility. *American Philosophical Quarterly* 38:37–51.

McKenna, M. 2008. A Hard-line Reply to Pereboom's Four-case Manipulation Argument. *Philosophy and Phenomenological Research* 77:142–159.

Mele, A. 2006. *Free Will and Luck*. Oxford: Oxford University Press.

Miller, A. 1990. Products Liability: Must the Buyer Beware? In *Contemporary Issues in Business Ethics*, 2nd ed., ed. J. R. DesJardins and J. J. McCall. Belmont, Calif.: Wadsworth. Excerpted from A. Miller, *Miller's Court*. Boston: Houghton Mifflin.

Nagel, T. 1976. Moral Luck. *Aristotelian Society: Supplementary Volume* 50:137–152.

O'Connor, T. 2000. *Persons and Causes: The Metaphysics of Free Will*. New York: Oxford University Press.

O'Shaughnessy, B. 1980. *The Will: A Dual Aspect Theory*, vol. 2. Cambridge: Cambridge University Press.

Pereboom, D. 2001. *Living without Free Will*. Cambridge: Cambridge University Press.

Quinn, W. 1989. Actions, Intentions, and Consequences: The Doctrine of Doing and Allowing. *Philosophical Review* 98:287–312. Reprinted in Quinn 1993.

Quinn, W. 1993. *Morality and Action*. Cambridge: Cambridge University Press.

Rachels, J. 1994. Active and Passive Euthanasia. In *Killing and Letting Die*, ed. A. Norcross and B. Steinbock. New York: Fordham University Press.

Smilansky, S. 2000. *Free Will and Illusion*. Oxford: Clarendon Press.

Strawson, G. 1986. *Freedom and Belief*. Oxford: Clarendon Press.

Thomson, J. 1976. Killing, Letting Die, and the Trolley Problem. *Monist* 59: 204–217. Reprinted in Thomson 1986 and Fischer and Ravizza 1992.

Thomson, J. 1985. The Trolley Problem. *Yale Law Journal* 94: 1395–1415. Reprinted in Thomson 1986 and Fischer and Ravizza 1992.

Thomson, J. 1986. *Rights, Restitution, and Risk: Essays in Moral Theory*. Ed. William Parent. Cambridge, Mass.: Harvard University Press.

Tooley, M. 1994. An Irrelevant Consideration: Killing Versus Letting Die. In *Killing and Letting Die*, ed. A. Norcross and B. Steinbock. New York: Fordham University Press.

Van Inwagen, P. 1983. *An Essay on Free Will*. Oxford: Clarendon Press.

van Inwagen, P. 1989. When Is the Will Free? *Philosophical Perspectives* 3: 399–422.

van Inwagen, P. 1998. The Mystery of Metaphysical Freedom. In *Metaphysics: The Big Questions*, ed. P. van Inwagen and D. Zimmerman. Oxford: Blackwell.

van Inwagen, P. 2000. Free Will Remains a Mystery. *Philosophical Perspectives* 14: 1–19. Reprinted in Kane 2002.

van Inwagen, P. 2004. Van Inwagen on Free Will. In *Freedom and Determinism*, ed. J. Campbell, M. O'Rourke, and D. Shier. Cambridge, Mass.: MIT Press.

van Inwagen, P. 2008. How to Think about the Problem of Free Will. *Journal of Ethics* 12:327–341.

Watson, G., ed. 2004. *Agency and Answerability*. Oxford: Oxford University Press.

Williams, B. 1973. A Critique of Utilitarianism. In J. J. C. Smart and B. Williams, *Utilitarianism: For and Against*. Cambridge: Cambridge University Press.

Williams, B. 1976. Moral Luck. *Aristotelian Society: Supplementary Volume* 50: 115–136.

Zimmerman, M. 1997. Moral Responsibility and Ignorance. *Ethics* 107:410–426.

2 A Reappraisal of the Doctrine of Doing and Allowing

David K. Chan

Warren Quinn[1] and Philippa Foot[2] have both given versions of the Doctrine of Doing and Allowing (DDA) that justify a moral distinction between doing something to bring about harm and doing nothing to prevent harm. They argue that whereas it is justified to allow one person to die so that one can save a larger number of people, it is not permissible to kill one person to achieve the same purpose. They defend the distinction on the basis of an account of positive and negative rights. Consequentialist moral philosophers, on the other hand, hold that if killing and letting die have the same consequences, there is no moral difference between the two acts.[3] Thus, the DDA's role seems to be to undercut the consequentialist position by using a moral distinction between doing and allowing to support a moral distinction not found in consequentialist thinking between killing and letting die. In justifying the DDA, the non-consequentialist must do two things: explain what difference the DDA captures, and show that its application has intuitive results through the use of examples.

In this essay, I shall show that the examples typically used to support the DDA do not in fact do so. Contrary to the deontological ethics supported by the DDA, I argue that it can be justified to minimize harm by killing a smaller number of people, in preference to letting a greater number die. But unlike for the consequentialist, my position is that the distinction between killing and letting die does have moral significance. I shall examine what other nonconsequentialist considerations, besides the appeal to positive and negative rights, could account for the distinction, and will suggest a middle position between the deontological and consequentialist approaches to the ethics of killing.

1   Harmful Agency

Not anyone who fails to prevent harm is allowing harm to occur. The person who allows harm is an *agent*. He is aware that he is in a position to prevent a certain harm to one or more other persons, but he decides not to do what he can to prevent the harm. He can carry out his decision by inaction, or by getting out of the way, or by doing something else, or he may have to actively refrain from actions that would prevent the harm. On the other hand, someone who is unaware that he is able to prevent a harm, or who has not decided about whether to prevent the harm, or who fails to carry out a decision to prevent the harm (because of weakness of will, or an unsuccessful attempt), will also have failed to prevent harm. But he would not be an agent who allows harm in the relevant sense.[4]

Judith Jarvis Thomson has pointed out that the moral relevance of the distinction between bringing about and allowing harm has to be judged using examples where "choice is presumably in question" (Thomson 1986a, 79). Thomson famously devised the Trolley examples, in which a driver or bystander has to choose between letting a runaway trolley cause the deaths of five people, or diverting the trolley onto a sidetrack where one person will be killed.[5] These and similar examples have drawn conflicting accounts of what the right choice is and why it is right to choose in that way. If the examples capture a moral distinction, what exactly is the distinction and why is it morally significant?[6]

Quinn is well aware that the DDA does not make a straightforward distinction between acts and omissions. The distinction that Quinn carves out is between what he calls (harmful) positive and negative agency. He holds that the DDA discriminates in favor of negative agency and against positive agency, where the result of the agency is that someone is harmed (Quinn 1993, 153). *Rescue I* is his example of the favored kind of agency. The rescuer has to choose between saving five people from drowning in one place and a single person in similar danger in another place. It seems justified to save the five and fail to save the one. *Rescue II* illustrates the disfavored positive agency. The rescuer can save the five only by driving over and killing someone who is trapped on the road. It is not justified to proceed with the rescue of the five.

Quinn's distinction does not correspond with the distinction between action and inaction. In his example of *Rescue III*, the rescuer is in the driver's seat of a special train on an urgent mission to rescue five persons in imminent danger of death. The rescue would be aborted if the train were to stop. Someone is trapped on the track and will be killed if the rescuer does not put on the brakes. The rescuer is not required to do anything to let the train continue. Quinn thinks that this is a special kind of inaction that counts as positive agency. According to him, "the train kills the man *because* of [the rescuer's] intention that it continue forward," and "the combination of control and intention in *Rescue III* makes for a certain kind of complicity" (Quinn 1993, 162).[7] Just as in *Rescue II*, the rescuer is obligated to stop the train—the death of the five persons who are not rescued counts as negative agency.

A further example is provided to show that a rescuer who does *not* intend that the train continue forward is permitted to save five persons in preference to stopping the train to prevent it from running over the person on the track. In *Rescue IV*, there are five badly wounded passengers at the back of the train after an explosion. The rescuer is attending to them when he learns that someone is trapped on the track. Stopping the train is a complicated business that would render it impossible to save the wounded passengers. Quinn thinks that the rescuer should not stop the train, as his failure to stop the train is, unlike in *Rescue III*, negative agency.

Quinn obviously needs to show why there is a difference in intention between *Rescue III* and *Rescue IV*. First, he defines an agent's "most direct contribution" (MDC) to a harmful consequence of his agency as the contribution that most directly explains the harm. Where harm comes from an active object such as a train, an agent may contribute to its harmful action by either his action or inaction. In *Rescue II*, the rescuer's MDC is his act of driving over the person trapped on the road. In *Rescue III*, his MDC is his failure to stop the train. According to Quinn, the rescuer "fails to [stop] it because he wants some action of the object that in fact leads to the harm" (Quinn 1993, 163). He intends an action of the train that in fact causes the man's death, namely, its passing over the spot where he is trapped. And he intends this because the train must pass that spot for the five others to be saved.

Does this work? Fischer and Ravizza have asked why it is not the case that the rescuer in *Rescue IV* intends the train to continue forward, given that he intends to refrain from leaving the five wounded passengers and rushing back to the controls of the train. They suggest that a principle that restricts intention transfer is needed that permits the transfer of intentions only across "elements in the causal chain that are necessary to the chain's resulting in the harm" (Fischer and Ravizza 1992, 350). It may then be argued that as the five passengers are in the relevant sense causally isolated from the movement of the train, the rescuer need not be attributed with an intention about the train.

I will not go any further into the debate about intention transfer.[8] Suffice it to say that we are getting not only an account of positive and negative agency that differs from the everyday notion of doing and allowing,[9] but also an account of intention that is far from intuitive.[10] Instead of providing criteria for distinguishing between positive and negative agency, and identifying an agent's intentions, prior to using the distinction to make moral evaluations, the criteria themselves are adjusted to fit our moral intuitions about the examples discussed.[11] These adjustments, designed to make the account fit the examples, seem ad hoc, and it is not obvious that the DDA defended by Quinn is the real basis of our moral intuitions regarding his examples. Because Quinn uses the rescuer's intention to distinguish between positive and negative agency, and then uses that distinction to explain why there is a moral difference between killing and letting die, it would be circular reasoning to use our moral intuitions regarding cases of killing and letting die to decide what the rescuer's intentions are unless something else about the situation is doing the moral work. Let us look at the examples again to see if the latter is the case.

2 Rescuing Intuitions

Quinn's use of *Rescue III* as an example to elicit moral intuitions has been criticized on the grounds that the example is underdescribed: "If we suppose that you are a mere bystander who played no role in the initiation of the rescue mission . . . then Quinn's intuition that you must stop the train from crushing the one seems fairly weak and unreliable" (Rickless 1997, 566). I think that the example is indeed underdescribed, but this does not mean that Quinn had gotten his intuitions wrong. What I reject, however, is Quinn's idea that the basis of the intuition rests on the rescuer's intention regarding the train.

Notice that Quinn assumes that the five persons who are to be rescued will die if the train is stopped and will be saved if it is not. Thomson's Trolley examples, frequently used in the debate on whether killing is worse than letting die, also involve the assumption that the consequences of acting and not acting are clear and known to the agent.[12] I think that our intuitions regarding these examples depend on whether we keep this assumption in mind. If you put yourself in the place of Quinn's rescuer, do you think that the five are as certain to die if you stop, as the one who is about to be run over by the train if you don't? If you so think, it is not clear that your intuition favors stopping the train. But it is difficult to make the assumption.[13] The five who are in danger are at a place that you have to travel to. Perhaps someone else will rescue them before you get there. Perhaps the danger will pass. We are also assuming that it is certain that you will succeed in saving them. Perhaps you will arrive too late. Perhaps you will get there but will not have the power to save them. In comparison, you can be certain that the decision to stop the train will make an immediate life-and-death difference to the person on the track.[14]

In *Rescue IV*, the certainty of the five's demise should you stop the train is much easier to keep in mind. You are already attending to them. We suppose they will drop dead if you stop. So our intuitions do not favor stopping the train. The difference, that the extent to which death is fore-seeable makes, is also applicable to the Trolley examples. The driver of the runaway trolley has to choose between letting the trolley continue on a track on which five persons are trapped, and switching the trolley onto a sidetrack where only one person is trapped. Our intuitions favor switch-ing tracks. Why should we favor killing one over letting five others die? Quinn implausibly claims that "the driver's passive option, letting the train continue on the main track, is really a form of positive agency," and that "his choice is really between two different positive options—one passive and one active" (Quinn 1993, 166–167).

Consider what our intuitions are when we do not assume that the five persons on the main track are certain to die. They are fifty miles away, whereas the one on the sidetrack is lying clearly in view. I do not think our intuition still favors switching tracks. Note, however, that it is not the distinction between killing and letting die that makes the difference. Suppose instead that the one person clearly in view is on the main track, and the five persons are fifty miles down the sidetrack. Should the driver do nothing to divert the trolley to the sidetrack? It seems to me that he should switch tracks, as he cannot be sure that the five on the sidetrack cannot be freed, or the trolley stopped, before it gets to the place where they are trapped. If I am right, the Trolley example shows that when the deaths of five on one track and the deaths of one on the other are equally certain, then other things being equal, the driver should choose the track where the fewer number of persons will die. Whether he is letting die through inaction, or killing through an act of switching tracks, does not make a crucial difference.

Another consideration that affects our intuitions about the examples is the role of prior commitments. In *Rescue IV*, the rescuer is already engaged in saving the lives of the five passengers. To rush off to stop the train will be to abandon his efforts to save them. This consideration affects our intuitions independently of the comparative numbers of people who can be saved, as illustrated by another example (*Freeze*):

Suppose I have always fired up my aged neighbor's furnace before it runs out of fuel. I haven't promised to do it, but I have always done it and intend to continue. Now suppose that an emergency arises involving five other equally close and needy friends who live far away, and that I can save them only by going off immediately and letting my neighbor freeze.[15]

To avoid complications, let us assume that I am absolutely certain that I can save my faraway friends, and that nobody else can save them. Despite their larger number, it is not clear that I am permitted to go off to save them, as I am already engaged in an effort to keep my neighbor alive.[16]

It may be said that the rescuer in *Rescue III* also has a prior commitment to save five lives. Is stopping the train not tantamount to abandoning the rescue of the five? However, unlike in *Rescue IV* and *Freeze*, it is possible that in *Rescue III* the five persons in danger can be rescued by others. As I have pointed out, the example presents a situation where the rescuer need not be certain about the demise of the five if he were to stop the train. But once we make the assumption that the five will die unless they are saved by the rescuer on the train, our intuitions no longer seem to favor stopping the train. Again, if we remove the assumption in *Freeze* that only I can help my neighbor, then it seems permissible to go away to rescue the five friends. Prior commitments are not irrevocable, but they do impose an obligation to find a replacement to relieve oneself in an emergency. Similarly, the rescuer in *Rescue III* is obliged to radio back for another team to take over if he stops the train.

I take it that it is a difference in the likelihood of harm and the presence of prior commitments, rather than the DDA, that grounds our intuitions regarding Quinn's examples.[17] In the absence of these two factors, should the rescuer then decide simply on the basis of the comparative numbers of people harmed? That is, would the best way to justify the intuitions rest on a consequentialist counting of lives? But if there are nonconsequentialist reasons to think that killing is worse than letting die, so that numbers would not be the only consideration, the consequentialist position need not follow.[18] Let me say something here about why it is important that the consequentialist position not be the default position.[19] It's not just that consequentialism has been criticized for its possible commitment to unjust acts, such as punishing the innocent, and to unjust institutions and practices, such as discrimination against minorities. It's that in the very examples we have been considering, assuming that the likelihood of harm is equally certain and that there are no prior commitments toward protecting or saving any of the lives at stake, it seems false that all that matters is the number of lives at stake, considered in consequentialist fashion. I have suggested that all other things being equal, when one is confronted with a choice between one person on one track, and five on the other, it is intuitively right to go down the track with the one person whether, in doing so, one has to divert the trolley or to just let the trolley continue on its way. But if all that matters is the number of lives at stake, then one would have no preference between the world in which one diverts the trolley and the world in which one lets the trolley continue. Yet even if it's the right thing to do, it's harder to choose to kill the one person than to choose to let the one person die,[20] which seems to indicate that there is a moral reason not to kill that has to be overridden before one can choose to kill a person to save a larger number of lives. In the next section, I will suggest that there is a nonconsequentialist moral basis for a shared intuition that it is worse to kill. If successful, I will have answered those who would argue that consequentialism, despite the many problems identified by critics, is still the best account of how to make decisions in situations of moral conflict, such as in the Trolley examples.

3 What Makes Killing Worse from a Nonconsequentialist Perspective

Suppose that there is exactly one person trapped on each track. A consideration that seems to favor doing nothing rather than switching tracks is that to do nothing is to let the one die, whereas to switch tracks is to actively engage in killing the other. Even the consequentialist may say this. Killing may impose a greater burden of guilt, and it may undermine human sensibilities that normally restrain us from acts that harm society. Quinn and Foot are nonconsequentialists who justify the DDA by appeal to an account of positive and negative rights. Killing violates negative rights against harmful intervention, whereas letting die violates positive rights to assistance. And negative rights "take precedence over" positive rights.[21] Unlike for consequentialists, the duty to avoid killing is an absolute duty, so it trumps any consideration of the numbers of people who are allowed to die.[22] This leads to the counterintuitive claim that it is preferable to allow very large numbers of innocent persons to die when one can save them by killing one person.[23]

Consequentialists, on the other hand, are too ready to use numbers to decide. Perhaps they may think that we should allow three to die rather than kill two persons, given the harmful effects on society of acts of killing. But it doesn't take many more at risk of letting die to turn the calculations in favor of killing. Moreover, consequentialists seem to miss out on what is wrong about killing. It cannot be just the harmful effects of the particular acts of killing, for killing can be wrong even when it is not harmful overall. And because they only consider the harmful effects, consequentialists do not give independent weight to whose agency brings about the harms. One morally significant difference between killing and letting die is that some other agent, human or natural, causes death when one lets die.

It seems that neither an account that makes it an absolute duty not to choose killing over letting die, nor an account that relies solely on comparing the numbers of people harmed, can satisfactorily reflect our moral intuitions. In response, one could view the project of formulating a wholly satisfactory and precise distinction between doing and allowing as far too complex, with too many rival distinctions to adjudicate between. According to Scheffler, it can be shown that "some distinction between what one does and what one allows is an ineliminable feature of any conception of normative responsibility," but "the contours of the distinction are likely to remain both imprecise and contested."[24] My objective in the remainder of this essay is, however, to stake out a middle position that takes both the harmful effects and the greater wrongness of killing into account. Although I can only provide a sketch here, I hope to say something about the wrongfulness of killing from a nonconsequentialist perspective that differs from other such accounts that have focused on the rights of the persons affected by what is done or not done.[25] On my account, what should be morally significant are the *agent*'s attitudes toward killing and saving lives that determine the choices that she makes in the Rescue and Trolley examples.

I begin with a famous example used to critique utilitarianism: Jim is faced with the choice of killing one Indian or allowing twenty Indians to be executed by soldiers (Williams 1973, 98–99). A utilitarian is expected to calculate that he can minimize harm by killing one Indian. According to Williams, even if the utilitarian choice is the correct one, the solution should not be reached by considering utility alone, without taking seriously the "distinction between my killing someone, and its coming about because of what I do that someone else kills them" (ibid., 117). He suggests that the utilitarian requirement that Jim kills the Indian puts Jim's integrity at risk, for he is compelled to set aside his personal projects owing to the impact of someone else's (the captain of the soldiers) projects on him. This idea of Williams can be developed in the following way.[26]

Consider that a person's commitment to projects contributes to her flourishing human life, and her choice of projects and the way that she carries them out are constitutive of her character. Suppose (as seems reasonable) that a disposition to avoid killing is part of a virtuous state of character. Suppose also (as seems equally reasonable) that a disposition to save others from death is also part of a virtuous state of character. In a morally perfect world, a person may be able to act in accordance with both of these dispositions. But in a world of forced choices, is it preferable to avoid killing or to save others from death? The answer to this question can be found by considering which of the two dispositions is more important for a virtuous state of character. But can we tell which disposition is more important without first determining what constitutes human virtue and goodness? Specifying human good is a challenge to virtue ethics on which consensus is unlikely. I propose here a shortcut that involves the following thought experiment: If we compare two persons, each of whom has one of the dispositions but not the other, which is the better of the two defective characters?

Jimmy has a disposition to avoid killing, but no disposition to save others from death. James, on the other hand, has a disposition to save others from death, but no disposition to avoid killing. We might say that although Jimmy seems to respect human life, he unfortunately lacks the virtue of compassion. People like Jimmy are not uncommon, as there are, for instance, many people who will not stop to help out at the scene of a road accident, but who wouldn't "hurt a fly." What can we make of James's character? He is someone who is likely to kill if he thinks circumstances merit it, but he is also likely to save others when they are at risk of being killed. There seems to be some incoherence in this combination of dispositions: wouldn't he try to save the person that he is willing to kill? But such persons do exist, though they are not common. They are like the cowboys portrayed in the movies of Clint Eastwood, people who have no qualms about killing when protecting the vulnerable from harm.

The comparison of characters is meant to motivate the following points, which I will not fully defend here. First, the character of Jimmy seems closer to virtue than the character of James. Second, most of us have both the disposition to avoid killing and the disposition to save others from death, but in less than ideal combinations. Third, a person's considered choice between killing and letting die is influenced by the strength of each of the two dispositions (assuming that no other dispositions are relevant). That is, the stronger her disposition to avoid killing, the fewer the situations in which she would choose to kill in order to save lives. Fourth, given that the character of Jimmy is more virtuous, a person is better for having a stronger disposition to avoid killing. And fifth, it follows that a person who is in a situation where killing a lesser number of people is necessary to save a greater number of others from death would be closer to virtue in choosing in a *nonconsequentialist* way that is reflective of dispositions that give greater weight to the undesirability of killing. Her choice differs from the consequentialist in that she may opt not to kill the lesser number of people, except where the number of people whose death can be prevented is significantly larger.

If I am right, when faced with a forced choice between killing and letting die, where numbers are close to being equal, a virtuous agent will choose to let die. However, where the number of persons who will die without her intervention is significantly higher than the number of persons she will kill by intervening, she may choose to kill the smaller number. I suspect that the figure that marks a significant difference is higher than that which will sway the consequentialist in favor of killing,[27] since the choice of the virtuous agent will reflect appropriate dispositions regarding the act of killing in itself, and not simply the consequences in terms of number of lives affected.

The earlier *Freeze* example also provides another reason why my position can differ from that of the consequentialist. The consequentialist position favors saving the five friends, thus leaving my neighbor to freeze. Although my past behavior may have engendered reasonable expectations that I will continue to keep my neighbor from freezing, and there are costs involved in disappointing such expectations, the benefits of saving the five will more than outweigh them. As a virtuous agent, I may, however, choose to stay to keep the neighbor alive. If I have made it a project of mine to keep my neighbor from freezing,[28] there is a failure in virtue if I simply drop the project. Imagine, for instance, a doctor with unique life-saving skills. He is engaged in saving the lives of a number of patients. He is told that if he moves immediately to another part of the world, there is a much larger number of persons whose lives he will save. Is it ethical for him to stop saving the lives that he is engaged in saving? He would fail to act virtuously if he were to do that. Beyond disappointing the expectations of others, and not carrying out his obligations to others, he has simply failed to do what virtue requires.

There is, I think, more to consider than consequences in acting as a virtuous agent would. Since there are many dimensions to a flourishing life, and virtues are manifested in desires not to kill, to save the lives of others, and to fulfill projects that one has prior commitments to, consequentialism fails to take into account all that is relevant in choosing between lives, whether it be by killing or by letting die.[29] But an approach to choices between killing and letting die, such as Quinn's, that ignores any comparison of the number of deaths resulting from each option, when the deaths are foreseen with certainty, is also one that leaves out something of obvious moral significance.

4   The Redundancy of DDA

My account recognizes the following moral difference between killing and letting die: In choosing between two courses of action only one of which can be successfully carried out, one a killing and the other a failure to prevent deadly harm, an ideally virtuous agent will be guided by a strong but defeasible aversion to killing. The mere fact that the consequences of killing are better, for instance, a smaller number of deaths, does not always lead the virtuous agent to a choice of killing. But given that she also has a desire to save lives, the smaller number of deaths can be a relevant consideration in favor of killing. It is possible that the virtuous agent may choose to kill to save a larger number of lives because a virtuous agent will be guided by both a disposition to avoid killing and a disposition to save lives (and other relevant dispositions).

It is, I believe, a fact about human beings that they lead better lives[30] by making rational choices as agents based on a set of dispositions that include an aversion to killing that is strong enough to justify a choice not to kill even when a larger (though not a lot larger) number of people could be saved by killing. It is in this sense that killing is worse than letting die, and not in the sense that killing exemplifies doing something to bring about harm whereas letting die exemplifies doing nothing to prevent harm. Where then does that leave the Doctrine of Doing and Allowing? We have already seen in the first section that in applying the DDA, the only way to preserve moral intuitions in the Rescue examples involves distorting what doing and allowing normally mean, which gives us a good reason to reject the DDA. Now, with an alternative basis to account for killing being worse than letting die, there is no good reason to accept such a doctrine.

Philosophical interest in DDA stems from an assumption that the moral distinction between killing and letting die is reflective of a moral distinction between the broader categories of doing and allowing, so that the best way to explain the former is in terms of the latter (McMahan 1993, 250).

What makes the assumption of a link between the two distinctions particularly attractive is the possibility of defining the categories of doing and
allowing in nonmoral terms. Philosophical work on DDA involves showing
that killing is impermissible because it involves doings that bring about
harm, whereas the same harm resulting from letting die may be permissible
as an instance of allowing a harm to occur. It is quite a stretch, however,
to show this, as the efforts of Foot, Quinn, and other philosophers have
demonstrated. Convinced that some form of the DDA is necessary to show
killing to be worse than letting die, they end up with complicated analyses
of what counts as doing and as allowing that are developed by considering
moral intuitions regarding cases of killing and letting die.[31]

But I would argue that, if we are going to rely on our moral intuitions
in fleshing out the DDA, the doctrine becomes redundant. Focusing instead
on what, concerning killing and letting die, virtuous agents would be
disposed to do has provided a basis for a moral distinction between killing
and letting die without appeal to the DDA. Since what the virtuous
agent actually chooses to do depends on how various dispositions of hers
balance out when she does her practical reasoning, there is room for her
to choose killing over letting die. Deontologists whose accounts make
killing always a worse choice than letting die[32] have to either deny our
intuitions, or make ad hoc moves such as allowing exceptions or redefining
doing, allowing, killing and letting die. The latter options end up compli-
cating the DDA with qualifying clauses, and this ultimately undermines
the doctrine's appeal. Should deontologists instead be willing to go against
our intuitions regarding the forced choices in the various examples of
choosing to kill or to let die? If they do this, they lose an advantage they
have over utilitarian consequentialists, who are often criticized for their
counterintuitive claims.

Virtue ethics has usually been attacked for its alleged lack of a decision-
making procedure for moral agents. It is claimed that we do not really
know what an ideally virtuous person would choose, and that practical
wisdom seems to be a matter of intuition instead of reason.[33] But not only
is it the case that the DDA has itself to be crafted with an eye on what
moral intuition says regarding the hard cases;[34] it is also the case that, if
accounts of the morality of killing and letting die are full of complexities,
then they would not amount to any useful decision-making guide that can
be applied without relying on intuition.[35] Thus, the criticism here of virtue
ethics applies also to the deontological accounts: it is simply not the case
that the DDA provides a basis for the moral distinction between killing
and letting die that can work without appeal to intuition.

In the account of moral decision making given by Rosalind Hurst-house,[36] virtue ethics fares no worse in providing guidance than deonto-logical rules and fares better than the oversimplified procedure of utilitarianism. It may in fact be objected that my account of the choice between killing and letting die has detracted from virtue ethics in two ways. First, Hursthouse asserts that there are irresolvable dilemmas where there are no moral grounds for favoring doing one action over another (Hursthouse 1999, 63). Should not the virtue ethicist treat many of the examples of choosing between killing and letting die as irresolvable dilem-mas? Second, Hursthouse eschews the ranking of virtues (ibid., 56). Now, I do not make any claim about the possibility in general of ranking all virtues such that any conflict between what different virtues require can be resolved. However, I do think that my comparison of Jimmy and James shows that doing away with the virtue consisting of a strong aversion against killing human beings does more damage to a person's character than doing away with the virtue of a strong desire to save the lives of human beings. Since it is too big a project to specify the whole of human good, this is the only ranking of virtues that I envisage in this essay. And returning to the first objection, it is because the virtues in question are the two that I have ranked that the dilemmas in the examples in this essay are resolvable. I do not need to claim that all dilemmas are resolvable.[37] Even the "resolution" that I propose here retains the qualities of ethical thinking found in virtue ethics, lacking the precise boundaries between the permis-sible and the impermissible associated with either consequentialism or the deontological application of the DDA, since I do not think it can be speci-fied in advance how many more people must it be that one can save before one is justified in killing one person.

Another criticism of my virtue approach that may arise is that the moral distinction between killing and letting die should be concerned with action, not with the agent. The distinction is meant to help us decide what to do, not what kind of person to be. Would not the requirement that agents choose on the basis of the right dispositions be overly demanding, compared to simply deciding that one should not do an action given that it is a killing? What the DDA does is to explain why, as a killing, the action should not be done. Did I change the subject when I rejected the DDA in favor of an explanation in terms of what a virtuous agent is disposed to do? I do not think so. The account of the dispositions of an ideal agent provides the *moral criterion* for the rightness of choosing letting die over killing, when the numbers do not justify killing. But an agent may make the actual choice of action without having the right balance of dispositions. In the examples we have considered, one can intuitively tell what the right thing to do is, and if one cannot so tell, one can follow someone who can. On the other hand, a moral criterion is introduced at a level of thinking in which concern with the agent's dispositions and character is not inappropriate. The moral criterion provides the explanation and justification for the right choice, showing that the use of intuition is not subjective. It is possible to be wrong in one's intuition. But by and large, we have reasonably good intuitions about the examples we have discussed, so much so that, as we saw earlier, if one relies on the DDA, one would have to adjust what one means by doing and allowing to ensure that the doctrine has intuitive results in its application. If my approach is less ad hoc and more consistent with moral intuition than the DDA, then it is the better account. And I believe that it is more reflective of intuition, given that it stakes out the middle ground between the less intuitive alternatives of always choosing letting die over killing, and always choosing by the number of lives.

5 Summing Up

In the Rescue examples, the moral difference between killing and letting die seems to rest on extrinsic considerations,[38] rather than on the mere fact that one is a doing and the other an omission. Quinn and Foot see the rationale for DDA in terms of the precedence of negative rights and the duty not to cause harm by intervention, over positive rights and the duty to provide aid. But the Rescue examples, since they rely also on assumptions about the foreseeability of harm, fail to show that killing is always worse than letting die. Moreover, Quinn has to stretch the meaning of positive agency to preserve intuitions about the examples. Consequentialists, on the other hand, play down the moral significance of the killing/letting die distinction by weighing the choice between killing and letting die only in terms of the number of people affected.

From the nonconsequentialist perspective of virtue ethics, the disposition to avoid killing seems more important in the character of a virtuous agent than the disposition to save others from death. I have sketched an approach that suggests how a virtuous agent is one who may choose to let the greater number of people die in circumstances where the consequentialist would choose otherwise. And since I have provided an account of the moral distinction between killing and letting die in terms of the dispositions or attitudes of a virtuous agent toward killing and letting die, my approach effectively renders the DDA redundant and avoids the convoluted attempts to redefine doing and allowing so as to preserve moral intuitions regarding the examples we have considered in this essay.

Acknowledgments

I wish to thank the two anonymous referees of this volume for their comments and suggestions, and the editors for their work on the volume. Thanks are also due to Harry Silverstein for his comments on my essay at the Inland Northwest Pacific Conference, James Sage who read the essay at the INPC on my behalf, and Lori Alward, who was commentator at the 2002 APA meeting in Philadelphia at which I had presented an earlier version of this essay.

Notes

1. See Quinn 1993. This was originally published in 1989 in the *Philosophical Review* 98: 287–312.

2. See Foot 1978, 1984, 1985.

3. Consequentialism, a broader category than utilitarianism, comprises those ethical theories that specify an action to be right insofar as it promotes the best consequences (however defined), and wrong insofar as it does not. Nonconsequentialists are not precluded from taking consequences into account, but do not make them the only criterion of right and wrong. In this essay, "consequentialism" refers to the set of views that deny any moral difference between killing and letting die that is not a matter of a difference in consequences, and "nonconsequentialism" refers to the set of views that suggest other considerations such as moral duties and rights, and virtues, may make a moral difference.

4. This is not to deny that someone may be subject to moral criticism for failing to be aware of her ability to prevent harm, or for indecisiveness, or for weakness of will. But this is a different moral failure from that of being an agent of harm.

5. The Trolley Problem is the subject of many articles on killing and letting die, in particular Thomson 1986a,b, but as Thomson acknowledged, Foot devised the first version of the example in Foot 1978, 23.

6. Scheffler (2004) suggests that distinctions such as that between doing and allowing, acts and omissions, and positive and negative agency are alternative formulations of the distinction between primary and secondary manifestations of individual agency, and that "in general, the norms of individual responsibility attach much greater weight to the primary than to the secondary manifestations" (216).

7. Quinn goes on to expand the definition of "harmful positive agency," saying that "where harm comes from an active object or force, an agent may by inaction contribute to the harmful action of the object itself" (1993, 163).

8. Fischer and Ravizza (1992) produce a counterexample to undermine the restricted transfer principle, while Rickless (1997) rejects the counterexample but produces another counterexample to Quinn's DDA.

9. An anonymous referee has suggested that 'positive agency' and 'negative agency' are technical terms used in an explanation of ordinary judgments and it is not an objection to Quinn that his use of the terms is unintuitive. But does that leave Quinn free to say whatever he likes about them, and how do we decide whether Quinn or Fischer and Ravizza have given the right account of positive and negative agency? In fact, Quinn's use of the terms is guided by intuitions: the moral kind that he draws from his examples. In my view, it is more appropriate for him to be guided by nonmoral intuitions about the difference between doing and allowing, given that the DDA is couched in those terms and serves to explain our moral intuitions.

10. If the agent knows and is certain that an effect will result from his action, and he took this into consideration in making his choice, it is not intuitive to say that he does not intend to bring about the effect. This is the criterion of closeness suggested by Foot (1978), 21–22.

11. Isaacs (1995, 362) has made a similar criticism of Jeff McMahan's (1993) distinction between killing and letting die.

12. Quinn (1993, 166) briefly discusses the Trolley examples.

13. The attempt by an anonymous referee to invent a test case where the survival of the five is solely determined by whether the rescuer gets to help them (and nothing else) only illustrates how difficult the assumption is. It is suggested that the five are clearly visible across a short bridge and only need some breathing equipment that has to be transported by the train. But will the breathing equipment work? Will the train make it across the bridge? The only way to make the situation of the five comparable to that of the person tied to the track is to imagine that they would be saved the instant the train runs over the one on the track and not otherwise. In that regard, the Trolley examples seem to provide better test cases than Quinn's examples, as my discussion below demonstrates.

14. Peter Singer has made a similar point using a railroad example, about how the difference in proximity of victims affects moral choice regarding famine relief in faraway places. Certainly, our responsibility for saving lives is conditioned by our effectiveness at doing so, and the possibility of others intervening. Both of the latter are affected by spatial and temporal distance.

15. This example originates from Quinn (1993, 160) and was used by Quinn to criticize Foot's version of DDA. Quinn surprisingly thinks that it is justified to abandon the neighbor to save the five.

16. Rickless (1997, 559) argues that there is a special obligation here that arises not from a promise but from an unspoken understanding.

17. These and the Trolley examples are notoriously difficult to get a grip on, and there will be those who do not share the intuitions that I appeal to here. The only thing one can do is to produce further examples to show what someone with different intuitions would be committed to, and who may thereby be led to change her views. In this essay, I limit myself to persuading those who do agree with the intuitions elicited by Quinn's examples, to show that the basis of those intuitions is not found in his account of positive and negative agency but the factors I have identified here.

18. Another way to avoid the consequentialist position is to defend the moral relevance of numbers *without recourse to consequentialist reasoning*, which is the subject of a debate engaged in by those responding to John Taurek's seminal (1977) paper. A good discussion is found in Wasserman and Strudler 2003. I shall not directly engage in this debate, although my nonconsequentialist approach in this essay allows me to say *both* that killing is worse than letting die and that the number of lives is morally relevant.

19. Harry Silverstein correctly drew my attention to the importance of not leaving the reader with the impression that consequentialism is the view to fall back on when faced with the difficulties of making nonconsequentialism work.

20. An anonymous referee has pointed out that the difficulty in choosing to kill may be psychological. It probably is, but is it merely psychological? The way for me to make a case that there is a moral reason at work is to provide an account of what this reason is and why it has the psychological force that it does.

21. Quinn 1993, 167–168; Foot 1978, 27–28.

22. Perhaps, as an anonymous referee suggests, there can be a kind of deontologist who is not an absolutist but who weighs rights against each other. But is such weighing of rights consistent with respect for persons? And if the right of one not to be killed can be outweighed by the (lesser) right of many others to be saved, is deontological ethics very different from consequentialism? Wouldn't such a deontologist have to reject the DDA?

23. Rickless (1997, fn. 4) shows awareness of this problem when he makes the qualification that "it is not clear that Foot's theory entails that you must choose B [allowing harm] over A [initiating harm] when the number of individuals who will suffer harm as a result of B is *astronomically* greater than the number of individuals who will suffer harm as a result of A." Why should astronomically greater numbers

make a difference if large numbers do not, and why can the duty not to kill be overridden by consideration of the numbers of people harmed if negative rights always take precedence?

24. Scheffler 2004, 239. On p. 217, he suggests that the project of formulating a precise distinction has "proven fiendishly complex" and perhaps "there is more than one such distinction that plays an important role in our moral thought."

25. These accounts include Thomson's, which differs from Quinn's and Foot's, and which I haven't discussed here. The "victim-focused" account in Kamm 1989 would make for interesting discussion that I do not have space for here. On her Principle of (Im)Permissible Harm (p. 232), "if an event [such as turning the trolley] is more intimately causally related to the harm than to the good," then achieving the greater good in this way is morally problematic. I would argue that the relevance of "degree of causal intimacy" to what is permissible in the Rescue and Trolley examples reflects how the likelihood of the harm or good occurring affects our intuitions, thus reinforcing my point in the previous section.

26. Williams's paper and the point he makes about integrity has been criticized by those who think that his position represents a narcissistic concern with the agent's own moral purity. But Williams does not actually endorse the position that Jim should not kill the one Indian to save the remaining nineteen. I do not use the example here to make any point about the DDA, but rather to draw on the idea that a person's commitment to projects contributes to her flourishing human life, which I develop in the rest of this section. On this point, it should be noted that such projects do not have to be narcissistic but could reflect compassion and a concern for the lives and well-being of others for their own sake. Thanks to Harry Silverstein for motivating me to add this note of clarification.

27. The Trolley examples use the magic figure of five persons being allowed to die compared to one person being killed. I think the consequentialist will choose to kill when the difference is much smaller, whereas the virtuous agent will not go as low.

28. The project may be a personal one (it's important to me that I am saving *my* neighbor), or an impersonal one (I am acting as a public-spirited citizen).

29. Consequentialists may take into consideration the strength of the agent's desire not to kill insofar as it is beneficial to society. But this desire is valued above a desire to save lives only because killing is considered worse than letting die on consequentialist grounds. If it is of greater benefit to save more lives by killing some, a desire not to kill will not be valued. On my account, the desire is valued for its own sake as an integral component of a virtuous character.

30. Although it is too much of a digression from the topic of this essay to go into details about what my account of virtue and character looks like, the reader

may recognize that my approach is largely Aristotelian. Thus, a better life is one that is closer to achieving the good that is the natural ideal for humans, and the virtues are dispositions that motivate human choice and action in the ideal human agent.

31. In some cases (e.g., McMahan 1993, 267), the complexities are carried over to the accounts given of what counts as killing and as letting die.

32. An anonymous referee has drawn my attention to the deontological position of Malm (1989), who argues that in simple conflict examples involving one situation and one agent, killing can be worse than letting die without appeal to the DDA. What makes killing worse in such situations is that it involves changing who lives and who dies, while the act of letting die does not (245), and this violates the duty to respect persons and not treat them as objects (249). But Malm's approach is not able to save the intuition that one may choose to kill one person to save a large (enough) number of persons who would otherwise be let die. (She focuses only on a case of interchanging one person for another, but it would equally violate the duty to respect persons to interchange one person for many others.) I do not therefore think that there is a deontological alternative to my account that stakes out the middle position that I set out in this essay.

33. This, I believe, is a false dichotomy as it assumes that choosing by intuition does not involve reason.

34. Kamm (1989, 227) is explicit in stating, "my aim is to find a principle which accounts for what I take to be 'common-sense' moral intuitions."

35. As McMahan (1993, 276) writes, "there are instances in which we intuitively discern an important moral difference between cases but are unable to determine what the difference is." Such cases provide support for Aristotle's view that ethics is uncodifiable.

36. Hursthouse 1999, part I. On pp. 53–54, Hursthouse makes the point I just made that deontological ethics is like virtue ethics in requiring the exercise of judgment or intuition.

37. Some may well be resolvable by rankings of virtues that I have not argued for, or by other means such as those explored by Hursthouse. Others may remain irresolvable. Hursthouse's example of an irresolvable dilemma seems to involve conflicting actions that are specifications of the *same* virtue, which cannot be resolved by ranking virtues.

38. These are what Frances Kamm (1983) calls contextual (as opposed to definitional) factors. These are factors that should be held equal in constructing "standard" comparable cases of killing and letting die. Yet Kamm in her list of factors that need equalizing (ibid., 298) does not take account of probability of foreseen harm. Interestingly, just as for the DDA, discussion of the Doctrine of Double Effect

similarly makes frequent use of cases for comparison that do not emphasize the importance of keeping the probability of harm constant, as I have pointed out elsewhere (Chan 2000, 408).

References

Chan, D. K. 2000. Intention and Responsibility in Double Effect Cases. *Ethical Theory and Moral Practice* 3:405–434.

Fischer, J. M., and M. Ravizza. 1992. Quinn on Doing and Allowing. *Philosophical Review* 101:343–352.

Foot, P. 1978. The Problem of Abortion and the Doctrine of the Double Effect. In *Virtues and Vices and Other Essays in Moral Philosophy*. Berkeley: University of California Press.

Foot, P. 1984. Killing and Letting Die. In *Abortion: Moral and Legal Perspectives*, ed. J. L. Garfield and P. Hennessey. Amherst: The University of Massachusetts Press.

Foot, P. 1985. Morality, Action, and Outcome. In *Morality and Objectivity*, ed. T. Honderich. London: Routledge & Kegan Paul.

Hursthouse, R. 1999. *On Virtue Ethics*. Oxford: Oxford University Press.

Isaacs, T. L. 1995. Moral Theory and Action Theory, Killing and Letting Die. *American Philosophical Quarterly* 32:355–368.

Kamm, F. 1983. Killing and Letting Die: Methodological and Substantive Issues. *Pacific Philosophical Quarterly* 64:297–312.

Kamm, F. 1989. Harming Some to Save Others. *Philosophical Studies* 57:227–260.

Malm, H. M. 1989. Killing, Letting Die, and Simple Conflicts. *Philosophy and Public Affairs* 18:238–258.

McMahan, J. 1993. Killing, Letting Die, and Withdrawing Aid. *Ethics* 103:250–279.

Quinn, W. 1993. Actions, Intentions, and Consequences: The Doctrine of Doing and Allowing. In *Morality and Action*. Cambridge: Cambridge University Press.

Rickless, S. C. 1997. The Doctrine of Doing and Allowing. *Philosophical Review* 106:555–575.

Scheffler, S. 2004. Doing and Allowing. *Ethics* 114:215–239.

Taurek, J. 1977. Should the Numbers Count? *Philosophy and Public Affairs* 6:293–316.

Thomson, J. J. 1986a. Killing, Letting Die, and the Trolley Problem. In *Rights, Restitution, and Risk*, ed. W. Parent. Cambridge, Mass.: Harvard University Press.

Thomson, J. J. 1986b. The Trolley Problem. In *Rights, Restitution, and Risk*, ed. W. Parent. Cambridge, Mass.: Harvard University Press.

Wasserman, D., and A. Strudler. 2003. Can a Nonconsequentialist Count Lives? *Philosophy and Public Affairs* 31:71–94.

Williams, B. 1973. A Critique of Utilitarianism. In J. J. C. Smart and B. Williams, *Utilitarianism: For and Against*. London: Cambridge University Press.

3 Killing John to Save Mary: A Defense of the Moral Distinction between Killing and Letting Die

Helen Frowe

1 Introduction

This essay considers Michael Tooley's argument that initiating a causal process is morally equivalent to refraining from interfering in that process. Tooley develops the Moral Symmetry Principle in order to show the moral irrelevance of whether a person causes, or merely allows, some outcome to occur. Tooley argues that the Moral Symmetry Principle is not vulnerable to the objection that it equates actions that are morally distinct. By distinguishing between preventative actions that interfere with another agent's action from preventative actions that do not, we can resist the inference that I am just as responsible for stopping you from initiating some causal process as I am for not initiating that process myself.

I argue that Tooley cannot offer any plausible ground for this allegedly significant notion of interfering in the actions of others such that it has sufficient force to overturn the objection of equating actions that are morally distinct. When it comes to preventing the initiating of causal process that will eventuate in serious harm, that one must interfere in another person's actions is not a morally salient feature. Even if Tooley were able to offer some rationale for this principle of noninterference, its inclusion substantially restricts the number of cases to which his Moral Symmetry Principle applies. It thus fails to serve any useful purpose as a principle of morality.

In addition to his more technical objection to the distinction between killing and letting die, Tooley advances a separate line of argument to undermine the idea that it matters, morally, whether we kill a person or let him die. Our conviction about the moral significance of this distinction is said by Tooley to be the result of distortion of our moral sense by the "external variables" that surround instances of killing, compared to those that typically surround instances of letting die.

I suggest that one of the most effective ways to support the relevance of the killing/letting die distinction in these "neutral" cases is by considering what each party can permissibly do in self-defense. Tooley's position, properly spelled out, would permit the use of lethal force against a bystander in order to induce that bystander to save one's life, even at the cost of another innocent person's life. This gives us further reason to reject the Moral Symmetry Principle.

2   Causing versus Failing to Interfere

The Moral Symmetry Principle

Michael Tooley argues that it makes no moral difference whether one initiates a causal process leading to an event E, or one merely fails to interfere in that same process to prevent E occurring. This, he claims, shows the absence of any morally significant distinction between killing and letting die. Tooley calls this the "Moral Symmetry Principle":

Let C be a causal process that normally leads to an outcome E. Let A be an action that initiates process C, and B be an action that stops process C before outcome E occurs. Assume further that actions A and B do not have any other morally significant consequences, and that E is the only part or outcome of C which is morally significant in itself. Then there is no moral difference between performing action A, and intentionally refraining from performing action B, assuming identical motivation in the two cases. (Tooley 1994, 104)

So, we have action A, which leads to outcome E. Doing A will cause E. The performance of action B will prevent E occurring. Intentionally not doing B will count as letting E occur.

Tooley illustrates the Moral Symmetry Principle using *Poisoned Whiskey*.

Poisoned Whiskey: Two brothers decide (independently of each other) to kill their wealthy father. The first brother poisons his father's whiskey. The second brother catches the first in the act. The second brother had been planning to poison the whiskey himself. Now he merely fails to warn his father that the whiskey has been poisoned, and also refrains from giving him an antidote to the poison.

Tooley claims "that the actions are morally equivalent, since . . . the moral symmetry principle . . . is sound" (Tooley 1994, 104).

So, we have a comparison between intentionally *initiating* a causal process leading to the father's death and intentionally *letting* the father's death occur. In the context of *Poisoned Whiskey*, Tooley's analysis seems fairly compelling. It is hard to pick out a moral distinction between the different actions of the two brothers. Tooley concludes that *Poisoned Whiskey* demonstrates the insignificance of the killing/letting die distinction.

The Traditional Objection

However, Tooley does acknowledge that there is a traditional objection to denying the significance of the killing/letting die distinction. The distinction might not seem to matter in *Poisoned Whiskey*. But there are many cases in which we *do* think it matters whether an agent kills or lets die. A universal acceptance of the Moral Symmetry Principle, therefore, will commit one to equating actions that are intuitively different.

An objection along these traditional lines tends to be illustrated by cases like *Enemy Torture*.

Enemy Torture: A captured spy refrains from divulging information to his enemy captor, despite the fact that the captor will torture a child as long as the spy says nothing. (Tooley 1994, 104–105)[1]

This seems relevantly analogous to *Poisoned Whiskey*. The second brother refrains from administering the antidote to his father, despite knowing that his father will be killed as long as he does nothing. The spy refrains from revealing his information, despite knowing that the child will be tortured as long as he says nothing. The antidote and the information are both ways of interfering to prevent some event occurring. Tooley equates the actions of the two brothers in *Poisoned Whiskey*. But we do not seem to want to equate the actions of the spy and his captor.

In anticipation of this sort of objection, Tooley offers the following clarification of the Moral Symmetry Principle. Properly understood, it will become clear of *Enemy Torture* that "this example is just not relevant to the moral symmetry principle" (Tooley 1994, 105). Tooley argues that

The moral symmetry principle states, very roughly, that it is as wrong intentionally to refrain from interfering with a causal process leading to some morally significant result as it is to initiate the process. It does *not* assert that it is as wrong to refrain from *preventing someone else* from initiating a causal process as it is to initiate it oneself. (Ibid.)

The Moral Symmetry Principle would fall prey to counterexamples like *Enemy Torture* only if it were committed to equating a failure to stop *others* from initiating a causal process with initiating the causal process oneself. And, Tooley claims, this is not something to which the Moral Symmetry Principle is committed.

It matters for Tooley, then, that in *Enemy Torture*, the spy fails to interfere to prevent the *captor* from *initiating* a causal process of torture. In

Poisoned Whiskey, however, the second brother fails to interfere in an *existing* causal process of poisoning. The idea seems to be that it is not as important to stop other people initiating causal processes as it is to stop existing causal processes (assuming that one is able to do so). So, the Moral Symmetry Principle equates failing to stop the existing process of poisoning with poisoning the whiskey. But it does not equate failing to prevent the *initiation* of the poisoning with poisoning the whiskey. Nor does it equate failing to prevent the captor from initiating the torture of the child with torturing the child oneself. The Moral Symmetry Principle, it seems, can resist the traditional objection to denying a moral difference between killing and letting die.

This is what Tooley's position looks like:

(1) Initiating the causal process

is equivalent to:

(2) Failing to interfere with the existing causal process.

But (1) is *not* equivalent to:

(3) Failing to prevent someone else from initiating the causal process.

But we need only tweak *Enemy Torture* very slightly to show the problem with this position. Imagine that in *Revised Enemy Torture* the captor is *already* torturing the child, and will not stop unless the spy divulges his information. Citing a lesser responsibility to interfere with the *initiation* of a causal process is not going to resolve the problem posed by *Revised Enemy Torture*. Divulging the information in this case no longer counts as interfering with the *initiation* of a process, but as interfering with an *existing* process. Not divulging information once the captor has begun torturing the child will still come out as equivalent to torturing the child oneself.

To try to solve this problem, we need to know why Tooley thinks there is a difference between failing to prevent the continuation of an existing causal process and failing to prevent the initiation of that process. Tooley suggests that there is a prima facie reason not to equate these two actions:

the intuitive feeling of most people would surely be that the mere fact that when one prevents someone else from doing something one is interfering with someone's action, whereas when one merely refrains from doing something oneself one is not, is a morally relevant difference. Thus there is a prima facie reason against any extension of the moral symmetry principle that would have the consequence that intentionally refraining from preventing someone else from doing something is morally equivalent to doing it oneself. (Ibid.)

So, whether one fails to prevent the continuation or the initiation of a process is not in *itself* the important difference. This difference matters only because of some *further* fact about the initiation of causal processes. This further fact is that in order to prevent the initiation of a causal process one would have to interfere with another person's actions.

Tooley is surely right that we do not equate my failing to prevent your initiating a causal process with my having initiated a causal process myself. But can the Moral Symmetry Principle support this intuition?

Note that the point at which Tooley requires the second brother to act in *Poisoned Whiskey* is *after* the first brother's actions have stopped. Poisoning is a self-sustaining process. Once he has added the poison to the whiskey, the first brother need do nothing else to bring about his father's death. Stopping the process, then, will not require the second brother to interfere in anyone else's actions. The second brother can either warn his father that the whiskey has been poisoned, or administer the antidote once the poison has been imbibed. He can do this without interfering with his brother's actions. His failure to do so, therefore, makes him as culpable as if he had added the poison himself.

The same is not true of *Revised Enemy Torture*. Torturing the child may well involve continued action on the part of the captor.[2] The spy, we can imagine, would have to stop the captor from *doing* something. But the first brother in *Poisoned Whiskey* is no longer doing anything with which the second would have to interfere if he is to stop his father's death. This, Tooley suggests, gives us a reason not to equate these actions. But is this a sufficient difference to mark out a moral distinction between a failure to interfere in *Poisoned Whiskey* and a failure to interfere in *Revised Enemy Torture*?

Interfering with Other People's Actions

Why would the fact that a particular part of a causal process involves another person's actions make a moral difference to our obligation to interfere with that process? How is Tooley going to motivate this principle? In an earlier paper, Tooley's formulation of the Moral Symmetry Principle specifies that interference in an existing causal process should involve only "a minimal expenditure of energy" (Tooley 1972, 58). And interfering with other people's actions does tend to involve a greater expenditure of energy than not doing so. However, this caveat is notably absent from the version of the principle that Tooley offers in the later article that I am discussing here. I think we should look at why this clause has been removed.

If Tooley specifies that refraining from saving is equivalent to killing only if saving would require very little effort on the part on the agent, this is going to substantially restrict the number of situations to which his principle can apply. And as the principle applies to fewer and fewer cases, we can ask legitimate questions about its plausibility.[3] Why, if we can posit a morally significant distinction in so many other cases, would we deny the distinction's relevance in these limited cases to which Tooley's principle can apply?

We might also wonder why one would be permitted to allow a causal process if preventing it would require a large expenditure of energy. We don't generally think that it would be permissible for me to *cause* harm if not doing so would require that I expend great energy. To suggest that it is morally better to allow harm in cases of large effort rather than to allow harm in cases of minimal effort, when the same is not true of causing harm, seems to undermine, rather than affirm, the asymmetry that Tooley is trying to establish.

I suspect that this is why Tooley has removed the clause about minimal expenditure of energy. It is hard to see how one could support this claim without reference to the difference between the things we do and the things we allow. And we generally want our moral principles to be wide in scope, not restricted to carefully specified cases. If Tooley wishes to maintain that interference in other people's actions really is a morally relevant difference, he will need some rationale other than energy expenditure that will generalize more easily.

The only other candidate for this rationale seems to be something like a principle about interfering with other people's autonomy. But we do not generally regard this as a reason to stop a person from doing something very wrong. Whatever reasons the spy might have for failing to prevent the captor from torturing the child, a reluctance to interfere with the captor's autonomy should not be one of them. It just doesn't seem to matter when we think about whether we ought to interfere in some very wrongful causal process (like torture) that doing so will involve interfering in the autonomy of an agent who is acting wrongly.[4]

Sustaining Causal Processes

So I'm not sure how Tooley can ground this intuition about the significance of interfering in other people's actions such that it can do the work that he needs it to in supporting the Moral Symmetry Principle. But let's look at what happens even if we grant Tooley the importance of this principle.

Assume, as Tooley does, that all cases of interfering with the initiation of a causal process will involve interfering with someone else's actions. This seems pretty plausible—after all, the point is that someone else is *causing* the process. Tooley suggests a distinction between a case in which one has to interfere with someone else's actions, and a case in which one does not. But what happens when we consider cases where not only the *causing* but also the *sustaining* of a causal process involves someone else's actions? Can Tooley plausibly draw a further distinction between self-sustaining processes like poisoning and processes that essentially require the continued action of another agent?

Compare the following two causal processes, one of which requires sustained action on the behalf of the initiator, and one of which does not.

Pram

(A)   Anna intentionally pushes a baby's pram, which then freewheels down a hill where it will land in a lake if not stopped. Betty watches, and does nothing.

(B)   Anna intentionally pushes a baby's pram across a flat park. Anna will push the pram into a lake if not stopped. Betty watches, and does nothing.

In (A), no sustained action is required on Anna's behalf. In (B), however, the causal process essentially requires sustained action to bring about the same result. But surely it cannot be the case that it is morally better for Betty to stand idly by in (B) than in (A)? It seems to me that Betty's actions in both cases are on a moral par. Doing nothing is (A) is equal to doing nothing in (B).

Yet if Tooley were to add a clause about interfering with an agent's action, he would be committed to drawing a moral distinction between Betty's noninterference in (A) where the pram is freewheeling, and Betty's noninterference in (B) where the pram is actively pushed. In addition, in (A) Tooley will have to equate idle Betty, who does nothing, with Anna, who deliberately causes the pram to freewheel down the hill. But in (B) he cannot equate idle Betty with Anna who deliberately pushes the pram across the park. Betty's inaction in (B) will somehow have to be morally better than her inaction in (A).

Not only does this asymmetry seem unintuitive to me as an advocate of the distinction between killing and letting die; it also seems that it would be unappealing to a critic of the distinction. Why would someone who sees no difference between letting a person die and killing a person want to draw such a fine-grained distinction as that between inaction when a pram is deliberately freewheeled into a lake, and inaction when a pram is deliberately pushed into a lake?

Even if Tooley could offer some kind of rationale for this principle, it would be another step altogether to make it appealing. If "the mere fact that when one prevents someone else from doing something one is interfering with someone's action . . . is morally relevant," it should be relevant in cases like *Pram*. And if it isn't, we need some explanation of *why* it isn't.

3   Reconstructing the Moral Symmetry Principle

So where is all this going? To remind ourselves: Tooley's conception of events looked like this:

(1) Initiating the causal process

was equivalent to:

(2) Failing to interfere with the existing causal process.

But (1) was *not* equivalent to:

(3) Failing to prevent someone else initiating the causal process.

But Tooley's attempt to distinguish (2) and (3) via "interference in another agent's actions" has proved unsuccessful. It seems that (2) is equivalent to (3) after all, on Tooley's account. But of course, if (1) is equivalent to (2), and (2) is equivalent to (3), (1) must also be equivalent to (3). So,

(1) Initiating the causal process

is equivalent to

(3) Failing to prevent someone else initiating the causal process.

What follows from equating a failure to prevent someone else from, for example, poisoning the whiskey with poisoning the whiskey oneself? Why does Tooley want to resist this identity? Well, if (1) and (3) are equivalent, then the converse should similarly correspond.

(1*) Not initiating the process of poisoning the whiskey

is equivalent to

(2*) Preventing someone else from initiating the process of poisoning the whiskey.

If there is a moral obligation not to poison people, and this obligation is morally equivalent to an obligation to prevent *other people* from poisoning people, it looks very much as if I have just as stringent a duty to stop other people carrying out poisonings as I have not to carry out poisonings myself.

This is not a position that Tooley wants to endorse. Being just as responsible for the things that other people do as we are for the things we do ourselves is not an attractive view, and it certainly is not a view for which Tooley has argued.

Tooley does acknowledge that if the Moral Symmetry Principle could not distinguish between (1) initiating a process oneself, and (3) failing to prevent someone else initiating that process, then this kind of agent-neutrality would indeed be implied by his view. Of his use of the prima facie importance of interfering in another's actions, he says the following:

> I certainly do not wish to assert that this prima facie case cannot be overcome. However, any argument that succeeded in overthrowing it would ipso facto give one reason to reject the contention that it is "monstrous" to treat actions [of the spy and the captor] as morally equivalent. (Tooley 1994, 105)

This seems plainly false. If one refutes the importance of interfering in another's actions, one is still left with the intuition that it is implausible to equate the actions of the spy and his captor. And the only remaining salient difference between these two actions seems to be that one constitutes torturing the child, and one constitutes allowing the child to be tortured. Showing that there is no difference between cases that require interference with another's actions, and those that do not require such interference, simply invites us to revert back to the original intuition that the actions of the captor are worse than those of the captor because the captor causes the torturing of the child. Given a choice between this and the agent-neutrality that is the conclusion of Tooley's Moral Symmetry Principle, there seems no reason at all to opt for the latter.

4 External Variables

Tooley also defends the Moral Symmetry Principle by adopting a strategy of argument similar to that employed by James Rachels his seminal paper "Active and Passive Euthanasia" (Rachels 1994). Rachels offers a variety of cases that purport to show the irrelevance of the killing/letting distinction. Both Tooley and Rachels argue that properly considered, it will become apparent that those who defend the killing/letting die distinction have confused the wrongness of external factors, like motivation, with the comparative wrongness of killing and letting die themselves. These external factors might make cases of killing *appear* to be worse than cases of letting die. But we should not take this appearance to show a more fundamental distinction between the two.

Tooley's Machine Case

Tooley claims that we ought to consider the following two questions:

(1) Is the distinction between killing and intentionally letting die morally significant *in itself*?

(2) Are there *other factors* that make it *generally* the case that killing someone is more seriously wrong than intentionally letting die?

The answer to the second question is surely yes. In the first place, the motive of a person who kills someone is generally more evil than the motive of a person who merely lets someone die . . . the alternative to letting someone die—saving his life— may involve considerable risk to the agent, or a very large expenditure of society's resources. . . .While one merely refrains from saving someone's life, there is often a substantial chance that she will survive in some other way. . . . It is these factors that make the difference, rather than the difference between killing and letting die. (Tooley 1994, 107)

Tooley gives the following "neutral" example in which all external variables are held constant between a case of letting die and a case of killing. We will call this *Machine*.

Machine: Two children, John and Mary, are trapped inside a machine, each in separate chambers. Above Mary is a canister of lethal gas, which will soon be released into her chamber. However, by pushing a button, Passerby can alter the machine so that the canister switches to John's chamber.[5]

Tooley describes the position as follows.

If one pushes a button, John will be killed, but Mary will emerge unharmed. If one does not push the button, John will emerge unharmed, but Mary will be killed. In the first case one kills John, while in the second case one merely lets Mary die. Does one really wish to say that the action of intentionally refraining from pushing the button is morally preferable to pushing it, even though exactly one person perishes in either case? The best action, it seems to me, would be to flip a coin to decide which action to perform, thus giving each person an equal chance of surviving. But if that isn't possible, it seems to me a matter of indifference whether one pushes the button or not. (Ibid., 108)

His claims about *Machine* suggest that Tooley thinks it permissible to redirect a harm onto an innocent person in order to save another innocent person who will otherwise be similarly harmed. But the fact that John has physical proximity to Mary doesn't seem like a good enough reason to allow Passerby to kill him to save Mary's life. By putting John in the machine, Tooley's example implies that John is somehow involved in the lethal sequence of events that threaten Mary's life. This might suggest to us that it is not unfair to include John in our moral equation. We are permitted to weigh Mary's interests against John's, since both are in this terrible predicament, in which only one can survive.

But John is *not* part of the lethal sequence of events that will cause Mary's death. As things stand, the gas canister poses a threat to Mary's life, and to her life alone. John's physical proximity to Mary does not somehow make him a legitimate alternative target, whom we can kill in the process of eliminating the risk of harm to Mary.

Harm, and Risks of Harm

To see the problem with Tooley's argument, we need to consider the distinction between being able to avoid *a harm*, and being able to avoid being *at risk* of that harm. According to Tooley, we can permissibly reduce the risk to Mary by transferring some of that risk to John. We ought to toss a coin to decide whether or not to press the button. But there is a difference between randomizing a harm between John and Mary when *both* Mary *and* John are at risk of harm, and randomizing a harm when only Mary is at risk.[6]

Compare *Disease* with *Diseased Mary*:

Disease: John and Mary both have a fatal disease. There is only one dose of antidote. Neither John nor Mary has any prior claim upon the antidote. A third party must decide who gets the antidote.

Diseased Mary: Mary has a fatal disease. She can save herself only by manufacturing a particular gas. The fumes from the gas will kill healthy John, who is in the next room.[7]

In *Disease*, one ought to toss a coin to see who gets the last dose of antidote. In this case, randomizing seems appropriate. But in *Diseased Mary*, one should not toss a coin to see whether Mary can permissibly infect John. This is true despite the fact that tossing the coin in *Diseased Mary* would give the children an equal chance of survival.

One way that we can explain the difference between *Disease* and *Diseased Mary* is by thinking about the courses of action that we could justify to John. In *Disease* it is reasonable to think that both John and Mary would agree to a third party's tossing the coin, because they both have an interest in getting the antidote. It also seems reasonable that they would prefer that the choice be made fairly, if they have no indication of how the third party would otherwise choose. At least tossing the coin gives each child a fifty–fifty chance of getting the antidote.

But in *Diseased Mary* John has no reason to agree to a third party's tossing the coin to decide whether Mary can manufacture the gas. He can gain no benefit from the randomization, but might suffer a very grave harm. We might sometimes require a person to suffer a lesser harm in order that some innocent person be saved from a greater harm. But in *Diseased Mary*, the harm that will be suffered by John should he lose the toss is equal to the harm that is currently directed at Mary. It seems to me that it would be wrong in *Diseased Mary* to force John to take on a risk of great harm when he can derive no benefit from that risk.

Machine seems much more closely analogous to *Diseased Mary* than to *Disease*. In both cases, Mary defends herself against a threat to her life in a way that kills John. Of course, in *Diseased Mary*, Mary introduces a new harm that kills John. In *Machine*, Mary redirects an existing harm. But I do not see how this difference could account for different permissions in the two cases. And we can easily tweak *Machine* so that there are separate canisters of gas above each child. Say that the machine has only enough power to trigger one canister's release mechanism. So, if John's canister is triggered, Mary's cannot release its lethal gas. In this case, pressing the button to save Mary would introduce a new harm to John. But I doubt that Tooley, or any one else, would think this difference affects the permissibility of pressing the button.[8]

Permissible Redirecting

I have suggested that in *Machine*, pressing the button is impermissible since it redirects harm toward John, and John is not part of the lethal sequence of events that threatens Mary's life. For now, we will refer to people like John as bystanders, since this is how conventional morality would describe John.[9]

An objector to my claim that pressing the button is impermissible might argue that there are some cases in which it *would* be permissible to defend oneself against a threat to one's life by redirecting harm onto a bystander. Consider *Body Armor*:

Body Armor: Aggressor is shooting at Victim. Bystander is in the vicinity of Victim, and can protect herself by putting on protective clothing. Bystander refuses to put on the clothing, because protective clothing is unflattering. Victim can save himself only by deflecting a bullet toward Bystander.

I agree that it is permissible for Victim to intentionally deflect the bullet toward Bystander if this is the only way Victim can save his own life. The difference between *Machine* and *Body Armor* is that in *Body Armor*, Bystander not only has a chance to avoid harm, but a "prior" fair chance to avoid even being *at risk* of harm. If Bystander declines to take that chance, it is permissible for Victim to redirect harm toward Bystander in defense of his life.[10]

There are questions about what counts as a "fair chance" to avoid being at risk of harm. I am not going to attempt here to demarcate exactly what counts as fair, but rather suggest that there are some chances that are clearly fair, and some that are clearly not. I admit that there will be plenty of cases where it is hard to establish whether a person has had a fair chance: the scope of the gray area will be substantial. But there will also be cases on either side of the gray area where it is *not* controversial that a person either had, or did not have, a fair chance to avoid harm. If a person is informed of a likely risk of harm, and can take steps to avoid exposing herself to this risk at little cost to herself, this seems to count as her having had a fair chance to avoid being at risk of harm.

I am not suggesting that given that one can, for example, avoid traffic accidents by staying at home, all voluntary pedestrians can be viewed as having failed to avail themselves of fair chances to avoid being at risk of traffic accidents. The cost of never leaving the house is sufficiently great that we cannot regard those who decline this option as having declined a *fair* chance to avoid being at risk of harm.

We might also think that although traffic accidents are a risk, they are not, in many circumstances, a *likely* risk. It is sufficient to support my point that there are *some* occasions when people do have a fair chance to avoid harm and know the possible implications of not doing so. Their failure to avail themselves of such chances has implications for how others may treat them.

This difference in treatment can be justified by the fact that by voluntarily exposing themselves to a risk of harm, a bystander can place additional burdens on other agents. The presence of a bystander can reduce the morally permissible options that are open to a person who is under threat of some harm. If the bystander had no chance to avoid her position, however, it is impermissible to kill the bystander in the course of self-defense.[11]

But it seems wrong that a "willing" bystander—that is, one who could have avoided her position but did not, should be afforded the same immunity as a bystander who had no chance to avoid her position. We might still think that if in *Body Armor* Victim could deflect the bullet in a different direction, away from the willing Bystander, then Victim ought to do so. The willing Bystander still merits this much consideration. But if Victim can make the alternative deflection only at much greater risk to himself, I do not think that he is required to do this. Victim should not be required to bear a significantly greater burden than he would have had to bear had Bystander taken her fair chance of avoiding being at risk of harm.[12]

So, it seems to me that tossing the coin in *Machine* would be like tossing a coin to determine whether Mary can permissibly gas John in *Diseased Mary*. In both cases, John has no fair chance to avoid being at risk of harm, and no reason to agree to the randomizing of the harm. Tooley's suggestion of tossing a coin to even the odds is out of place here. One can permissibly kill only those bystanders who had a fair chance to avoid being *at risk* of harm. One cannot permissibly kill bystanders who have only a fair chance of avoiding the harm itself.

Even if pushing a button that will kill John is the only way that Mary can save her own life, it is impermissible for her to do so. And it cannot be permissible for Passerby to kill John on Mary's behalf if it is impermissible for Mary to kill John herself. If *she* cannot push a button to redirect a threat to her life toward a bystander, it cannot be that case that someone else can push it for her.

This, I think, casts some serious doubt on Tooley's claim that it is a matter of moral indifference whether or not I push the button. Redirecting a lethal threat toward an innocent bystander is never a matter of moral indifference. But it may not be obvious that a prohibition on killing bystanders supports a distinction between killing and letting die. We could have other reasons for believing in the wrongness of killing bystanders that do not rest upon the killing–letting die distinction. With this in mind, we turn to consider what John and Mary might be permitted to do in self-defense.

5   Reestablishing the Distinction

Self-defense

One of the most effective ways that we can show the relevance of the killing/letting die distinction to *Machine* is by thinking about what John and Mary can permissibly do in self-defense. Imagine that Passerby decides to push the button that will kill John. However, John, being a forward-thinking person, has a shotgun concealed about his person. Can John permissibly shoot Passerby, who poses a lethal threat to him, in order to prevent Passerby from pressing the button? It seems to me that he can.

Now consider whether it is permissible for Mary to use harmful means to force Passerby to *push* the button. Killing Passerby wouldn't do Mary much good. But shooting at Passerby's knee, with the threat of further attacks, might well induce Passerby to push the button. Is this use of force morally permissible?

If, on the one hand, we answer that Mary can use force against Passerby, in order to preserve the similarity between John and Mary, we are committed to the implausible claim that one may use seriously harmful means to force a person to come to one's aid at the cost of an innocent person's life.

If, on the other hand, we answer that Mary may not use such force, this supports a significant difference between killing and letting die. John is permitted to use potentially lethal force to defend himself against a person who is going to kill him, *even though* someone else (Mary) will die as a result. But Mary is *not* permitted to inflict even lesser harms against a person who intends to let her die, *especially* if someone else will die if she succeeds.[13]

Bear in mind that this claim does not commit us to the further claim that it is wrong in general for a person to threaten to harm someone who refuses to save him or her. It may even be permissible to exact some harm upon someone who is refusing to save your life when doing so will not involve his incurring some comparable cost. But that you may not do *as much* against someone who refuses to save you as you may do against someone who is going to kill you is sufficient to support the killing/letting die distinction.

Responsibility

We can further support the relevance of the killing/letting die distinction by envisaging *Revised Machine*.

Revised Machine: John and Mary are again in separate chambers, but now Passerby cannot see the gas canister. Thus, Passerby does not know at which chamber the canister is currently pointed. Passerby knows only that pushing the button will cause the canister to *switch* chambers.

So, Passerby has no idea whether pushing the button will kill John or kill Mary. The proviso against tossing a coin still holds in the revised case, and

I think that intuitions against pushing the button are perhaps clearer here than in the original *Machine* case.

Given that Passerby does not know which child will die either way, it seems better that he do nothing. For what he *does* know is that in pushing the button he will kill a child, whereas in not pushing the button he will let a child die. It seems implausible that one would opt for *causing* a child's death over *allowing* a child's death if one does not know which child will be killed. This is true despite the fact that in terms of the number of deaths that result, it makes no difference whether or not Passerby pushes the button, since one child will die either way.

Where it does make a difference whether or not Passerby presses the button is in terms of the responsibility that he will bear for a child's death. We can hold constant all the variables that Tooley cites as important, such as motivation and outcome, and still point to a difference between the case where Passerby kills John, and the case where he lets Mary die. If he kills John, Passerby breaches a more serious responsibility that he owes to John than he would breach if he were to let Mary die.

That killing John breaches a more serious responsibility than letting Mary die seems to stem from the fact that John would have survived had Passerby been absent. Whether some event would have occurred whether or not I had been present seems, at least prima facie, to bear on my responsibility for that event.[14] In Frances Kamm's words:

In dying, the [victim of letting die] loses only life he would have had via the agent's help. By contrast, the standard [victim of killing] . . . loses life he would have had independently of the killer. (Kamm 1996, 23)

I think that we can be more specific about the difference that Kamm highlights. If Passerby lets Mary die, Mary is no worse off for Passerby's presence than she would have been for his absence. Indeed, Mary has a possible lifeline only *because* of Passerby's presence. Thus, Passerby cannot be said to make Mary worse off by being there and failing to save her. But if Passerby were to kill John, John is undeniably worse off for Passerby's presence. Passerby would place John before a risk of harm that John would not otherwise face. But Passerby bears no such responsibility for the harm facing Mary. That Passerby has a more stringent duty not to cause harm to John than he does to save Mary from harm seems clear.

6 Conclusion

I have argued that Tooley's account of the moral symmetry between doing and allowing fails. Tooley's attempt to distinguish acts by reference to the importance of interfering with the actions of others does not succeed. Without this notion to distinguish between actions, Tooley will be committed to the implausible claim that I am as responsible for causal processes that you initiate as I am for causal processes that I initiate myself. This in turn leaves the Moral Symmetry Principle vulnerable to the traditional objection to denials of the doing/allowing distinction. The Moral Symmetry Principle will equate actions that seem morally different, like the actions of the spy and his captor.

I rejected Tooley's contention that there is no moral difference between letting Mary die and killing John in *Machine*. I argued that we must distinguish between bystanders who have a fair chance to avoid harm and bystanders who have a fair chance to avoid being *at risk* of harm. Only those bystanders who have a chance to avoid being at risk of harm are liable to be killed in self-preservation. Tossing a coin in *Machine* places John at risk of a harm that he had no opportunity to avoid.

I also argued that John is permitted to use lethal force against Passerby to prevent Passerby from pushing the button in *Machine*. But Mary is not permitted to use even nonlethal force to induce Passerby to push the button. Mary cannot permissibly harm a person who refuses to save her if saving Mary will involve the killing of John. That John is made worse off by Passerby if Passerby presses the button is also significant. Passerby does not make Mary worse off by his presence if he fails to save her. It is only *because* Passerby is present that Mary can be saved at all. The difference between what John can do to someone who will kill him, and what Mary can do to someone who will fail to save her, results from the moral worseness of killing John compared to letting Mary die.

Acknowledgments

I am particularly grateful to Brad Hooker, Russ Payne, and Andrew Williams for detailed comments on earlier drafts of this essay. I owe thanks to the two referees for helpful comments. Thanks also to Peter Cave, Adrian Moore, Charlie Pelling, Harry Silverstein, Philip Stratton-Lake, Galen Strawson, Jussi Suikkanen, and Mark Young for comments on an earlier draft of this essay.

Notes

1. We can assume that both the spy's country and his captor's country are pursuing morally similar aims.

2. Tooley can employ this distinction only if he has a broad nonphysical conception of what counts as interfering with a person's actions, such that the spy's revealing of his information counts as such an interference.

3. See Trammell 1976 for a discussion of the limiting nature of Tooley's qualifications of the Moral Symmetry Principle.

4. In fact, it might actually make us more likely to, say, lethally intervene to stop the captor if we knew that his torturing of the child proceeded from his agency. Compare this captor to Hypnotized Captor, who has been manipulated into torturing the child. That the torturing of the child does not proceed from Hypnotized Captor's autonomy might make us less inclined to use lethal force against him. So considered, the fact that the captor acts autonomously seems to give us additional reason to interfere in his actions. It certainly doesn't give us any reason to refrain from interfering.

5. I have fleshed out Tooley's example a little, in order to make it clearer. The original example states that pressing the button will kill John, and not pressing the button will be to let Mary die, but does not specify the method of gas canisters.

6. I take it to be the case that only Mary is at risk because, as things stand, the probability that Mary will be killed is 1 and the probability that John will be killed is 0.

7. Based on Philippa Foot's case in Foot 1994, 276.

8. Indeed, either version of the machine is compatible with Tooley's own description.

9. I say "for now" because I think that we ought to adopt a narrower definition of 'bystander' than that currently dictated by convention. Under this revised definition, John will not count as a bystander, but rather an innocent, indirect threat. However, the points I make here stand whether or not John qualifies as a bystander.

10. I count *Body Armor* as an example in which the bystander had a chance of avoiding being at risk of harm, since in putting on the armor the bystander would no longer have been at risk. This seems different from *Diseased Mary*. If a third party decides to toss a coin, John finds himself at risk of being harmed without having had a fair chance to avoid that risk. I argue that we cannot kill bystanders who had only the chance to avoid the harm—they must also have had the chance to avoid the risk.

11. An anonymous referee pointed out to me that anyone who thinks that Third Party can flip the switch in a trolley problem, such that the trolley kills one instead of two, will think that Third Party can do this even if the one has no chance to avoid being at risk of harm. I do not think that Third Party is permitted to flip the switch in this case, since I take the killing/letting die distinction pretty seriously. We are not permitted to kill one innocent person even if it will save two innocent

lives. There is insufficient scope here to expound my view on the trolley problem. But, briefly, those who think that flipping the switch is permissible might think about whether Third Party ought to flip the switch in a case of one versus one. If Third Party should not, this suggests that what is really going on in the two versus one case is a principle about numbers *overriding* principles about killing and letting die, and permissible redirection. It does not show that the killing/letting die distinction is irrelevant, or that redirection is generally permissible.

We might also compare what the two and one can do to Third Party in self-defense. It seems to me that it would be impermissible for the two to shoot Third Party to make his body fall on the switch, altering the course of the trolley toward the one. But it would *not* be impermissible for the one to shoot Third Party in self-defense if Third Party moves to flip the switch to alter the trolley's course so that it will kill the one. See section 5 below for more on this idea. Importantly, our intuitions in these cases seem to be radically altered if we add that the one saw the trolley approaching the two but wandered onto the alternative track anyway because it was quicker than using the bridge. Here, the one had a fair chance to avoid being at risk of harm, and has placed great burdens on those whom the trolley approaches. That it seems much clearer that in this case we can permissibly redirect the trolley away from the two toward the one supports my claim that there is a difference between chances to avoid harm and chances to avoid being at *risk* of harm.

12. There might be a case for claiming that a willing bystander as described in *Body Armor* is not really a bystander at all, on the grounds that she culpably reduced the potential victim's morally permissible options. But this adjustment will not affect my thesis here—it will still support the claim that we can kill Bystander only if she had a chance to avoid being at risk of harm (whether we call her a bystander or not).

13. Frances Kamm advances a similar line of argument against Warren Quinn in Kamm 1996, esp. 76–79, 101–104, although she does not explore it as fully as I do here.

14. I say "prima facie" because we could think of cases in which, say, you promise to shoot Victim unless I shoot Victim. That Victim would have died whether or not I had shot him does not seem to alter the fact that I am responsible for his death if I do shoot him. But these tricky cases of overdetermination are, I think, insufficient to undermine the general principle.

References

Foot, P. 1994. The Problem of Abortion and the Doctrine of Double Effect. In *Killing and Letting Die*, ed. A. Norcross and B. Steinbock. New York: Fordham University Press.

Kamm, F. 1996. *Rights, Duties, and Status*, vol. 2: *Morality, Mortality*. New York: Oxford University Press.

Rachels, J. 1994. Active and Passive Euthanasia. In *Killing and Letting Die*, ed. A. Norcross and B. Steinbock. New York: Fordham University Press.

Tooley, M. 1972. Abortion and Infanticide. *Philosophy and Public Affairs* 2:37–65.

Tooley, M. 1994. An Irrelevant Consideration: Killing versus Letting Die. In *Killing and Letting Die*, ed. A. Norcross and B. Steinbock. New York: Fordham University Press.

Trammell, R. 1976. Tooley's Moral Symmetry Principle. *Philosophy and Public Affairs* 5:305–313.

4 Making Up One's Mind

Randolph Clarke

Often, on the basis of practical reasoning, one makes up one's mind to do a certain thing. In so doing, one comes to have an intention to do that thing. As well, one often engages in theoretical reasoning and, on that basis, makes up one's mind how things stand in some matter, thereby coming to have a certain belief.

Making up one's mind in either of these types of case is sometimes called *deciding*: in the first type of case, *practical deciding* (Mele 2000, 82)[1] or *deciding-to-do* (O'Shaughnessy 1980, 297); in the latter, *cognitive* (Mele 2000, 82) or *doxastic* (Watson 2004b, 139) *deciding* or *deciding-that* (O'Shaughnessy 1980, 297). And both processes of reasoning leading to one's making up one's mind may fairly be called *deliberation* (cf. Audi 2001, 93). In both cases, there is some question or uncertainty in one's mind, and one seeks a resolution by engaging in the appropriate sort of reasoning. If one succeeds at what one is trying to do, one takes a stand, therein coming to have a certain psychological attitude on the basis of one's reasoning.

The acquired attitudes, too, are in important respects similar. Both intending and believing are a matter of being committed, in the first case to performing an action of a certain type, in the second to things' being a certain way. And both are "judgment-sensitive" attitudes, attitudes that, in a rational being, are responsive to that individual's assessments of reasons favoring or disfavoring these attitudes (Scanlon 1998, 20). Individuals may be subject to criticism for failures to follow certain norms in forming intentions and beliefs. And the relevant norms, in both cases, include norms of rationality as well as ethical norms.[2] In important respects, coming to have the attitudes one acquires when one makes up one's mind differs from coming to have a headache or becoming hungry.

Despite these similarities, there are important differences. An obvious one, already suggested, is that in standard cases, one makes up one's mind what to do on the basis of practical reasons, whereas one makes up one's mind how things stand on the basis of evidence or epistemic reasons.

Here I'll draw attention to what appear to be two further—and interrelated—differences, one phenomenological, the other conceptual. These apparent differences underwrite the widespread view that there is a fundamental dissimilarity with respect to our agency in the two kinds of case. I examine these differences in the first section below and set out a prima facie case for dissimilarity.

In the final two sections, I address two alternative views on which making up one's mind what to do and making up one's mind how things stand are on a par with respect to our agency. On one of these views, although one may in either case actively try to decide, in both cases the culmination of any such effort—the final making up of one's mind—is essentially inactive; on the other view, the culminating event is active in both cases, and in the same sense. Defusing the arguments offered for these views supports the position that these two forms of making up one's mind are, as regards our agency, fundamentally dissimilar.

I won't have much to say here about *why* practical deciding and cognitive deciding differ with respect to our agency. It's easy enough to say that the answer has something to do with the kinds of reasons for which one may intend, on the one hand, and believe, on the other; but it's far from easy—and something I'm not sure anyone has succeeded in doing—to fully explain this difference. My aim here is more modest. There is a prima facie difference between these two kinds of case of making up one's mind; I aim to exhibit this apparent difference and rebut two denials of its reality.

1   Intentional Control

Consider a typical episode in which you're unsure how things stand in some matter, you conduct an inquiry with the goal of making up your mind, and on the basis of reasoning you come to have a firm belief about how things stand. Suppose, for example, that you've long been puzzled about what moved the jurors to acquit O.J., and you want now to settle the question. Was it their standing distrust of the police, the botched exhibition of the gloves, Fuhrman's racism, or Cochran's wit? You review accounts of the trial, read subsequent interviews with the jurors, discuss the matter with friends, and settle on a view, becoming fully convinced, say, that Cochran's closing argument was the decisive factor.

At various stages of this process, you're active in the fullest sense: you seek out and collect written accounts, attend to what you read, focus on how it bears on your question, raise the matter and discuss it with friends, and so forth. These portions of the process *seem* to you to be fully active; their phenomenology is that of agency. The appearance of the culminating event—that of coming to fully believe that it was Cochran's close—is otherwise. Your agential control, your active guidance of what you're doing, doesn't seem to extend through the occurrence of this event. You act, trying to make up your mind, trying to settle on a view, and then the conviction comes. It comes rationally, of course—it's based on the epistemic reasons you've found in your enquiry—but it doesn't appear to you that you actively form it. It seems to be a product of "the natural causality of reason" (Strawson 2003, 232), unlike a headache or a feeling of hunger, but also unlike an ordinary action such as raising your arm. At least, that is the way episodes of this sort typically seem to me.

Consider, in contrast, a case of making up your mind what to do. You wonder, for example, whether to buy a new car later this year. You consider the age of your current car, the cost of the needed repairs, your resources, how much better the new car would be, and so on, and you make your decision, say, to buy. Again, various earlier stages of the deliberative process seem to you to be fully active, as you focus on the practical question, seek relevant facts, and think about how these facts bear on your question. In a typical case of this sort, however, you may well feel as though your agency covers the process through to the end, that you directly control the formation of the intention to buy this year, that the guidance you exercise in this process includes your active authorship of this specific intention. At least, that is the way such episodes often seem to me.

The distinctive phenomenology of agency has been characterized in various ways. When you act, it's said, typically there's something of what you do that seems to you as if you're directly making it occur, producing it, determining it (Ginet 1990, 13). It seems to you that you, *qua* agent, generate your doing (Horgan, Tienson, and Graham 2003, 329). You're aware of your doing as your own, and aware, when you act, that you're trying to do something (Peacocke 2003, 98). I've characterized the appearance as its seeming to you that you're guiding or actively controlling what you're doing in some degree of specificity; in the case of practical deciding, that control includes actively forming the specific intention that is acquired.

I don't wish to rest much weight on any particular description of the phenomenology of agency. It should suffice for my purposes to remind you of it. You know it from your own case, and I trust that, reflecting on what you know, you'll agree that a practical decision of the sort I've described typically has this characteristic appearance, whereas the kind of cognitive decision I've described lacks it.

Together with this phenomenological difference, there is, apparently, a conceptual one. As you try to make up your mind about what moved the O.J. jurors, many of the things you do, you do intentionally. You intentionally try to think where you can find pertinent information, intentionally collect the information, and intentionally attend to it. You might even be said to intentionally make up your mind in the matter. But you don't intentionally make up your mind that it was Cochran's close. Coming to have that particular conviction, with that specific content, is not something that you intentionally do.

In contrast, you intentionally decide to buy a car this year. Again, earlier stages of the deliberative process involve intentional actions. You intentionally focus attention on the question, intentionally seek relevant facts, and so on. And you intentionally make up your mind. But there is this further fact: that you intentionally make up your mind to buy the car. In a typical case of this sort, your forming that particular intention, with that specific content, is itself something that you do intentionally.

So it's thought, by both many and many of the wise. Evidence regarding the latter can be found, for example, in the literature on free will. A great deal of this work takes choices, or practical decisions, to be paradigms of free action;[3] and, of course, the central cases of free action are things done intentionally. In part, what I'll try to determine here is whether the writers whose work I'll subsequently examine show either that this view of practical deciding as intentional action is untenable or that cognitive deciding, too, is intentional action.

In a standard case of intentional action, the phenomenological and the conceptual features that I've noted are closely interrelated.[4] When you decide to buy a car, you mean then not just to be making up your mind, but to be making up your mind to buy. It is, in this case, at least partly because you so mean to be doing just this that your forming the intention to buy seems to you to be, itself, an exercise of your agency—something in the doing of which you are directly exercising control—and not just a rational result of your prior agency. Your feeling that your active control extends through the making of this specific decision, with this particular content, is intertwined with your meaning to be deciding to buy. And conversely, the feeling that you don't directly actively control your coming to have the specific belief that it was Cochran's close that made the difference with the jurors is closely tied to the fact that, although you may intentionally make up your mind on this matter, you don't intentionally make up your mind that it was the close.

Several points of clarification are in order. First, I said that when you decide to buy a car, you mean to be making this specific decision. I aim in so saying to emphasize the fact that, as it seems, you intentionally decide to buy.

There is a somewhat different claim that might be made: that you intend to decide to buy. However, we may suppose that there is no time (not even an instant) prior to the decision at which you have an intention to decide to buy.

There are two ways to accommodate this supposition consistently with saying that you intentionally decide to buy. One is to reject the position (known as the *Simple View*) that intentionally A-ing requires intending (or having an intention) to A. Moved by arguments against the Simple View, Alfred Mele (1997, 243) takes it that although, necessarily, practical decisions are intentional actions, the appropriate production of a decision to A by, for example, an intention to decide whether to A can suffice to make it the case that one has intentionally decided to A; no intention to decide to A need figure in the story.[5] (I'll describe later some of the considerations that have led Mele and others to reject the Simple View.)[6]

Hugh McCann accepts the Simple View and takes a second way to avoid commitment to a prior intention to decide specifically as one does. When one decides to A, he holds (McCann 1998, 163–164), one intends to decide to A. But McCann insists that one's so intending is neither a matter of the content of the intention that is formed in deciding nor a matter of one's having any further intention in addition to the one formed in making the decision. One's so intending is just a matter of a decision's being, by its very nature, an act that the agent means to be performing, a matter of the intrinsic intentionality of deciding. Though I favor Mele's way of handling this issue, either strategy is consistent with my position here.

Second, although I take practical decisions to be intentional actions of intention formation, I don't claim that every intention is acquired actively. Sometimes an intention arises directly from a momentary desire; walking on a path in the woods, one might spontaneously reach for a sprig of berries (Audi 1993, 64). The intention to pick the berries arises from a desire that comes to one just then, and there is no intentional agency involved in the acquisition of the intention (though there is in executing it). An intention-acquisition of this sort will not have the distinctive phenomenology of agency; indeed, in a typical case of this sort the agent will not even be aware of the intention.

Practical deciding occurs only when there is some question or uncertainty about what to do.[7] Typically, such uncertainty leads one to deliberate, but not always; sometimes the question is no sooner asked than it is answered. And even when one does deliberate, the commitment to a specific course of action need not always be active. If it becomes clear that the only sensible thing to do is to A, and one has no strong competing motivation, it may be that no intentional agency is required for one to come to intend to A; a judgment that one ought to A might straightaway bring it about that one intends to A. (Again, such nonactive acquisitions of intentions will typically not seem to be fully active.)

Nevertheless, I claim, cases in which intentions are actively formed are common. Although one might employ the phrase "practical decision" to cover all intention-acquisitions, or all those that settle practical uncertainty, I use it here to pick out only some of these events, those that have the intentionality (and typically also the phenomenology) I have noted. It is these that I claim are exercises of our agency.

A third point concerns the cognitive deciding that I take to be inactive. It is, specifically, standard cases of coming to believe on the basis of theoretical reasoning that are my target. I allow that there are other cognitive attitudes—other species of acceptance—that one might come to have, and with respect to which one might exercise the same form of agency that we exercise in practical deciding. One might, for example, accept some proposition as a basis for practical reason and action without believing it (Bratman 1999), and one might be fully active in so accepting it—in taking that attitude of acceptance toward it. And we can suppose or pretend things at will. It is only the formation of belief that I wish to contrast with practical deciding.

Even with respect to forming a belief, there are writers who maintain a voluntarist view. Typically, they restrict active belief-formation to special cases, for example, those of self-fulfilling beliefs, or those where the individual has significant nonepistemic reasons for coming to have a certain belief. Although I doubt that the voluntarist position is correct even when so restricted, my thesis here can allow for it. For I'm concerned here with cases of cognitive deciding on the basis of epistemic reasons.

2 Practical Deciding

Brian O'Shaughnessy (1980, 297–299) agrees with the view taken here of cognitive deciding. Trying to make up one's mind how things stand in some matter, he accepts, is an active process; but the event of cognitive commitment that occurs when one succeeds in making up one's mind—the event that is a cognitive deciding—is essentially inactive. However, in conflict with the position taken here, O'Shaughnessy (1980, 300–302) argues that practical deciding is exactly analogous. Trying to make up one's mind what to do is an active process, but the practical deciding that occurs when one succeeds in so making up one's mind is essentially inactive.

What seems to be the crux of O'Shaughnessy's argument is his remark (1980, 300) that "there is no order: 'Decide to raise your arm.'" At any rate, he takes the nonexistence of such a command to confirm his position that practical deciding is not an action.[8]

Decision commands are indeed odd, but they are not always nonsensical. It might sometime make sense to tell someone not just to make up her mind on some practical matter but to make it up in some specific way—not just to decide whether to A, but to decide to A. It might make sense to do this in a case with the following features: first, a decision with some specific content will yield certain benefits, benefits not available from decisions with different content, and benefits yielded whether or not the decision is carried out; second, the commanded agent already has good enough reason to do what, in obeying the command, she would decide to do; and third, once so decided, the commanded agent will have best reason to act as decided.

Here is an illustration. Sam is driving his roommate Dave crazy with his vacillating, out-loud deliberations about whether to ask Mary out on a date. Sam's reasons pro and con are fairly evenly balanced. Dave doesn't care whether Sam asks Mary out or not, but he very much wants Sam to stop pestering him. Dave expects that a decision by Sam to ask Mary out would remain firm and give him—Dave—considerable relief, whereas a decision not to ask her out would likely be annulled and followed by further annoying deliberation. And Dave rightly expects that once Sam has decided to ask Mary out, he'll have a tie-breaking reason to do so—namely, that Dave would tease him mercilessly were he not to carry out the decision. Dave might tell Sam just to ask Mary out; but it would make as good sense for him to tell Sam to do what he, Dave, cares to have Sam do—namely, decide to ask Mary out. And since Sam realizes that such a decision would relieve his roommate, he might find the latter command quite sensible.[9]

Deciding is forming an intention, and intentions are commitments to perform certain actions. Ordinarily, a commitment to A is made for reasons that favor A-ing. But forming an intention can have autonomous benefits, benefits to be obtained independently of whether one acts as intended.

Autonomous benefits of deciding can provide one with autonomous reasons for deciding, reasons for deciding to A that aren't also reasons to A.[10] Because intending to A is being committed to A-ing, autonomous reasons for deciding to A will generally be ineffective when the agent expects to have little or no reason to A, and particularly when she expects to have overwhelming reason not to A.[11]

A decision command can provide one with an autonomous reason for deciding. As just noted, in many cases such a reason will be ineffective. In such cases, there will be no sense in issuing a decision command. But, as Sam's case illustrates, not all cases are of this sort.

One might wonder whether cognitive commitments can also be commanded, as when McCartney implores his darling, "Believe me when I tell you, I'll never do you no harm." It's likely that such entreaties are better understood as something other than imperatives.[12] In any case, I don't take the existence of sensible commands in the case of practical decisions to be what shows that we are active in making such decisions. My aim here is, rather, to rebut an argument that relies on a denial of such commands. It is not to an asymmetry in the existence of decision commands that I appeal in maintaining that practical decisions differ from cognitive decisions with respect to our agency. I appeal to the manifest differences in phenomenology and intentionality to support that claim. The apparent difference is not shown to be merely apparent by the mistaken denial of sensible decision commands.

O'Shaughnessy (1980, 298) also observes that, when one makes up one's mind that p, there is no intention to make up one's mind that p. One might intend, rather, to make up one's mind whether p. He takes this fact to imply that cognitive deciding, deciding-that, is not active. But likewise, generally, when one makes up one's mind to A, there is no preceding intention to make up one's mind to A. One might intend, rather, to make up one's mind whether to A. Should we take this fact to imply that practical deciding, deciding-to-do, is not intentional action?

I claimed that when one decides to A, one intentionally decides to A. The fact observed in the preceding paragraph could be shown to undermine this claim by showing that the Simple View is correct *and* showing that practical decisions are not intrinsically intentional. For establishing both of these points would rule out Mele's and McCann's strategies of reconciling the intentionality of practical deciding with the (general) absence of prior intentions to make specific practical decisions.

O'Shaughnessy rejects McCann's strategy, maintaining that intentional actions require intentions that cause them, but he doesn't defend the

Simple View. As he sees it, intentionally *A*-ing requires that one's *A*-ing be caused either by an intention to *A* or by an intention to try to *A*.[13] We might call this the *Nearly Simple View*. If there were good reason to accept this view, then there would be good reason to deny that decisions to *A* are generally intentional actions, since they are not generally caused either by intentions to decide to *A* or by intentions to try to decide to *A*.

O'Shaughnessy's sole argument for the Nearly Simple View appears to be the claim that an intentional *A*-ing must give expression to a desire to *A*, which desire causes one or another of the required intentions.[14] But the premise here is at best dubious. Some cases casting doubt on the premise don't also directly challenge the Nearly Simple View, but some do.

When grocery shopping, you might select one of several indistinguishable cans of beans, say, the one to the left of the others. You might desire to pick up a can of this kind of beans, and then intend to pick up the can on the left. It does not seem that you must first desire to pick up the can on the left before coming to so intend, in order to intentionally pick up the can on the left.

Indeed, ordinary instrumental intentional actions, though they might often result from a desire that meets O'Shaughnessy's requirement, don't seem to require such a desire. Suppose that Ann desires to *B*, and it occurs to her that *A*-ing is a satisfactory way to *B*; she therefore decides to *A*, and she then intentionally *A*s. Ann might have acquired, along the way, a desire to *A*, which then issued in her intention to *A*. But such a desire seems unnecessary; she might have gone straight from her desire to *B* and her instrumental belief to her intention to *A*.[15] It might be thought that a desire to *A* would be needed as motivation if her *A*-ing is to be intentional. But intentions themselves encompass motivation,[16] and her intention might be motivated by the desire to *B*, together with the instrumental belief.

Some cases that directly challenge the Nearly Simple View also cast doubt on O'Shaughnessy's premise. Some instances of routine subsidiary action do so. Consider an example from Mele (1997, 242–243): when Al walks to work, he takes a number of individual steps. He may intend to walk to work, but he wouldn't ordinarily intend to take (or to try to take) an entirely routine individual step that he takes along the way. Still, not only is Al's walking to work intentional, but, apparently, the step in question is as well. Likewise, it seems, although Al might well desire to walk to work, he wouldn't ordinarily desire to take the step in question.

A case from Carl Ginet has a similar impact. Here is his presentation:

I confront a set of double doors through which I wish to go. I know that the doors open only one way, either toward me or away from me, but I do not know which. I am in a hurry, so I simultaneously push away from me on one of the doors and pull toward me on the other. Suppose that I open the door I push on. In pushing on it I am trying to push it open, and I succeed. So I open it intentionally. If it were the other door, the one I pull on, that opened, then I would open *it* intentionally. But for neither door can we say that I have the intention to open it. We cannot suppose that I have *both* intentions, the intention to push open the one door and the intention to pull open the other, for it would be quite irrational of me to intend to accomplish both of these ends while knowing that it is impossible to do so. But it is not irrational of me to *try* both courses of action simultaneously while knowing that at most one can succeed, given that I do not know which one will succeed. And it would be arbitrary to attribute one of the intentions to me rather than the other. Therefore, neither intention can be attributed to me. (Ginet 1990, 76-77)[17]

Ginet holds that the content of the agent's intention in this case is "only the disjunction of the alternative ends and not any one alternative by itself" (ibid., 77), something on the order of: to open either the one door or the other. The agent *could* intend to try to open the one door *and* intend to try to open the other. But those intentions to try seem unnecessary in order for the eventual opening to be intentional; the intention with disjunctive content would seem to suffice. Likewise, the agent need not desire to open the door that eventually opens. A desire with disjunctive content— to open either—would seem to suffice.

There is no more to be said for the Nearly Simple View than there is for the Simple View. And given that both are rather suspect, the fact that a decision to *A* is generally not preceded either by an intention to decide to *A* or by an intention to try to decide to *A* does not undermine the view that practical deciding is an intentional action.

But if deciding to *A* is an intentional action even though not typically preceded by an intention to decide (or to try to decide) to *A*, why can't deciding that *p* be an intentional action, despite not typically being preceded by an intention to decide (or to try to decide) that *p*? I noted earlier a doubt that anyone has fully explained why practical and cognitive deciding differ in the way they do as regards our agency, and my doubt extends to answering the question here. Still, the fact that practical deciding is, but cognitive deciding is not, so apparently intentional action is, I contend, part of a prima facie case (the difference in phenomenology being another part) for the view that the two differ importantly with respect to our agency. This part of the case would be undermined were it shown that intentionally *A*-ing required either of the prior intentions to which O'Shaughnessy alludes, but he hasn't shown that to be so.

O'Shaughnessy further notes that practical deciding need not be preceded by any active process of deliberation. "A man can go to bed undecided and wake to a state of decision. . . . All that may be required is that the mental dust should settle," he says (1980, 301). I have observed that a practical question may be answered, by a decision, as soon as it is asked, without the need for deliberation. And I accept that one may go to bed undecided about whether to *A* and awake intending to *A*. But if no act of intention-formation occurred, then no decision occurred. One can come to have an intention nonactively, without making a decision.

3   Cognitive Deciding

In a fascinating paper on the will, Gary Watson (2004b) largely takes it for granted that practical deciding is an exercise of agency.[18] However, he maintains that deciding-that is active in the same sense, and he challenges those who would accept the agency of practical deciding but deny that of cognitive deciding to justify the distinction.

Decidings of both types are active, Watson (2004b, 140–141) maintains, because they are alike instances of assenting or rejecting, instances of commitment. I don't find that he offers any understanding of assent or commitment that would sustain an effective argument here.

On a widely held conception, intending to *A* is being settled on or committed to *A*-ing. As this view has it, commitment to pursuing a certain course of action is common to all intentions, whether they are actively formed or nonactively acquired. Commitment, then, isn't a distinguishing mark of the active. Even if cognitive decisions are commitments, in some similar sense, to the truth of certain propositions, that fact would not show that these decisions are active.

I've maintained that intentions can be nonactively acquired, and Watson (e.g., in Watson 2004b, 126) seems to allow that this is so. He suggests that "it is appropriate to speak of intentions as practical commitments only in case the creature has *formed* those intentions, as distinct from acquiring them in other ways" (ibid., 143, n. 49). But the suggestion raises two difficulties. First, it leaves us in need of some account of what, if not commitment to performing a certain type of action, is common to both actively formed and nonactively acquired intentions. More to our purposes here, reserving the term 'commitment' for cases of agency renders the claim that cognitive decisions are commitments question-begging.

A similar difficulty arises with the appeal to deciding as assenting or rejecting. One can come to be committed to performing a certain action without actively assenting to so acting, and one can come to be committed to the truth of a certain proposition without actively assenting to it. Whether cognitive deciding involves any active assent is just the question at issue, and thus appealing to assent can't help settle that question.

The second consideration—and perhaps the main one—that Watson raises in support of the similarity of practical and cognitive deciding concerns responsibility. We are, he holds,

as responsible for the judgements we make as for the intentions we form. In both cases I am open to normative appraisal and answerable for my commitments. It makes sense to press me on my reasons, and to say of me, "You should have reached a different conclusion (formed a different intention)." (2004b, 150)

A belief that I form by making a cognitive decision is, he says, "up to me" (ibid., 147), subject to my decision-making powers, to my normative competence. What is up to me in this sense is what I am responsible for. The decision wherein I form this belief is attributable to me, Watson argues, because it is appropriately related to my rational capacities. And attributability of this sort, he maintains, is sufficient for the kind of agency that is common to cognitive and practical deciding.

Responsibility is a large topic. I'll focus here only on issues that bear directly on my main thesis in this essay.

A number of writers take it that to be responsible for something (some psychological attitude, some state or occurrence, or some action) is for that thing to be attributable to you as a basis for moral assessment of you. Several who endorse this conception of responsibility (e.g., Scanlon [1998, 18–22] and Smith [2005]) argue that we are thus responsible for psychological states and occurrences that are "judgment-sensitive," those that, in a rational person, respond to that individual's assessments of reasons favoring or disfavoring them. Since such states and occurrences are responsive to our normative judgments concerning reasons, they are up to us, they leave us answerable to requests for justification, and they open us up to criticism when we've violated the relevant norms.

Pertinent to the discussion here is the fact that it is not just practical and cognitive decisions that are attributable to us in the way that is held, on this view, to suffice for responsibility. For one, we also make what can be called conative decisions, deliberating and forming preferences on the basis of that deliberation, and conative decisions are equally attributable to us, in the sense at issue. Further, such attributability covers not only those intentions, beliefs, and desires that we acquire on the basis of deliberation, but others as well, some arrived at inferentially, others noninferentially (such as beliefs that arise in perception).[19] And, as the authors just mentioned point out, it covers a wide variety of other psychological attitudes, including fear, anger, gratitude, contempt, and admiration. If attributability of this sort is the mark of agency, then mental agency is widespread indeed.

Of course, many writers hold that it is widespread.[20] I know of none, however, who take coming to fear, coming to admire, and so on, to be intentional actions. What we do intentionally is active in a more robust sense than is much of what is, on the view under consideration, attributable to us as a basis for moral assessment. That one's *A*-ing is intentional reflects the fact that one is actively controlling it, *qua A*-ing. An intentional action has its specific *telos* because that is the agent's *telos*. Practical deciding, I contend, is active in this robust sense, whereas cognitive deciding is not.

Though Watson takes cognitive deciding to be active, he doesn't say that it is intentional action. There may, then, be little real disagreement between us. But he doesn't say, either, that practical deciding is intentional action. To overlook this difference would be to miss a significant difference, as regards our agency, between decidings of the two types.

Watson (I think correctly) doesn't take attributability to be the whole of responsibility. As he sees it, attributability concerns the appropriateness of judgments about what kind of person someone is, about his or her excellences or faults, as these are manifested in thought and conduct— what Watson (2004a) calls *aretaic judgments*. A second aspect of responsibility, he holds, is accountability, which involves the idea that agents may deserve adverse treatment in response to things they do. Although responsibility for cognitive deciding involves a kind of accountability, Watson concedes that "we have notions of culpability and guilt that don't apply to responsibility for belief" (2004b, 151). Perhaps, he suggests, accountability of this further sort requires a kind of control that goes beyond responsiveness to reasons.

Watson notes that a capacity for counternormative agency—knowingly deciding, or otherwise acting, contrary to one's own judgments regarding what it is best to do—is sometimes said to be just the further type of control that is required. But short of this capacity (or liability), the fact that practical deciding is, in its specific content, intentional, whereas cognitive deciding is not, constitutes a difference in the active control that is exercised in the two cases that can ground a difference in the type of accountability that we might have for these two forms of making up one's mind.[21]

Watson concludes: "I have found no convincing reason to think that adopting intentions and making judgements belong on different sides of a line dividing our agency from what merely happens to us" (2004b, 152). With agency construed broadly, I might agree. There are mental states and occurrences that are not at all directly responsive to a rational agent's assessments of reasons. Headaches and feelings of hunger are examples. With respect to such things, we are in an important sense entirely passive: they merely happen to us. Granted, we can intentionally do things that are aimed at, and succeed at, causing ourselves to enter these passive states. We are not, however, active in entering them.

Many other psychological occurrences that are not intentional doings are, insofar as we are rational, nevertheless directly responsive to our assessments of reasons. Often, in undergoing these occurrences, we are exercising our rational capacities. But we are not as fully active in undergoing these changes as we are when we do things intentionally.

Cognitive deciding falls on the same side of the line separating the entirely passive from what we do intentionally as does practical deciding. The two forms of deciding are nevertheless importantly different with regard to our agency. It matters little whether we extend the term "active" to cover all that is judgment-sensitive. It does matter that we distinguish within this class those doings that are intentional actions from those that aren't.

Unlike cognitive deciding, practical deciding often has the phenomenology of agency; and apparently, whereas one intentionally decides to A, one does not intentionally decide that p. These manifest differences support the view that, as regards our agency, these two forms of making up one's mind are fundamentally different. O'Shaughnessy and Watson make them out to be the same, but neither writer offers good reason to reject the apparent difference.

Acknowledgments

I wish to thank Rick DeWitt, Al Mele, and the audience at the 2006 Inland Northwest Philosophy Conference for thoughtful comments on earlier versions of this essay.

Notes

1. Mele follows Kaufman (1966, 25) in using 'practical' and 'cognitive' to distinguish these two forms of making up one's mind.

2. For example, in many instances, it would be not just a fault of rationality but a moral fault to conclude that the Holocaust is a fraud.

3. Indeed, some writers take practical decisions to be the only directly free actions, with the freedom of any other actions deriving from that of free decisions. For a sustained defense of this view, see Pink 1996.

4. This is not to say that they cannot come apart. Some cases of automatism, such as automatic writing, may be instances of intentional action that lack the characteristic phenomenology of agency; indeed, the agent may sincerely deny that she is doing what is being done. And an agent may have an illusion of control, feeling that she is doing something that she is not in fact doing. Wegner (2002) presents an interesting discussion of both phenomena.

5. Mele (2000, 90–92) allows that in unusual cases, there might be such prior intentions to make specific decisions.

6. Bratman (1987, 113–119), Ginet (1990, 75–77), and Harman (1997, 151–152) also reject the Simple View.

7. Watson (2004b, 125–126) denies that active intention-formation need be preceded by any uncertainty about what to do. He describes a case in which, while walking along carrying some packages, he notices an elderly person in need of help. With the thing to do immediately clear to him, he straightaway settles on the action of helping the old person. Although Watson doesn't insist that we call what occurs here deciding, he does maintain that it is the formation of an intention, and an instance of agency.

Watson convincingly notes the need to distinguish here between coming to intend to help and attempting to help (the latter may begin sometime after the former, as the helper must first set down his packages). But he offers no argument—only an assertion—that the intention in this case is actively formed, rather than nonactively acquired. Hence, the example fails to undermine the view that actively forming an intention occurs only when the agent is first uncertain about what to do.

8. O'Shaughnessy apparently assumes here, what he states later (1980, 324–325), that "*the decisive test* of action" is whether the thing in question is "the type of item which *it makes sense to ask someone to do*." Some care would be needed to advance this requirement, for there appear to be nonactions that one can sensibly request or command ("Go to sleep") and actions or action-series that it makes little sense to request or command ("Decline all requests"). Pink (1996, especially chs. 5 and 8) argues that practical decisions are actions even though (he accepts) they can't be sensibly commanded.

9. I'm grateful to John Elia for suggesting this example.

10. I defend this claim in Clarke 2007.

11. Prizes offered for intending have the same feature. See Kavka 1983.

12. In this case, McCartney seems to be not just asserting that he won't harm, but giving his assurance on the matter, staking his credibility on his claim, thereby (at least ostensibly) giving stronger evidence of its truth. The grammatical imperative is aimed at persuading.

13. "[T]o perform an intentional φ-doing one need not have an intention to do φ; but one must at least harbour an intention of trying to do φ" (O'Shaughnessy 1980, 326). For the requirement that the intention in question cause the action, see p. 327.

14. "[A]ll intentional φ acts must give expression to an intention-producing desire to φ; and therefore must give expression to an intention whose act content is φ, which is to say *either* to an intention of doing φ *or* to an intention of trying to do φ *or* both; which must in turn cause a striving to do φ that is successful" (O'Shaughnessy 1980, 329).

15. Curiously, O'Shaughnessy (1980, 307–308) himself seems to allow that there can be such cases.

16. On this point, see, e.g., Brand 1984, 45–46, and Mele 1992, 130–131.

17. The case resembles, and is inspired by, Bratman's video game case; see Bratman 1987, 113–115.

18. Largely, but not entirely. He replies (Watson 2004b, 142–143) to O'Shaughnessy's denial of the activeness of practical deciding, claiming that a practical decision is active because it is an instance of assenting or rejecting. In the text below I discuss Watson's parallel claim regarding cognitive deciding.

19. Although such beliefs aren't produced by reasoning, nevertheless, as Scanlon (1998, 22) observes, "as continuing states these attitudes are 'up to us'—that is, they depend on our judgment as to whether appropriate reasons are present."

20. See, e.g., Moran 2001, especially 114. Smith also holds that "I am active, and responsible, for anything that falls within the scope of evaluative judgment (i.e., anything that is, or should be, sensitive to my evaluative judgments and commitments)" (Smith 2005, 263), though she allows that nothing much hinges on using the word "active" here.

21. The claim is not that the fact that what was done was done intentionally suffices to render the agent liable to sanctions (given that the deed was a misdeed). The deed must have been done freely if there is to be this sort of accountability. Still, it is no coincidence that paradigm cases of free action are cases of intentional action. The fact that an action was intentional is already an important fact about the type of active control that was exercised in performing that action.

References

Audi, R. 1993. Intending. In *Action, Intention, and Reason*. Ithaca, NY: Cornell University Press.

Audi, R. 2001. Doxastic Voluntarism and the Ethics of Belief. In *Knowledge, Truth, and Duty: Essays on Epistemic Justification, Responsibility, and Virtue*, ed. M. Steup. New York: Oxford University Press.

Brand, M. 1984. *Intending and Acting: Toward a Naturalized Action Theory*. Cambridge, MA: MIT Press.

Bratman, M. 1987. *Intention, Plans, and Practical Reason*. Cambridge, MA: Harvard University Press.

Bratman, M. 1999. Practical Reasoning and Acceptance in a Context. In *Faces of Intention: Selected Essays on Intention and Agency*. Cambridge: Cambridge University Press.

Clarke, R. 2007. Commanding Intentions and Prize-Winning Decisions. *Philosophical Studies* 133:391–409.

Ginet, C. 1990. *On Action*. Cambridge: Cambridge University Press.

Harman, G. 1997. Practical Reasoning. In *The Philosophy of Action*, ed. A. R. Mele. Oxford: Oxford University Press.

Horgan, T., J. Tienson, and G. Graham. 2003. The Phenomenology of First-Person Agency. In *Physicalism and Mental Causation: The Metaphysics of Mind and Action.*, ed. S. Walter and H.-D. Heckman. Exeter: Imprint Academic.

Kaufman, A. S. 1966. Practical Decision. *Mind* 75:25–44.

Kavka, G. 1983. The Toxin Puzzle. *Analysis* 43:33–36.

McCann, H. J. 1998. The Formation of Intention. In *The Works of Agency: On Human Action, Will, and Freedom*. Ithaca, NY: Cornell University Press.

Mele, A. R. 1992. *Springs of Action: Understanding Intentional Behavior*. New York: Oxford University Press.

Mele, A. R. 1997. Agency and Mental Action. *Philosophical Perspectives* 11:231–249.

Mele, A. R. 2000. Deciding to Act. *Philosophical Studies* 100:81–108.

Moran, R. 2001. *Authority and Estrangement: An Essay on Self-Knowledge*. Princeton: Princeton University Press.

O'Shaughnessy, B. 1980. *The Will: A Dual Aspect Theory*, vol. 2. Cambridge: Cambridge University Press.

Peacocke, C. 2003. Action: Awareness, Ownership, and Knowledge. In *Agency and Self-Awareness: Issues in Philosophy and Psychology*, ed. J. Roessler and N. Eilan. Oxford: Clarendon Press.

Pink, T. 1996. *The Psychology of Freedom*. Cambridge: Cambridge University Press.

Scanlon, T. M. 1998. *What We Owe to Each Other*. Cambridge, MA: Harvard University Press.

Smith, A. M. 2005. Responsibility for Attitudes: Activity and Passivity in Mental Life. *Ethics* 115:236–271.

Strawson, G. 2003. Mental Ballistics or the Involuntariness of Spontaneity. *Proceedings of the Aristotelian Society* 103:227–256.

Watson, G. 2004a. Two Faces of Responsibility. In *Agency and Answerability: Selected Essays*. Oxford: Clarendon Press.

Watson, G. 2004b. The Work of the Will. In *Agency and Answerability: Selected Essays*. Oxford: Clarendon Press.

Wegner, D. M. 2002. *The Illusion of Conscious Will*. Cambridge, MA: MIT Press.

5 Conscious Intentions

Alfred R. Mele

Anthony Marcel writes: "Oddly, many psychologists seem to assume that intentions are by their nature conscious" (Marcel 2003, 60). Daniel Wegner asserts that "*Intention* is normally understood as an idea of what one is going to do that appears in consciousness just before one does it" (Wegner 2002, 18). If this allegedly normal understanding of "intention" is treated as a *definition* of "intention," then, by definition, any item that does not "appear in consciousness" is not an intention, and intentions are "by their nature conscious." Is the connection between intentions and conscious-ness this tight? And why might scientists find themselves disagreeing about this? In sections 1 and 2, I lay some groundwork for an examination of these questions. In section 3, I offer some answers. ·

The measure of subjects' consciousness of their intentions in scientific studies is their reports—reports subjects make to the effect that they had conscious intentions at certain times. In the words of Richard Passingham and Hakwan Lau, "the operational index of consciousness is the ability to report" (Passingham and Lau 2006, 67). (One who does not realize that the operational index of the ability to report is an actual report may misread the quoted claim.) Now, consciousness may be layered in such a way that some occurrences or states that properly count as conscious for the ordinary adult human beings who are the loci of those occurrences or states are not reportable by those human beings. Unreportable conscious-ness is not my concern here. It is consciousness (or awareness) that is high-level enough to be measured by reports that concerns me; for it is consciousness of this kind, or in this sense, that is at issue in the dispute between Marcel and his opponents about whether "intentions are by their nature conscious." I call it *report-level consciousness (or awareness)*. In the remainder of this essay, I write simply in terms of consciousness (or aware-ness) and count on the reader to remember that report-level consciousness (or awareness) is at issue.

1   Intentions and Questions

Intentions are a topic of discussion in a variety of fields, including neuro-science, philosophy, law, and several branches of psychology. It should not be assumed that the term "intention" is understood in the same way in all these fields. Nor should it be assumed that there is a uniform understanding of the term within each field.

Here is a representative account of intention from the neuroscience literature:

Intention is an early plan for a movement. It specifies the goal of a movement and the type of movement. . . . We can have intentions without actually acting upon them. Moreover, a neural correlate of intention does not necessarily contain information about the details of a movement, for instance the joint angles, torques, and muscle activations required to make a movement. . . . Intentions are initially coded in visual coordinates in at least some of the cortical areas within the PPC [posterior parietal cortex]. This encoding is consistent with a more cognitive representation of intentions, specifying the goals of movements rather than the exact muscle activations required to execute the movement. (Andersen and Buneo 2002, 191)

This account is similar in some respects to my own account of intentions—more specifically, occurrent intentions (see below)—as executive attitudes toward plans (Mele 1992). The account is based primarily on functions assigned to intentions in various bodies of literature (see section 3). In my account, plans—which range from simple representations of prospective "basic" actions to complex strategies for achieving remote goals—constitute the representational content of intentions.[1] What distinguishes intentions to A from other practical attitudes—for example, desires to A—is their distinctively practical nature.[2] According to an influential view of representational attitudes—for example, Al's belief that p, Beth's desire that p, Carl's desire to A, Donna's intention to A—one can distinguish between an attitude's representational *content* and its psychological *orientation* (Searle 1983). Orientations include (but are not limited to) believing, desiring, and intending. On my view, the executive dimension of intentions is intrinsic to the attitudinal orientation *intending*. We can have a variety of attitudes toward plans: for example, we might admire plan x, be disgusted by plan y, and desire to execute plan z. To have the intending attitude toward a plan is to be settled (but not necessarily irrevocably) on executing it.[3] The intending and desiring attitudes toward plans differ in that the former alone entail this settledness.

How is deciding to A related to intending to A? Like many philosophers, I take deciding to A to be a mental action of forming an intention to A (see Mele 2003, ch. 9; also see Frankfurt 1988, 174–176; McCann 1986, 254–255; Pink 1996, 3; Searle 2001, 94). As I have observed elsewhere, many of our intentions seem to be acquired without being formed in acts of deciding. For example, "When I intentionally unlocked my office door this morning, I intended to unlock it. But since I am in the habit of unlocking my door in the morning and conditions . . . were normal, nothing called for a *decision* to unlock it" (Mele 1992, 231). If I had heard a fight in my office, I might have paused to consider whether to unlock the door or walk away, and I might have decided to unlock it. But given the routine nature of my conduct, there is no need to posit an action of intention-formation in this case. My intention to unlock the door may have been acquired without having been actively formed. If, as I believe, all decisions about what to do are prompted partly by uncertainty about what to do (Mele 2003, ch. 9), in situations in which there is no such uncertainty, no decisions will be made. This is not to say that, in such situations, no intentions will be acquired.

My aim in the preceding paragraphs was to set the stage for a question. If intentions are items of the kind or kinds described there, must they be "conscious" in order for any of the following to play a significant role in producing intended actions: intentions, acquisitions of intentions, the persistence of intentions, or the neural correlates of any these things? (As shorthand for what follows the colon in the preceding sentence, I will use the expression "intentions or their neural correlates.") A clearer formulation of this question—question Q—would facilitate discussion. Obviously, if an intention is conscious, it is not conscious in the way in which I am conscious now. At the moment, I am conscious of the feel of my keyboard, the presence of my computer monitor, and a slight pain in my left elbow, among other things; and, of course, intentions are not conscious of anything. Is what is meant by a "conscious intention" of mine an intention of mine of which I am conscious? Wegner seems to mean something like this.[4] Recall his assertion that "*Intention* is normally understood as an idea of what one is going to do that appears in consciousness just before one does it" (2002, 18). He accepts this allegedly normal understanding and argues that intentions play no role in action initiation.

Wegner's account of what intentions are is unacceptable, as I will explain shortly. My present concern is to get a grip on question Q. Here is one variant of it: (Q1) Must I be conscious (or aware) of my intention to A in order for it or its neural correlate to play a significant role in producing an intentional A-ing? And here is another: (Q2) Must I be aware that I intend to A in order for my intention to A or its neural correlate to play a significant role in producing an intentional A-ing? An agent's being aware that he intends to A entails that he has a concept of intention. Someone who has no concept of paradox or counterfeit dollar bill—say, a normal two-year-old child—cannot be aware that his mother has just described a paradox to his sister or that he is holding a counterfeit bill. Similarly, someone who has no concept of intention—perhaps the same child—cannot be aware that he intends to A.[5] However, one can, in principle, be conscious (or aware) of an intention to A that one has without having a concept of intention and without being aware that one intends to A, just as one can be conscious (or aware) of a counterfeit bill without having a concept of counterfeit bill and without being aware, for example, that what one is looking at is a counterfeit bill. A young child who intends to pick up a toy that is lying on the floor a few feet away may, in principle, be conscious of something that we would describe as an intention to pick up the toy even though he is in no position to describe—or conceive of—what he is conscious of in this way. $Q1$ and $Q2$ are both targets of investigation here.

A distinction between two kinds of intentions is relevant to my present concerns for reasons that will emerge shortly. Some of our intentions are for the nonimmediate future and others are not. I might have an intention on Tuesday to attend a lecture on Friday, and I might have an intention now to phone my father now. The former intention is aimed at action three days in the future. The latter intention is about what to do now. I call intentions of these kinds, respectively, *distal* and *proximal* intentions (Mele 1992, 143–144, 158). Proximal intentions also include intentions to continue doing something that one is currently doing and intentions to start A-ing (e.g., start climbing a hill) straightaway.

Return to Wegner's assertion that "*Intention* is normally understood as an idea of what one is going to do that appears in consciousness just before one does it" (2002, 18). This assertion plainly does not apply to distal intentions. Nor does it identify a sufficient condition for something's being an intention. As you are driving, another driver cuts you off. The following idea of what you are "going to do . . . appears in consciousness just before" you hit his car: "Oh no! I'm going to hit that car." The idea expresses a prediction, not an intention; and "intention" definitely is not normally understood in such a way that this idea is an intention.

Perhaps what Wegner means is that proximal intentions, as normally understood, are ideas of what one is *intentionally* "going to do" that appear "in consciousness just before one does it" (in those cases in which one succeeds in doing what one proximally intends). Readers who do not *identify* proximal intentions with such ideas have some options about how to read Wegner's expression "conscious intention." They may read it as referring to an intention that appears in consciousness *as an intention* or instead as referring to an intention some important aspect of which appears in consciousness. On the second reading, the aspect would apparently be some "idea of what one is going to do." Because the second reading is more modest, it is more charitable. One who thinks of occurrent intentions as executive attitudes toward plans may regard the content of the "idea of what one is going to do" that is supposed to appear in consciousness as including the content of a proximal intention or some important part or expression of the content. (Again, on this view, the content of an intention is a plan.)

I ask myself now, at noon on Sunday, what I intend to do tomorrow. Reflection on this question may prompt me to form some new intentions, and it may prompt me to recall having formed intentions to do various things on Monday. I recall that I decided on Friday to call my travel agent on Monday to make plane reservations for a trip to Idaho and that I decided to reserve a hotel room there once I ordered my plane tickets. I am now aware that I intend to do these things tomorrow.

Is it possible for me to intend to do these things tomorrow without being aware that this is so? Consider my condition ten minutes before noon—ten minutes before I asked myself about my intentions for tomorrow. Might I have intended then to call my travel agent on Monday even though I was not aware of that intention?

Attention to a familiar distinction between *occurrent* and *standing* desires or wants (Goldman 1970, 86–88; see also Alston 1967, 402) will prove useful as background for an attempt to answer this question.[6] Alvin Goldman writes: "An occurrent want is a mental event or mental process; it is a 'going on' or 'happening' in consciousness. A standing want . . . is a disposition . . . to have an occurrent want, a disposition that lasts with the agent for a reasonable length of time" (Goldman 1970, 86). For example, we can "say that John wants to be president of his company because he has a *disposition* to have occurrent wants to this effect. . . . This disposition is present . . . though it is not being manifested" (ibid.). A distinction of this kind is motivated partly by evidence about the ordinary notion of desire or wanting provided by common attributions of desires or wants. Ann, a graduate student, is deeply committed to pursuing a career in physics. As the verb "want" is standardly used, "Ann wants a career in physics" is true even while she is thoroughly absorbed in a conversation about her father's financial problems or is dreamlessly sleeping. When

Ann's supervisor finds himself inclined to tell a prospective employer that she definitely wants a career in physics, he need not phone her to learn whether she is awake before he can be confident that he will be speaking the truth. The quoted sentence also is true when Ann is crafting a cover letter for her job applications. In the latter case, but not the former, Ann has an occurrent want for a career in physics.

If there are standing desires, perhaps there are also standing intentions. Standing desires, if they exist, are such that agents can have a standing desire to A at times at which they are not aware that they desire to A and are not conscious of a desire to A. The same is true of standing intentions. If Ann has a standing intention to do her best to secure a career in physics, she has this intention at times at which she is not aware that she intends to do this and is not conscious of an intention to do this. Proponents of the view that "intentions are by their nature conscious" may either contend that there are no standing intentions or assert that their view is about occurrent intentions only.

If an "occurrent want" were defined, with Goldman, as a want that is "a 'going on' or 'happening' in consciousness" and occurrent intentions were understood on this model, the claim that all occurrent intentions are "conscious" would be true by definition. However, Goldman's way of drawing the distinction between standing and occurrent wants or desires is problematic.[7] An important part (at least) of what the distinction is supposed to mark is the difference between (1) desires to A (or for X) that are wholly constituted by dispositions to have desires to A (or for X) that manifest these dispositions and (2) desires that are functionally more closely connected to action than such dispositions are (Alston 1967, 402; Goldman 1970, 88). For example, the characteristic functional role of Ann's standing desire for a career in physics is to contribute to her having occurrent desires for a career in physics. Her standing desire's functional connection to action features its contributing to her having occurrent desires that manifest it. But not all desires with a more direct connection to action are present to consciousness—at least if common sense and clinicians may be trusted.[8] Bob might have spoken to Beth as he did because he wanted to hurt her feelings, even though he was not conscious at the time of a desire to do that. Bob might not have had a standing desire to hurt Beth's feelings. But if he did have one, and if it played the role characteristic of standing desires, it was manifested in a desire of another kind to hurt her feelings—an occurrent desire to do that. (If Bob did not have a standing desire to hurt Beth's feelings, then, of course, any occurrent desire to hurt her feelings that he had did not manifest a standing desire to do that.) Goldman implausibly makes being "a 'going on' or 'happening' in consciousness" an essential feature of occurrent wants or desires. An agent's being conscious of a desire is not required for the desire's playing a role in action production that suffices for its not being a standing desire and therefore suffices for its being an occurrent desire, if the distinction between standing and occurrent desires is exhaustive. I should add that occurrent desires, as I understand them (Mele 2003, 30–33), are not occurrences or events ("in consciousness" or otherwise): they are states.

As I understand *standing* desires, intentions, and beliefs, they are wholly constituted by dispositions of certain kinds to have corresponding occurrent desires, intentions, and beliefs. For example, a standing belief that *p* is wholly constituted by a disposition of a certain kind to have occurrent beliefs that *p*. These dispositions have no explicit representational content. They are accorded a content-supplying description in virtue of the content of the occurrent attitudes that manifest them. Having no explicit representational content, standing desires, intentions, and beliefs are not *explicit attitudes*.[9] Rather, they are dispositions to have explicit attitudes of a certain kind. They are, one may say, "implicit" attitudes.[10]

Might an agent have, at a time *t*, an occurrent intention to *A* without being conscious of it (or any part of it) at *t* and without being aware at *t* that he intends to *A*? In section 3, I will argue that the answer is *yes*. I will also argue that this is the correct answer even on a very thin understanding of "conscious intention" to be developed in the following section.

2   A Thin Understanding of "Conscious Intention"

Might one underestimate the frequency of "conscious" proximal intentions as a consequence of framing one's search for them in terms of such things as agents' awareness that they *intend* to *A* and their awareness of (some aspect of) their proximal *intentions* to *A*? Might it be useful to think in terms of agents' awareness (or consciousness) of being *about to A*, where that is not a predictive awareness of the sort present in the case of the driver who is aware that he is about to collide with the car that just cut him off?

Consider an artificial scenario. As I was sitting at my desk thinking about conscious intentions, I decided to raise my right arm later and to pay very close attention to what I am aware of and how things feel just before I begin to raise it. My plan was to count slowly and silently and to begin raising my arm when I got to 5. Some time later, I did this. I was aware that I was about to raise my right arm. Seemingly, that awareness was based at least partly on my awareness that I intended to raise my arm when I got to 5 and my awareness that I was approaching 5.

Wegner speaks of an "authorship emotion"—a "feeling of doing" (2002, 325). If there is such a feeling, there may also be an anticipatory feeling of being about to perform an action of a specific kind. Set yourself the task of slowly raising your right arm when you have slowly and silently counted to 5 and of paying very close attention to what you are aware of and how things feel just before you begin to raise it. Did you notice something that might reasonably be described as a *feeling* of being about to raise your arm?

Consider now a scenario that is not at all artificial. Normally, when I get home from work, I park my car in the driveway, walk to my side door, unlock it, open it, and walk into the kitchen, closing the door behind me. It is natural to say that all of these actions are intentional and intended. Normally, I am aware (conscious) of doing them and of my driveway, my door, and my keys. Is it also true that, normally, when I am about to unlock my door, I am aware that I am about to unlock it? Attention to some contrasting scenarios might help in articulating what this kind of awareness might be like.

Consider a scenario in which things proceed routinely until I try to turn my key in the lock. This time, the key does not move, and the door, consequently, is not unlocked. The lock is jammed. Now, "S is about to unlock his door" does not entail "S proceeds to unlock his door," as the following true story indicates: "Ann was about to unlock her door when she heard someone call her from the street. She immediately walked toward the street, keys in hand, to see who was calling." Since it is true that Ann was about to unlock her door even though she did not unlock it, the same may be true of me in the jammed lock scenario. This provides some guidance for someone seeking to understand what it means to say that I am aware that I am about to unlock my door. I will return to this suggestion after another contrasting scenario is in place.

As I am walking on a crowded sidewalk, the person in front of me suddenly stops. I am aware that I am about to bump into him even as I try to minimize the blow. My awareness here is based on my observation of external events and on my sense of how fast I am moving and how fast I can stop. On this basis, I *predict* the bump. My awareness that I am about to bump into the person in front of me is an instance of what may be termed *predictive awareness*. My awareness that I am about to sneeze also is a predictive awareness, even though that awareness normally is not even partly based on my observation of external events.

When, in a normal scenario, I am aware that I am about to unlock my door, on what is that awareness based? One may claim that it is based solely on nonintrospective observation: I see that I am approaching the door and I feel or see the keys in my hand; I infer from this that I am about to unlock my door. Is this plausible? Seemingly not; and on a thin reading of "conscious intention," the following is sufficient for my having a *conscious* proximal intention to unlock my door: my having a proximal intention to unlock my door together with an awareness that I am about to unlock it (*type 1 awareness*), which differs from what I called predictive awareness (*type 2 awareness*). If type 1 awareness is a real phenomenon, it has at least a partial basis in something other than nonintrospective observation. Possibly, if Wegner were to offer a position on the content of "idea[s] of what one is going to do" that he identifies with intentions, he would understand that content as the content of states of type 1 awareness. Partly because I have not offered an account of type 1 awareness, the proposed sufficient condition of my having a conscious proximal intention to unlock my door definitely is open to interpretation. I wish to leave open reasonable but relatively undemanding interpretations of the condition; for I want to show that even when the standards for a proximal intention's being a conscious intention are relatively modest, it is implausible that all proximal intentions are conscious. (Here, a reminder that the consciousness or awareness at issue is at the *report level* may be in order.)

A disjunctive alleged sufficient condition of an agent's having a conscious proximal intention to A may be constructed out of the various sufficient conditions for this suggested in this section: the agent's being aware of his proximal intention to A or of some appropriate part or expression of its content; the agent's being aware that he intends to A now; the agent's having a proximal intention to A together with an awareness that he is about to A that differs from what I called predictive awareness. Another disjunct may be added to the list: a proximal intention to A may be treated as a conscious proximal intention at a time if, at that time, the agent consciously makes a proximal *decision* to A.

3   Questions Answered: Functional Roles and Folk Theories

If there are proximal intentions, if they tend to be fit for execution, and if they play an important role in the production of intentional actions, then, in typical instances, agents begin executing their proximal intentions almost as soon as they acquire them.[11] If standing intentions to A are wholly constituted by dispositions to have occurrent intentions to A, then, because such dispositions are not executable, no executed intention is a standing intention. And simply in virtue of its being executed at a time, a proximal intention has a claim to being an occurrent intention at that time. (If the distinction between standing and occurrent intentions is exhaustive, then all executed intentions are occurrent intentions.)

Why might researchers disagree about whether all proximal intentions are conscious intentions, even on the broad disjunctive reading of "conscious proximal intention" that I sketched? One possible explanation is that, even setting aside the issue of consciousness, they disagree about what intentions are. A potential source of disagreement about what intentions are is disagreement about what does and does not count as an intentional action. If some theorists have a more restrictive conception of intentional action than others do, it might not be surprising that they also have a more restrictive conception of intention. In section 1, I briefly described my view (developed in Mele 1992) that occurrent intentions are executive attitudes toward plans. My route to that view starts with a canvassing of functions attributed to intentions (Mele 1992, ch. 8), or, more precisely, to intentions, their acquisition, their persistence, or neural correlates of these things. (Again, I will use the expression "intentions or their neural correlates" as shorthand for this.) The featured functions include (but are not limited to) initiating, sustaining, and guiding intentional actions. Someone who agrees that intentions or their neural correlates play these roles but disagrees with me about what counts as an intentional action may also disagree with me, accordingly, about what intentions are. And that disagreement may have a bearing on our respective views about the connection between intentions and consciousness.

The following assertion from Haggard and Clark (2003, 695–696) is interesting in this connection: "functional imaging studies of intentional actions typically show activation in the basal ganglia and supplementary motor area . . . while studies of externally triggered actions show activation in the cerebellum and premotor cortex." This assertion certainly suggests that "externally triggered actions" are not intentional actions. One study Haggard and Clark cite here compares subjects instructed to raise their right index finger whenever they wish without waiting more than four seconds between raisings with subjects instructed to do this whenever they hear a tone (Jahanshahi et al. 1995). (The tones are separated by no more than four seconds.) The first group is said to perform "self-initiated" finger raisings and the second to perform "externally triggered" finger raisings (Jahanshahi et al. 1995, 913). As I understand intentional action, the finger raisings of both groups are obviously intentional. But as Haggard and Clark understand intentional action, the finger raisings of the second group are not intentional.

How might this disagreement bear on a disagreement about the connection between consciousness and intention? Jahanshahi et al. infer that the greater activation of the dorsolateral prefrontal cortex in the first group "was associated with the additional requirement of *decision making* about the timing of the movement on each trial, or 'when to do' it" (1995, 930; my emphasis); and this is what motivates Haggard and Clark's claim about which finger raisings are intentional and which are not.[12] Now, Haggard and Clark surely would find it odd to say that although the subjects in the second group do not intentionally raise their index fingers, they *intend* to raise them. So they probably are equating intentions with decisions or thinking that the only way we acquire intentions to A is by deciding to A. If this is their view, then if my earlier claim that not all intentions are acquired in acts of decision making is correct, Haggard and Clark have an unduly restrictive conception of intention—a conception to which their restrictive conception of intentional action might have led them. Notice finally that if it is significantly more plausible that agents consciously make all of the decisions they make than that agents consciously acquire all of the intentions they acquire (including intentions not acquired in acts of decision making), theorists with a view of intentional action like Haggard and Clark's are more likely, other things being equal, to view intentions as being essentially conscious than are theorists with a broader—and, I dare say, more normal—conception of intentional action. One moral to be drawn from this is that one who wishes to appeal to what purport to be empirical assertions about intentions should try to get a firm sense of what the researchers making the assertions mean by "intention."

The main measure of awareness of intentions in scientific studies, as I have mentioned, is subjects' reports. For example, Benjamin Libet (1985) asks his subjects to report, after flexing a wrist, when they first became aware of a proximal intention to flex it (or some related state: see below). The subjects, instructed to flex whenever they feel like it, are watching a rapidly revolving spot on a clock and trying to keep track of where the spot was when they first became aware of a proximal intention to flex (or related states).

Suppose experienced drivers who are in the habit of signaling for the turns they make were asked to drive for an hour in an area used for drivers' training, to turn at whatever intersections they felt like turning at, using their turn indicators to signal the turns, and to report after flipping the indicator when they first became aware of their intention to flip it.

They are instructed to keep track of a rapidly revolving spot on a clock on their rearview mirrors as they drive, and to make their awareness reports in terms of where the spot was when they first became aware of the pertinent intentions. Such a study might generate many reports of intention awareness. The instructions would encourage subjects to search their minds, as it were, for intentions to flip the turn indicator. If they do become aware of proximal intentions to flip their turn indicators, one hypothesis is that what they become aware of are states of a kind— proximal intentions—that would have been present under normal circumstances without their being aware of them. In experienced drivers who are in the habit of signaling for their turns, the signaling is "overlearned" or "automatic" behavior: in normal circumstances, they are not aware of doing it, much less of being about to do it or of having a proximal intention to do it.[13]

The hypothesis I just mentioned is of special interest in connection with the central thesis of Wegner's (2002) *The Illusion of Conscious Will*. Wegner argues that "conscious will is an illusion . . . in the sense that *the experience of consciously willing an action is not a direct indication that the conscious thought has caused the action*" (2002, 2). He contends that "The experience of will is merely a feeling that occurs to a person" (14). More specifically, "conscious will . . . is a feeling of doing" (325). Wegner writes: "The new idea introduced here is the possibility that the experience of acting develops when the person infers that his or her own *thought* (read intention, but belief and desire are also important) was the cause of the action" (66). Collectively, these last three quotations suggest that his claim about illusion may be understood as follows: the feeling of doing "an action is not a direct indication that the conscious [intention to perform the action] has caused the action" (2).

Among the work to which Wegner appeals in defending his thesis about illusion is Libet's. In Libet's (1985) main experiment, subjects are instructed to flex their right wrists or the fingers of their right hands whenever they wish. Electrical readings from the scalp—averaged over at least 40 flexings for each subject—show a shift in "readiness potentials" (RPs) beginning about 550 milliseconds (ms) before the time at which an electromyogram shows relevant muscular motion to begin. Subjects are also instructed to "recall . . . the spatial clock position of a revolving spot at the time of [their] initial awareness" (529) of something, x, that Libet variously describes as an "intention," "urge," "wanting," "decision," "will," or "wish" to flex.[14] On average, "RP onset" preceded what the subjects reported to be the time of their initial awareness of x (time W) by 350 ms. Time W, then, preceded the beginning of muscle motion by about 200 ms. These results are represented as follows:

Libet's Results

–550 ms	200 ms	0 ms
RP onset	time W	muscle begins to move

(Libet finds independent evidence of a slight error in subjects' recall of the times at which they first become aware of sensations. Correcting for that error, time W is –150 ms.)

Wegner writes: "The position of conscious will in the time line suggests perhaps that the experience of will is a link in a causal chain leading to action, but in fact it might not even be that. It might just be a loose end—one of those things, like the action, that is caused by prior brain and mental events" (Wegner 2002, 55). By "the experience of will" here, Wegner means "the experience of wanting to move" (ibid.). He is suggesting that this is not a cause of the flexing. Here one must be careful. A subject's wanting to flex soon and his experience of wanting to flex soon are not identical. So to grant that a subject's experience of wanting to flex soon is not a cause of his flexing is not to grant that his wanting to flex soon also is not a cause of his flexing.

Move from wanting to intending. An intention to flex straightaway is a proximal intention. Suppose that Libet's subjects have many conscious intentions of this kind during the course of an experiment. Suppose also that neither their *experiences* of proximally intending to flex nor the neural correlates of those experiences are causes of their flexing actions. These suppositions leave it open that the subjects' proximal intentions or their neural correlates are causes of these actions; for their experiences of their proximal intentions are not identical with the intentions themselves.

Partly because they are told that they need to "recall . . . the spatial clock position of a revolving spot at the time of [their] initial awareness" of their urges (or wishes, intentions, etc.) to flex (Libet 1985, 529), Libet's subjects may interpret their instructions as including an instruction to wait until they feel—that is, experience—an urge to flex before they flex and to flex in response to that feeling. If they comply with the instructions, so understood, the feelings are among the causes of the flexings: the feelings serve as cues to begin flexing. This obvious point is a problem for Wegner's *statement* of his position—specifically, his claim that "the experience of wanting to move" in Libet's subjects is not "a link in a causal chain leading to action" (Wegner 2002, 55). However, Wegner's actual position is more subtle. It is that the basic causal process that leads to flexing in these subjects does not depend on consciousness of—that is, feeling—an urge to flex. The idea is that even if the subjects were not waiting to feel an urge as a cue for flexing—even if, as one might put it, they did not interpret an instruction to flex whenever they *feel* like it in a phenomenological way—flexing would be produced in the same basic way: the consciousness of the urge is "just . . . a loose end" in this process (ibid.), and the same is true of the consciousness aspect of any conscious proximal intention to flex that may emerge.

Suppose that Wegner is right about this. What would the upshot be? If, as Marcel (2003) maintains, nonconscious proximal intentions can produce corresponding intentional actions, an agent's conscious proximal intention to flex may produce a flexing action in a way that does not depend on the intention's consciousness aspect. If many proximal intentions produce actions without the intentions showing up in consciousness, this is not a terribly surprising result.

In an imaginary variant of Libet's main experiment in which subjects are asked to watch the clock and to flex whenever they feel like it but are not asked to report on their awareness of anything, would consciousness of a mental antecedent of flexing be a frequent occurrence? Recently, I was a subject of an experiment with the design of Libet's main experiment. I had just three things to do: watch the clock with a view to keeping track of when I first became aware of something in the ballpark of a proximal urge or intention to flex; flex whenever I felt like it (many times); and report, after flexing, where the spot was on the clock at the moment of first awareness. Because I found it difficult to locate a specific proximal urge or intention or a feeling of being about to flex, I hit on the strategy of saying "now" silently to myself just before beginning to flex. This is the mental event that I tried to keep track of with the assistance of the clock. I thought of the "now" as shorthand for the imperative "flex now!"—something that may be understood as an expression of a proximal decision to flex. (To make a proximal decision to flex is to form—actively—a proximal intention to flex.) Suppose that my task had been simply to flex whenever I felt like it (many times) while watching the clock. One might think that because the only salient practical question facing me during the experiment would be when to flex, I would be aware of some distinctive kind of occurrence that preceded the flexings. The thought, perhaps, is that I would be aware of a distinctive antecedent of the flexings because there is so little to attend to in this experiment. However, when I try this, I find that I am not aware of such an antecedent. I needed the silent "now" in the actual experiment to have some mental event that I could report, but I do not need it in the modified experiment. (If I were to hit upon the strategy of silently saying "now" to myself to answer my practical question about when to flex, how would I answer my practical question about when to say "now"?)

Suppose that in the imagined experiment, I were to produce RPs of just the sort I produced in the actual experiment. A proponent of Wegner's view may contend that the supposed result would indicate that proximal intentions to flex (and their neural correlates) are not involved in the production of my flexings in either experiment, even if I have a "conscious" proximal intention to flex in the actual experiment. One argument for this contention runs as follows: (1) the RPs are correlated with the causes of the flexing; (2) that the RPs match indicates that the causes at work in the two experiments are of the same kind; (3) given that intentions are essentially conscious, there is no proximal intention to flex in the imaginary experiment; and, obviously, absent intentions can do no causal work; so (4) given that the causes at work in the two experiments are of the same kind, my proximal intention to flex does no causal work in the actual experiment.

The argument is unconvincing, even if its first two premises are granted. The supposed result is consistent with the view that proximal intentions to flex (or their neural correlates) are at work in me in both experiments, provided that proximal intentions are not essentially conscious. The design of Libet's experiment may foster consciousness of proximal intentions to flex, and those intentions (or their neural correlates) might have done their action-initiating work independently of the subjects' consciousness of them. They may do the same work when agents are not conscious of them.

In my own case, as I mentioned, the design of Libet's experiment prompted me, in effect, to make conscious decisions about when to flex so that I would have a mental event to report. If to decide to A is to perform the mental action of forming an intention to A, then in proximally deciding to flex, I formed a proximal intention to flex. Insofar as I consciously made my proximal decisions to flex, the associated proximal intentions may be counted as conscious intentions. But, in principle, proximal intentions to flex that are acquired without being formed in acts of proximally deciding to flex may do the same basic work as these "conscious intentions."

Compare my unlocking my side door with a normal experienced driver's flipping the turn indicator for a turn he is about to make in utterly normal circumstances. When, in normal circumstances, I unlock my door and walk into my kitchen after driving home from work, the claim that I am aware of unlocking the door and walking into the kitchen certainly is significantly less controversial than the claim that I was aware of being about to do these things. Because experienced drivers seem typically not to be aware of flipping their turn signals in normal circumstances, the claim that they are aware of being about to flip them is on shaky ground. However, this places the claim that they have proximal intentions to flip them on similarly shaky ground only on the assumption that proximal intentions are essentially conscious, even on the modest disjunctive understanding of "conscious intention" that I identified. And that conceptual assumption is far from unassailable.

In an article defending the thesis that "most of a person's everyday life is determined not by their conscious intentions and deliberate choices but by mental processes that are put into motion by features of the environment and that operate outside of conscious awareness and guidance" (Bargh and Chartrand 1999, 462), John Bargh and Tanya Chartrand approvingly quote (468) the following passage from William James's *The Principles of Psychology*: "It is a general principle in Psychology that consciousness deserts all processes where it can no longer be of use . . . . We grow unconscious of every feeling which is useless as a sign to lead us to our ends, and where one sign will suffice others drop out, and that one remains, to work alone" (James 1890, vol. 2, 496). If James is right, by the time drivers have developed the habit of signaling for turns they are about to make, they no longer consciously form intentions to signal for turns (in normal circumstances) and no longer are conscious of being about to signal or even of signaling (in normal circumstances). Even so, in a straightforward sense of "intentional," their signalings are intentional actions; and, in light of this, it certainly is far from bizarre to suggest that they are intended.[15] Bargh and Chartrand write: "goals can become activated by means other than an act of will, and once activated, such goals operate in the same way, and produce the same effects, as when they are put into motion intentionally" (1999, 472). Similarly, a conscious and a nonconscious proximal intention to signal for a turn may "operate" in basically the same way and produce a signaling action. One who takes the position that all proximal intentions are conscious intentions produced by conscious "act[s] of will," as Bargh and Chartrand seem to do, will reject the preceding sentence. But what motivates this position seems to be its adherents' sensitivity to what they take to be a popular folk theory about intentions or the folk concept of intention, not empirical considerations. To the extent to which proximal intentions are conceptualized in terms of such roles as initiating, sustaining, and guiding intentional actions, such actions being understood as including normal experienced drivers' signaling for turns in normal circumstances, the postulation of nonconscious proximal intentions is attractive.

I opened this article with Marcel's assertion that "Oddly, many psychologists seem to assume that intentions are by their nature conscious" (2003, 60). He proceeds to produce what he regards as counterexamples, including the following:

> the expert acts intentionally but may be unaware of the specifics of tactical intentions, for example, in tennis whether one intends to play a drop volley or a drive volley even when the postural aspects of one's approach to the net is a selective preparation for one rather than the other. Indeed, this is why even when such experts sincerely claim unawareness of their intention, their opponent can anticipate the shot, though the opponent himself may not know how he did so. (Ibid., 61)

Marcel does not say here whether, when the player begins his stroke, he is still unaware of his intention to hit whatever sort of shot he intends to hit—a drive volley, say. But he is at least claiming, in effect, that as the player is running to the net, he has a proximal intention to put himself in a position to hit a drive volley without being aware of that. As I understand Marcel, the player does not have a conscious intention to do this in any of the senses of "conscious intention" that I identified: when the player starts moving toward the net, he is not aware of being about to begin putting himself in a position to hit a drive volley, and as he is moving toward the net he is not aware that he is putting himself in a position to hit such a volley.

Why does this seem right to Marcel? Because, unlike Wegner, Bargh and Chartrand, and others, he conceives of proximal intentions in terms of such functional roles as initiating, sustaining, and guiding intentional actions, and he does not take an agent's intentionally A-ing to require his being conscious (aware) of A-ing. It is not at all odd that scientists who conceive of intentions in this way would reject the assumption that "intentions are by their nature conscious." Nor is it odd that they would find their opponents' view odd.

Can an agent A intentionally without being aware of A-ing? If a driver can intentionally flip his turn signal without being aware of flipping it and a tennis pro can intentionally put himself in a position to hit a drive volley without being aware that he is putting himself in a position to do that, then the answer is *yes*. These examples are controversial in the present context, but others are not. Consider the following case (Mele 2001, 36).

Al knows that funny jokes about cows have consistently made his young daughter laugh. When he composes and sends a funny e-mail message about cows to his daughter with the intention of making her laugh, he is not aware that she is laughing and therefore is not aware that he is making her laugh. Suppose that when she reads the joke she finds it hilarious and laughs uproariously. Then it is very plausible that Al *intentionally* makes her laugh, given the other details of the case. To be sure, Al was aware of doing some of the things that he did intentionally in this story: for example, he was aware of composing a message about cows. But making his daughter laugh is not among the things he was aware of doing. One who claims that intentionally A-ing entails being aware of A-ing is considering too narrow a range of examples of intentional action.

Some neuroscientists are doing research with monkeys that is aimed at developing neural prostheses that will enable paralyzed people to move their limbs. They seek to record monkeys' intentions and to use the associated neural signals to move robot arms, for example (see Andersen and Buneo 2002; Musallam et al. 2004). Recall that the measure of awareness of intentions in scientific studies is subjects' reports. The monkeys in these experiments report nothing. Yet, in the articles I cited, the experimenters express no reservations about attributing intentions to them. Presumably, if they had shared Wegner's conception of intentions as essentially conscious, they would have sought evidence of the required consciousness.

4   Conclusion

In the opening paragraph of this essay I raised two questions: Are intentions "by their nature conscious"? And why might scientists find themselves disagreeing about this? In the scientific literature on intentions that I discussed, the focus is *proximal* intentions. Accordingly, I narrowed the focus of the first question to intentions of this kind. I identified various interpretations of "conscious intention," including a very modest one according to which the following is sufficient for an agent's having a conscious proximal intention to A: his having a proximal intention to A together with an awareness that he is about to A that differs from what I called predictive awareness. And I motivated the thesis that, given any of the interpretations offered, not all proximal intentions are conscious intentions.

My answer to the second question, in a nutshell, is this: some scientists conceive of proximal intentions in terms of such functional roles as initiating, sustaining, and guiding intentional actions, and they do not take an agent's intentionally A-ing to require that he is conscious (aware) of A-ing, whereas others conceive of proximal intentions in a way that is motivated by their sensitivity to an apparent folk theory about or folk concept of such intentions according to which they are conscious products of conscious acts of will. How one chooses to use the word "intention" should not be a matter of much concern—provided that one makes one's meaning clear. Unclarity can result not only in misunderstanding or puzzlement on the part of readers but also in misunderstanding the import of one's own data.

Whether layfolk conceive of proximal intentions as uniformly conscious products of conscious acts of will is testable. For example, researchers can ask one group of experienced drivers whether, when they signal for turns, they intend to do that; and they can ask other groups such questions as whether, in normal circumstances, they are aware of an intention to signal for a turn they are about to make, aware that they intend to signal, and aware of being about to signal. If it were to turn out that *yes* is the majority response to the first question and *no* is the majority response to each of the questions about awareness, that would be evidence that the folk concept of proximal intention does not treat proximal intentions as essentially conscious. But this imagined discovery about a folk concept—a discovery that would imply, for example, that Wegner has overestimated the extent to which layfolk link intentions to consciousness—is not a discovery about how actions are produced. If, as James says, "consciousness deserts all processes where it can no longer be of use" (1890, vol. 2, 496), and if many such processes survive the desertion, then perhaps it deserts some processes that include proximal intentions and corresponding intentional actions while those processes survive. Whether this is so does not depend on whether or not layfolk (or some researchers) happen to conceive of proximal intentions as essentially conscious.

Again, my reason for focusing on proximal intentions in this essay is that such intentions are the focus of the scientific work discussed here. Consider the claim that all occurrent *distal* intentions are, at some time or other, conscious intentions. There is more to recommend this claim than there is to recommend the corresponding claim about proximal intentions. Setting fanciful hypotheses aside, if a distal intention of mine to write a grant proposal next month, to send my sister a birthday card next week, or to buy a plane ticket to Berlin after I return home from Idaho were never a conscious intention, I would not act on it. Possibly, those who say that intentions are essentially conscious take occurrent distal intentions as their model of what intentions are, judge that all such intentions are (at some time or other) conscious intentions, and (tacitly) assume that, regarding consciousness, what is true of occurrent distal intentions is true of all occurrent intentions. However, empirical work focused on *proximal* intentions is well served by conceptual work on the same topic.

Acknowledgments

Earlier versions of this essay were presented at the 2006 Inland Northwest Philosophy Conference and at the universities of Maryland and Potsdam. I am grateful to my audiences, and especially to Michael Bratman and Philipp Hübl, for productive discussion.

Notes

1. Roughly speaking, *basic* actions differ from nonbasic actions in not being performed by way of performing another action.

2. How readers interpret the variable "*A*" should depend on their preferred theory of action individuation. Donald Davidson writes: "I flip the switch, turn on the light, and illuminate the room. Unbeknownst to me I also alert a prowler to the fact that I am home" (1980, 4). How many actions does the agent, Don, perform? Davidson's *coarse-grained* answer is one action "of which four descriptions have been given" (ibid.). A *fine-grained* alternative treats *A* and *B* as different actions if, in performing them, the agent exemplifies different act-properties (Goldman 1970). On this view, Don performs at least four actions, since the act-properties at issue are distinct. An agent may exemplify any of these act-properties without exemplifying any of the others. (One may even turn on a light in a room without illuminating the room: the light may be painted black.) *Componential* views represent Don's illuminating the room as an action having various components, including his moving his arm (an action), his flipping the switch (an action), and the light's going on (Ginet 1990). Where proponents of the coarse-grained and fine-grained theories find, respectively, a single action under different descriptions and a collection of intimately related actions, advocates of the various componential views locate a "larger" action having "smaller" actions among its parts. Readers should understand the variable "*A*" as a variable for actions themselves (construed componentially or otherwise) or actions under descriptions, depending on their preferred theory of action individuation. The same goes for the expressions that take the place of "*A*" in concrete examples.

3. In the case of an intention for a not-doing (e.g., an intention not to vote tomorrow), the agent may instead be settled on not violating the simple plan embedded

in it—the plan not to vote. On not-doings and attitudes toward them, see Mele 2003, 146–54.

4. For two occurrences of "conscious intention," see Wegner 2002, 20, 68.

5. Janet Astington and Alison Gopnik suggest that "at four or five years of age children begin to differentiate intention from desire" (Astington and Gopnik 1991, 47).

6. In the remainder of this paragraph, I borrow from Mele 2003, 30.

7. I use the nouns "want" and "desire" interchangeably.

8. For discussion of some relevant empirical work, see Vollmer 1993.

9. Gilbert Harman writes, "one believes something explicitly if one's belief in that thing involves an explicit mental representation whose content is the content of that belief"; later, he speaks of something "explicitly represented in one's mind" as "written down in Mentalese as it were, without necessarily being available to consciousness" (1986, 13–14). This is the general picture I mean to evoke with the expression "explicit attitudes," but I neither venture an opinion about *how* the contents of attitudes are explicitly represented nor claim that they are all represented in the same way (e.g., in a language of thought). Incidentally, my subsequent use of "implicit" in "implicit attitudes" does not parallel Harman's use of the term in his expression "implicit beliefs" (ibid., 13).

10. On the question whether standing desires are actually desires, see Mele 2003, 32–33.

11. In an atypical case, an agent dies a millisecond after he acquires a proximal intention to raise his right arm. If agents do not begin to execute intentions for arm raisings for some milliseconds after the intention is acquired, this agent did not begin to execute his intention. Incidentally, I am not assuming here that agents do not begin executing their intentions for overt actions until muscles begin to move. On this conceptual issue, see Adams and Mele 1992.

12. Notice that, as I understand deciding and intention acquisition (see sec. 1), we have here physical evidence of a difference between proximally deciding to *A* and otherwise acquiring a proximal intention to *A*. For a relevant caveat, see Jahanshahi et al. 1995, 930.

13. If the turn indicator were to become stuck, these drivers probably would notice that. But that does not entail that they were aware of (some aspect of) their intention to flip it or of being about to flip it or that they were aware that they intended to flip it. Awareness of these things may be prompted by encountering resistance. An agent may become aware that he intended to *A* or that he was about to *A after* he encounters resistance.

14. Libet et al. report that "the subject was asked to note and later report the time of appearance of his conscious awareness of 'wanting' to perform a given self-initiated movement. The experience was also described as an 'urge' or 'intention' or 'decision' to move, though subjects usually settled for the words 'wanting' or 'urge'" (1983, 627).

15. I am not suggesting that intentionally *A*-ing *entails* intending to *A*.

References

Adams, F., and A. R. Mele. 1992. The Intention/Volition Debate. *Canadian Journal of Philosophy* 22:323–338.

Alston, W. 1967. Motives and Motivation. In *The Encyclopedia of Philosophy*, ed. P. Edwards. New York: Macmillan.

Andersen, R. A., and C. A. Buneo. 2002. Intentional Maps in Posterior Parietal Cortex. *Annual Review of Neuroscience* 25:189–220.

Astington, J. W., and A. Gopnik. 1991. Developing Understanding of Desire and Intention. In *Natural Theories of Mind: Evolution, Development and Simulation of Everyday Mindreading*, ed. A. Whiten. Oxford: Blackwell.

Bargh, J. A., and T. L. Chartrand. 1999. The Unbearable Automaticity of Being. *American Psychologist* 54:462–479.

Davidson, D. 1980. *Essays on Actions and Events*. Oxford: Clarendon Press.

Frankfurt, H. 1988. *The Importance of What We Care About*. Cambridge: Cambridge University Press.

Ginet, C. 1990. *On Action*. Cambridge: Cambridge University Press.

Goldman, A. 1970. *A Theory of Human Action*. Englewood Cliffs: Prentice-Hall.

Haggard, P., and S. Clark. 2003. Intentional Action: Conscious Experience and Neural Prediction. *Consciousness and Cognition* 12:695–707.

Harman, G. 1986. *Change in View*. Cambridge, MA: MIT Press.

Jahanshahi, M., I. H. Jenkins, R. G. Brown, C. D. Marsden, R. E. Passingham, and D. J. Brooks. 1995. Self-Initiated versus Externally Triggered Movements. *Brain* 118:913–933.

James, W. 1890. *The Principles of Psychology*, vol. 2. New York: Henry Holt.

Libet, B. 1985. Unconscious Cerebral Initiative and the Role of Conscious Will in Voluntary Action. *Behavioral and Brain Sciences* 8:529–566.

Libet, B., C. A. Gleason, E. W. Wright, and D. K. Pearl. 1983. Time of Unconscious Intention to Act in Relation to Onset of Cerebral Activity (Readiness-Potential). *Brain* 106:623–642.

Marcel, A. 2003. The Sense of Agency: Awareness and Ownership of Action. In *Agency and Self-Awareness*, ed. J. Roessler and N. Eilan. Oxford: Clarendon Press.

McCann, H. J. 1986. Intrinsic Intentionality. *Theory and Decision* 20:247–273.

Mele, A. R. 1992. *Springs of Action*. New York: Oxford University Press.

Mele, A. R. 2001. Acting Intentionally: Probing Folk Notions. In *Intentions and Intentionality: Foundations of Social Cognition*, ed. B. Malle, L. Moses, and D. Baldwin. Cambridge, MA: MIT Press.

Mele, A. R. 2003. *Motivation and Agency*. New York: Oxford University Press.

Musallam, Sam, B. D. Corneil, B. Greger, H. Scherberger, and R. A. Andersen. 2004. Cognitive Control Signals for Neural Prosthetics. *Science* 305: 258–262.

Passingham, R. E., and H. C. Lau. 2006. Free Choice and the Human Brain. In *Does Consciousness Cause Behavior?* ed. S. Pockett, W. Banks, and S. Gallagher. Cambridge, MA: MIT Press.

Pink, T. 1996. *The Psychology of Freedom*. Cambridge: Cambridge University Press.

Searle, J. 1983. *Intentionality*. Cambridge: Cambridge University Press.

Searle, J. 2001. *Rationality in Action*. Cambridge, MA: MIT Press.

Vollmer, F. 1993. Intentional Action and Unconscious Reasons. *Journal for the Theory of Social Behaviour* 23:315–326.

Wegner, D. M. 2002. *The Illusion of Conscious Will*. Cambridge, MA: MIT Press.

6 Locke's Compatibilism: Suspension of Desire or Suspension of Determinism?

Charles T. Wolfe

Voluntary opposed to involuntary, not to necessary.
—John Locke[1]

The common notion of liberty is *false*.
—Anthony Collins[2]

Naturalistic theories of mind and action are typically considered to be recent arrivals on the philosophical scene, in contrast with theories that insist on a categorical separation between actions and events, such as agent causation, which is typically traced back to Aristotle, and can be found in medieval and early modern thinkers such as Francisco Suarez, Samuel Clarke, the Cambridge Platonists, Kant, and Reid, to name but a few. For example, Clarke declares, "When we say, in vulgar speech, that motives or reasons determine a man, 'tis nothing but a mere figure or metaphor. 'Tis the man, that freely determines himself to act."[3] The more naturalistically oriented species of theories tend to be associated with causal closure arguments derived from early twentieth-century physics, notably as mediated through the Vienna Circle. At most, some historical recognition will be given to Hobbes's determinism and Hume's compatibilism. In what follows I wish to show that an original form of compatibilism that acknowledges the complexity of mental life was presented by Locke and radicalized by his disciple Anthony Collins, in a way unlike either Hobbes before them or Hume after them. It may be hoped that a dose of conceptually motivated history of philosophy can have a place in contemporary discussions of action, whether it is as a presentation of possible "solutions," unthought-of "problems," or a rejection of the apparent simplicity of either.

In the chapter "Of Power" in his *Essay Concerning Human Understanding*, Locke uses the logic of ideas to construct a complex deflationary challenge to mainstream notions of freedom as autonomy or as a capacity associated with a distinct faculty called "the Will," understood as entirely separate from the rest of our cognitive functions (Locke 1975, Bk. II, ch. xxi). In a famous but mysterious formulation, he says there can be no such thing as free will because freedom and will are both "powers," and there can be no such thing as a power of a power. We are free to act or not act, but our actions are determined by our will; we are not free to will or not will:

[T]hat which has the power or not the power to operate, is that alone which is or is not free, and not the power itself. For *freedom, or not freedom, can belong to nothing but what has or has not a power to act.* (§19, emphasis mine)

Power is, like pleasure or pain, a simple idea of sensation and reflection (II.vii.1; xxi.2; xxii.10). In his early drafts for the *Essay*, Locke had actually alternated between "power" and "will" as one of the four simple ideas, along with thinking (or perception), pleasure, and pain. He ultimately ends up defining will as power *plus an act of the mind.*[4] In any case, by stipulating that there cannot be a "power of a power," Locke is ruling out a class of responses to the question "Is the will free?"—namely, ones that appeal to divisions within the mind or to higher-order evaluative attitudes (Yaffe 2000, 26).

If Locke had let the matter rest there, he would have contributed an interesting doctrine to the available "set" of compatibilist moral philosophies—ones that recognize the truth of determinism up to a certain point, but consider that this does not rule out the existence of goal-directed, intentional human action, and a fortiori action that responds to praise or blame, rewards or punishments, and thus is "responsible."[5] But in fact, the "Power" chapter is fraught with difficulties, which render it both less coherent and more interesting. It is the longest chapter in the *Essay*, revised significantly for each of the four editions of the book, without earlier versions always being removed, leaving many readers—from Edmund Law, Locke's editor in the eighteenth century, declaring of Locke that

Tho' he has inserted several Passages in the subsequent Editions, which come near to Liberty, yet he takes in the greatest part of his first passive Scheme, and generally mixes both together. This has occasioned the greatest confusion in the Chapter abovementioned, which cannot but be observ'd by every Reader[6]

to Leibniz, and today, Vere Chappell—with the feeling that Locke's account is incoherent or at least inconsistent, something Locke himself apologizes for at the end of the chapter (§72).[7]

I shall focus on Locke's account and its difficulties, but I shall supplement his account in my final discussion with its revision and deterministically directed critique as put forth by his own closest disciple, the deist

Anthony Collins,[8] in his *Philosophical Inquiry Concerning Human Liberty* (1717). Locke's account contains at least three distinct "theories of freedom"; I suggest below that Collins's reading of this situation and reinforcement of one of these theories (the most determinism-friendly one) is the most convincing.

Locke starts out with the intellectualist position that we are "determined by the Good," the greater Good, which we know through our understanding (II.xxi.29 in the 1st edition); this is a *perfection*. But in response to Molyneux's criticism that

you seem to make all Sins proceed from our Understandings . . . ; and not at all from the Depravity of our Wills. Now it seems harsh to say, that a Man shall be Damn'd, because he understands no better than he does[9]

Locke introduces a new concept in the second edition, as he writes to Molyneux; he now recognizes that "every good, nay every greater good, does not constantly move desire, because it may not make, or may not be taken to make any necessary part of our happiness; for all that we desire is only to be happy."[10] He is now focusing on the causal mechanisms of what determines the will and thus moves us to act, in other words, the "motivational triggers" of action; this will turn out to be "uneasiness."

How could we then seek out the Highest Good? How can we "feel" or "sense" that the Highest Good is, in fact, *our* good? Locke originally thought that the Highest Good did play a causal role in our actions, so that our desire would be "regulated" by the "greatness or smallness of the good,"[11] ("the greater Good is that alone which determines the Will" [§29]), but he gave up this view starting with the second edition, in which he adds the category of uneasiness: "*good*, the *greater good*, though apprehended and acknowledged to be so, does not determine the will, until our desire, raised proportionately to it, make us uneasy in the want of it" (§35). Thus

[Uneasiness] is the great motive that works on the Mind to put it upon Action, which for shortness sake we will call *determining of the Will* (§29)

and more explicitly,

what . . . *determines the Will in regard to our actions* is not . . . the greater good in view: but some (and for the most part the most pressing) *uneasiness* a man is at present under. (§31, 2nd–5th editions)

As my interest is the emergence of a determinist approach to action, Locke's addition of a hedonistic motivational psychology is noteworthy as a recognition of determinism, if only a "soft determinism."[12] Whether or not I can rationally judge X (say, a one-month intensive course in classical Greek, in a secluded desert setting) to be a greater good than Y (large amounts of chocolate and other sweets, several glasses of Cognac, a cigar), if obtaining Y removes the greater pressing uneasiness, I will choose Y. This is Locke's way of addressing weakness of will, confirmed by his quotation of Ovid's "Video meliora, proboque, deteriora sequor" (I see the better [path], but I choose the worse).[13] But in my view, uneasiness is not just an explanation for ataraxia; it is *Locke's* (2nd edition) *explanation for action as a whole*, and it is his recognition of "micro-determinism" at the subpersonal level of action. It's quite possible for me to choose X over Y, in fact, many people do; they simply had a greater pressing uneasiness in that direction. As for responsibility, it is unaffected, since God judges all of our actions at the time of resurrection, in any case.

Locke always rejects the thesis of the autonomy of the will, according to which the will is *self-determining*; he holds that the will *is always determined "by something without itself."*[14] This determination from "without" can either be from the Greater Good (1st edition), the most pressing uneasiness (2nd edition), or an interplay between this uneasiness and the last judgment of the understanding (2nd–5th editions), and since the Good is always defined as happiness (§42), and happiness is always defined as pleasure, the "hedonism" that commentators see appearing in the second edition is not absent from the first edition. This is why he denies the liberty of indifference—the absolute equilibrium of Buridan's ass, that is, the situation in which an agent is free if and only if, given all conditions for an act A, it can both A and not A, which Leibniz helpfully describes as "indifference of equilibrium"[15]—as directly contradicting his hedonism (§48). For Locke, it is both *impossible* to be genuinely indifferent, as we are always being swayed by one uneasiness or another, and *not a good idea to be indifferent*, as our ideas of good and evil, translating as they do into pleasure and pain, are "in us" for the purpose of our self-preservation:

our All-wise Maker, suitable to our constitution and frame, and knowing what it is that determines the *Will*, has put into Man the *uneasiness* of hunger and thirst, and other natural desires . . . to move and determine their *Wills*, for the preservation of themselves, and the continuation of their Species. . . . We may conclude, that, if the bare contemplation of these good ends to which we are carried by these several *uneasinesses*, had been sufficient to determine the *will* . . . we should have had in this World little or no pain at all. (§ 34)

He also claims that the existence of genuine indifference is an impossibility. It would be useless to be indifferent with regard to the understanding, because our actions would then be like "playing the fool" or better, being a "blind agent";[16] moreover, being determined in our choices by the last judgment of the understanding is a *good idea* in terms of our welfare and self-preservation.

Now, the actions of an agent who is never indifferent, and whose actions are never uncaused, are perfectly compatible with determinism. This overall "compatibility" means, I think, that Locke's vision of action and freedom can be understood simply as calling attention to our "reinforcement" of certain links in the causal chain, rather than insisting on a quasi-categorial distinction like that between "happenings" and "doings," in which a "happening" is merely a relation between an object and a property, whereas a "doing" expresses a stronger relation.[17]

However, Locke is about to modify his theory of action—if not, per se, of motivation—in an important way, resulting in a new theory of freedom, and in a step away from compatibilism, the very step Collins will challenge. Recall Locke's second (and crucial) account of what determines the will:

There being in us a great many *uneasinesses*, always soliciting and ready to determine the *will*, it is natural, as I have said, that the greatest and most pressing should determine the *will* to the next action; and so it does *for the most part, but not always*. (§47, emphasis mine)

"For the most part, but not always": this is the sign of the coming modification. Hedonistic determination of our will works most of the time, but not always; sometimes we can simply *stop the mechanism*. I quote Locke's new statement:

For, the mind having in most cases, as is evident in experience, a power to *suspend* the execution and satisfaction of any of its desires; and so all, one after another; is at liberty to consider the objects of them, examine them on all sides, and weigh them with others. In this lies the liberty man has; and from the not using of it right comes all that variety of mistakes, errors, and faults which we run into in the conduct of our lives, and our endeavours after happiness; whilst we precipitate the determination of our *wills*, and engage too soon, before due *Examination*. To prevent this, we have a power to suspend the prosecution of this or that desire; as every one daily may experiment in himself. This seems to me the source of all liberty; in this seems to consist that which is (as I think improperly) called *free-will*. For, during this *suspension* of any desire, before the *will* be determined to action, and the action (which follows that determination) done, we have opportunity to examine, view, and judge of the good or evil of what we are going to do; and when, upon due *Examination*, we have judged, we have done our duty, all that we can, or ought to do, in pursuit of our happiness; and it is not a fault, but a perfection of our nature, to desire, will, and act according to the last result of a fair *Examination*. (§47)

He confirms some sections later that suspension is the "hinge" on which the new theory of freedom "turns":

This is the hinge on which turns the *liberty* of intellectual beings, in their constant endeavours after, and a steady prosecution of true felicity,—That they can *suspend* this prosecution in particular cases, till they have looked before them, and informed themselves whether that particular thing which is then proposed or desired lie in the way to their main end, and make a real part of that which is their greatest good. . . . experience showing us, that in most cases, we are able to suspend the present satisfaction of any desire. (§52)

How did we get to suspension? Not by some casual intuition Locke suddenly remembered, about how we do stop and reflect about different goods frequently. Rather, Locke appeals to his distinction between active powers and passive powers. We know by experience that we have a power to change and a power to receive changes. In the realm of thinking, the power to receive ideas from without is the merely "passive" power, by the exercise of which we are patients and not agents. But we also have an active power, "to bring into view ideas out of sight, at one's own choice, and compare which of them one thinks fit" (§72). This quote from the end of the chapter, precisely in the portion that was added last, provides the conceptual justification for what may be Locke's key moral idea, the *suspension of desire.*

This active power applied to the moral realm is the power to suspend the "execution and satisfaction of [our] desires" (§47), in other words, the "prosecution" of an action. We are not necessarily compelled to attend to a present (and pressing) uneasiness, because we can reflect on the main source of this uneasiness, in order to know which object of desire we should pursue. This "suspension" of action is "the source of all liberty . . . which is (as I think improperly) called *Free will*" (§47). An action can be suspended until the will is determined to action; the will is determined to action by a judgment on which good we pursue. In other words, this "moment of freedom" occurs within a causal scheme in which we "desire, will and act according to the last result of a fair examination" (§48); this last result is very reminiscent of the final moment of deliberation that Hobbes compared to the feather which breaks the horse's back.[18]

A mitigated determinism, but still a determinism, then: we can suspend the mechanism of desire and uneasiness and deliberate on a course of action, that is, we can suspend the "prosecution" of an action, but once a course of action has been chosen, we have to follow it. If we hadn't noticed that this moment of suspension seems hard to reconcile with the rest of the hedonistic scheme, Collins will call attention to this flaw or inconsistency in Locke's explanation, and cast doubt on the possibility of our power to somehow *suspend a course of events*—in other words, the possibility that in a causal chain of actions, there might be a moment that is not itself within the causal chain. With his unmistakable clarity and precision, Collins says simply that "*suspending to will*, is itself an *act of willing*; it is willing to defer willing about the matter propos'd" (Collins 1717, 39); and since Collins does not accept a categorial separation between desire and will, which he finds to be a traditional (Aristotelian) residue in Locke, he will consider any suspension of the will, being "itself an act of willing," to still be determined by the causal mechanism of uneasiness.

Locke has moved from freedom as the power to do what one wills to do or not do, that is, not the freedom to *will* but to *act* (§§8, 23), to freedom understood as the ability to suspend desire, to keep it from provoking action (§§47, 52). If uneasiness turned out to be the only causal mechanism through which the Good can influence me, then for my actions to not be fully determined by this mechanism, I must be able to suspend the execution of my desires. Suspension is "the hinge on which turns the *liberty* of intellectual beings, in their constant endeavours after, and a steady prosecution of true felicity" (§52). It sounds a lot like a "second-order freedom" of the sort made popular by Charles Taylor and Harry Frankfurt in contemporary moral philosophy. But the early modern thinker who most prominently defends a doctrine of freedom as a derivative state in relation to more primary voluntary mental states is not Locke, but Leibniz.[19] For Locke, freedom as suspension is still not freedom to will; it is freedom to act in accordance with the will. It's natural to ask whether the suspension doctrine is a departure from determinism or not.[20] Indeed, in §56 of the "Power" chapter, which he added to the fifth edition, Locke says the following:

Liberty 'tis plain consists in a Power to do, or not to do; to do, or forbear doing, as we will. This cannot be denied. But this seeming to comprehend only the actions of a Man consecutive to volition, it is further inquired,—Whether he be at liberty to will or no? And to this it has been answered, that, in most cases, a Man is not at Liberty to forbear the act of volition: he must exert an act of his will, whereby the action proposed is made to exist or not to exist. But yet there is a case wherein a Man is at *Liberty in respect of willing*; and that is the choosing of a remote Good as an end to be pursued. Here a Man may suspend the act of his choice from being determined for or against the thing proposed, till he has examined whether it be really of a nature, in itself and consequences, to make him happy, or no. (Emphasis mine)

In sum, Locke's "Power" chapter contains not one but *three separate doctrines of freedom*:

(A) freedom is determination by the Good (1st edition);
(B) given the condition of uneasiness, freedom is the suspension of desire (2nd edition); this allows the Good and the understanding to be "reintroduced";
(C) liberty with respect to willing (5th edition), which seems to follow from suspension: once we suspend, we can choose one good over another, and once that choice is made, it raises our uneasiness accordingly.

Many commentators, Chappell most prominently, have worried about how to reconcile (A) with (B): how to reconcile a notion of the Good with a hedonistic motivational psychology. My response is that if we recall that the Good always means happiness, itself definable in terms of pleasure and the avoidance of pain, and the presence of the afterlife and its potential rewards and punishments *cannot be excluded from hedonistic considerations*, there seems to be almost no difficulties with reconciling these two doctrines. *However*, the situation appears to be different with doctrine (C), liberty "in respect to willing." The idea appears to be blatantly inconsistent with the rest of the chapter. Indeed, it's not just §56 that presents this difficulty; consider this statement:

Nay, were we determined by anything but the last result of our own Minds, judging of the good or evil of any action, we were not free; the very end of our Freedom being, that we may attain the good we choose. (§48)

This sentence can be simplified to read:

If our will were determined by something other than X, then it would not be free.

As Yaffe (2001) suggests, this can in turn be rewritten in this way (even if it's simply a matter of denying the antecedent):

If our will is determined by X, it is free.

If only in terms of Locke's own rhetoric in the early sections of the chapter, one cannot help but point out that he had claimed to be dispensing with the notion of free will, for good . . . and here he is entertaining a version of it, however revised. What should we make, then, of Locke's apparent insouciance?

The naively biographical approach would be to say that Locke first asserted (in a rather orthodox, Scholastic way) that we are determined by the Good; then he was radicalized in a hedonistic direction by reading

Gassendi during his stay in Montpellier (indeed, his first essays on pleasure and pain are exactly contemporary with this reading); lastly, frightened by the possible consequences of this doctrine, he jerry-rigs a device by which we are again "free" faced with the various micro-determinisms, whether hedonistic or just plain unconscious.[21]

In contrast to this approach, I would present a case for the "enduring" status of determination in his chapter (a more "determinist" reading of Locke, then) for two reasons, ranked in increasing order of importance:

(1) Suspension is not really the opposite or contrary of uneasiness, as one might think; rather, it *emerges out of uneasiness* (an emergence that would not have been conceivable or allowable for earlier suspension theorists; Locke, in contrast, allows that the stirrings of desire have not only intentional content but reflexive content). Thus it is not a mere grafting on of libertarian elements into a formerly compatibilist view. Because there are multiple stimuli, we need to be able to pick and choose between them; or, better put, suspension supervenes on the "multiple conative elements"[22] of uneasiness, and is thus not tantamount to "indifference," which is the contrary of uneasiness; it does not reintroduce true divisions in the mind. James Tully uses different language and emphasis to similarly nuance Locke's shift from determination-by-the-Good to hedonism as a motivational theory:

Locke argues that his first view cannot be true, because if it were everyone who has considered Christianity would be an unfailing Christian in practice. This is so since they would be aware that heaven and hell outweigh all other good and evil, and so they would be motivated to live a Christian life to gain infinite pleasure and avoid infinite pain. Yet it obviously is true that everyone who has considered Christianity is not a practising Christian, therefore the greater good in view does not determine the will. (Tully 1988, 47)

(2) Locke never ceases to deny freedom as indifference, which leads him to formulate a new part of his doctrine: the determination of our will by the last judgment of our understanding is a "perfection of our nature" (§47) rather than a "restraint or diminution of freedom" (§48). Much like the "practical" argument against indifference in terms of self-preservation, Locke thinks it is a *perfection* to be *determined*:

A man is at liberty to lift up his hand to his head, or let it rest quiet: he is perfectly indifferent in either; and it would be an imperfection in him, if he wanted that power, if he were deprived of that indifference. But it would be as great an imperfection, if he had the same indifferency, whether he would prefer the lifting up his hand, or its remaining in rest, when it would save his head or eyes from a blow he sees coming: *it is as much a perfection, that desire, or the power of preferring, should be determined by good, as that the power of acting should be determined by the will; and the certainer such determination is, the greater is the perfection.* (§48, emphasis mine)[23]

In sum, Locke has put forth both a powerful critique of mainstream theories of freedom and the will, with his concept of "uneasiness," *and* he seems to have retreated from the (hedonistic) deterministic implications of this concept, with his claim that there are moments when we can suspend all such determination and be free "with respect to willing." At the same time, partly owing to the theological overtones of his moral philosophy, he thinks it is a *perfection* that we are in fact determined in our actions, and an unavoidable one. Based on the textual complexities and variations in the "Power" chapter of the *Essay*, one could defend different versions of compatibilism in Locke. Namely, one could defend a moral theory in which we are determined by the Good; or one could view Locke as the originator of Frankfurt-style "second-order" freedom (although as I have noted, Leibniz is a better author to pin this doctrine on); lastly, one could focus on Locke's notion of uneasiness and show how it opens on to a coherent *and psychologically fine-grained* determinism. It is the latter theory that I find most compelling, and it was this approach that was taken by Locke's radical friend and disciple, Anthony Collins.

Collins seized upon Locke's notion of uneasiness, bolstered it metaphysically with various determinist arguments drawn from Hobbes, Spinoza, Leibniz, and Bayle (principally an "argument from experience" and an "argument from causality"), and challenged any type of "suspension" or "liberty with respect to willing" as being inconsistent with uneasiness. In doing so, he puts forth a powerful and original form of determinism that does not neglect the conceptual and empirical particularities of the world of action, contrary to most discussions in action theory or the philosophy of science, which tend to ignore one another—one may term Collins's position a "volitional determinism";[24] he himself speaks of "moral necessity," taking a term from the incompatibilist, libertarian vocabulary used notably by Samuel Clarke:

I contend only for what is called moral necessity, meaning thereby, that man, who is an intelligent and sensible being, is determined by his reason and his senses; and I deny man to be subject to such necessity, as is in clocks, watches and other beings which for want of sensation and intelligence are subject to an absolute, physical or mechanical necessity. (Collins 1717, preface, iii)

It is not possible here to go into further details about Collins's doctrine, which significantly anticipates the "Hume–Mill" thesis (later defended by thinkers such as Moritz Schlick, A. J. Ayer, and J. J. C. Smart[25]) according to which an agent is causally determined by her beliefs, desires, and other mental states, in a way that forms an adequate basis for a moral theory. Put differently, even if there are really are "rationality relations" between beliefs and desires on the one hand and behavior on the other hand, it does not follow that beliefs and desires do not cause behavior (Churchland 1986, 304); this is why our actions are not fully random. Quine, for one, credited Spinoza and Hume with this view:

Like Spinoza, Hume and so many others, I count an act as free insofar as the agent's motives or drives are a link in its causal chain. These motives or drives may themselves be as rigidly determined as you please. (Quine 1995, 199)

But most contemporary scholars and action theorists tend to attribute this view to "Hume and subsequent compatibilists"[26]; my point as regards this historical claim is that Locke actually first lays out the conditions for such a view, and that Collins expresses it in full, a generation before Hume.

In addition to the "character-causal" claim, Locke and Collins also make the classic deflationary point that our everyday ways of talking, in which we are not *caused* by the reasons for our action because we *reflected* on these reasons, so that "if a man's behavior is rational, it cannot be determined by the state of his glands or any other antecedent causal factors,"[27] are precisely just *façons de parler* and do not reflect any underlying "joints" of things. They would undoubtedly agree with Daniel Wegner that our experience of free will is "the way our minds portray their operations to us, not their actual operation" (Wegner 2002, 96). In this sense, Lockean–Collinsian volitional determinism could be true even if the universe as a whole is *not* deterministic, for example, at the quantum level: universal physical determinism plus supervenience of the mental on the physical entails psychological determinism, but the reverse does not hold.[28] Contemporary claims that compatibilism is inherently self-contradictory because determinism implies a total lack of control over any part of the universe and its laws, whether made in support of libertarian free will (van Inwagen) or of determinism (Galen Strawson), are impressive in their metaphysical coherence but, curiously for moral philosophy, seem to ignore those specific features of psychological life that these early modern philosophers took seriously, and which impact directly on moral considerations. They seem to ignore that "even in a deterministic world, not all thieves are kleptomaniacs," in Saul Smilansky's evocative phrase (Smilansky, this volume).

I have tried to outline the complexity of Locke's views on action and indicate how they formed the basis for a new and less-known form of determinism—a uniquely "volitional" determinism that recognizes the specific complexity of mental life, or psychological events, since after all, "determinism alone does not tell us what laws or kinds of laws take human acts as their dependent variables" (Goldman 1970, 173). The shift from the will understood as an autonomous, self-transparent faculty to the will as a "power" is also a kind of "psychologization" (understood as a form of naturalization), since the notion of a faculty implies a kind of autonomy and distinction from the natural world, whereas a power is a "Newtonian" concept, which applies equally to the physical and the psychological realms, as is evident in Locke's various examples.

Both Locke and Collins reject, preemptively, anything like agent causation, or a basic distinction between reasons and causes. Unlike a pure physicalistically driven determinist like Hobbes, they offer a fine-grained account of volitional determinism and other motivational "pressures." The suspension of desire is not, then, a suspension of determinism.

Acknowledgments

Some of this material is derived from my Ph.D. dissertation, "Locating Mind in the Causal World: Locke, Collins, and Enlightened Determinism," Department of Philosophy, Boston University (2006); it has been presented in different forms in Moscow (Idaho), Montréal, and New York. My thanks to Kenneth Winkler, Justin Steinberg, Meggan Payne, and the anonymous reviewers for helpful criticisms and suggestions.

Notes

1. Locke 1975, Book II, chapter xxi, §11. Unless otherwise indicated, all quotations from Locke are from this chapter and are simply given as section (§) numbers.

2. Collins 1717, 22.

3. Clarke 1738/1978, 723.

4. "Pleasure, Pain, the Passions," in Locke 1997, 244.

5. Of course, the term "compatibilism" is quite broad; thinkers as different as Spinoza and Leibniz (in addition to Locke) can both safely be described as compatibilists. In fact, what it meant to be a compatibilist in the early modern period was less specific than now, if it is the case that compatibilists "typically hold either that free will is compatible with deterministic causal laws at the psychological level, or

that even if there are no such laws, every psychological event is still causally determined through being token-identical with some physical event which falls under the laws of physics" (Borst 1992, 57).

6. Law, in King 1731/1739, 253ff., n. 45.

7. Locke had acknowledged how much he had revised the chapter in the "Epistle to the Reader": "I have found reason somewhat to alter the thoughts I formerly had concerning that, which gives the last determination to the Will in all voluntary actions" (11).

8. Collins was extremely close to Locke in the last years of his life, and their correspondence is both moving and filled with provocative insights, not least on theological matters. Locke wrote to Collins that "if I were now setting out in the world I should think it my great happiness to have such a companion as you who had a true relish of truth . . . and to whom I might communicate what I thought true freely"; as for strictly intellectual kinship, "I know nobody that understands [my book] so well, nor can give me better light concerning it" (Letters of October 29, 1703 and April 3, 1704, letters 3361 and 3504 in Locke 1976–1989, vol. 8, 97, 263).

9. Molyneux to Locke, December 22, 1692, letter 1579 in Locke 1976–1989, vol. 4, 600–601. (James Tully points out that the criticism was first suggested by William King, the Archbishop of Dublin, then relayed by Molyneux, who discussed it at length with Locke; see Tully 1988, 47.)

10. Letter 1655 (August 23, 1693), in Locke 1976–1989, vol. 4, 722.

11. Locke, "Pleasure, Pain, the Passions," in Locke 1997, 243.

12. That is, not hard determinism, in which "a complete description of the state of the world at any given time and a complete statement of the laws of nature together entail every truth as to what events happen after that time"(Ginet 1990, 92). A less fortunate definition of soft determinism is Paul Russell's "compatibilism plus the belief that determinism is true" (Russell 1995, 83 n. 20).

13. Locke 1975, II.xxi.35 (the quotation is from Ovid, *Metamorphoses*, VII, 20–21; it is Medea speaking, about killing her children). Descartes, Hobbes, and Spinoza also quote this passage.

14. §29, in the first edition only (p. 248n.); in the final edition, this phrase is the entry in the table of contents for §§25–27. See Vere Chappell's contribution to Sleigh, Chappell, and Della Rocca 1998, 1250–1251, and Chappell 1994, 201.

15. Leibniz to Coste, December 19, 1707 (the "letter on human freedom"), in Leibniz 1989, 194–195.

16. Locke to van Limborch, August 12, 1701, letter 2979 in Locke 1976–1989, 408.

17. Gideon Yaffe, in his elegant, thought-provoking but anachronistic work *Liberty Worth the Name* (Yaffe 2000), suggests the above distinction and appeals to it frequently but inconsistently. I disagree with Yaffe's reading of Locke on action, on a fundamental level: Yaffe's Locke holds that we are determined *by the Good*, whereas Locke as I read him places the emphasis on *determined*.

18. Hobbes 1839–1845, vol. 4, 247, and Hobbes 1999, 34. Collins uses the same image (Collins 1717, 49).

19. Vailati 1990, 226, n. 50. See Leibniz 1982, II.xxi.23.

20. Sleigh, Chappell, and Della Rocca 1998, 1250. Yaffe (2001, 387, n. 2) remarks nicely that suspension is really an idea Locke takes over from the libertarian or incompatibilist position, particularly Malebranche, whereas his initial doctrine of freedom as the absence of constraint on action was more compatibilist, closer to Hobbes. With respect to Collins's critique, this implies that, depending on which edition of the *Essay* one looks at, one finds a more or less determinist Locke; thus one could conceivably construct an alternate Locke who would not be (as) vulnerable to the reductionist "streamlining" offered by Collins.

21. One of Leibniz's chief criticisms of Locke's moral psychology is that he leaves out (or is unaware of) the entire unconscious dimension of mental life (see Leibniz 1982, II.xx.6). In fact, in various texts written parallel to the *Essay*, including his correspondence with Jean Le Clerc, Locke shows that he is quite aware of the subpersonal levels of uneasiness.

22. Borrowing this expression from Dretske (1988), p. 138.

23. In this sense Locke is closer to Calvinism than, notably, his friend and correspondent Philipp van Limborch, the head of the Remonstrant Arminian congregation in Amsterdam. (Remonstrants or Arminians were followers of Jacobus Arminius [1560–1609], who scandalized the Calvinists by claiming that our wills are at least sufficiently free that we can rationally be subjected to persuasion and punishment [hence salvation through works].)

24. I take this term from Chappell (1998, 86). He uses it to mean the thesis that we are not free in willing; I agree, but extend the term to mean a metaphysical thesis, a variant of determinism that focuses on volitions, and thereby action, and thereby the *mind*, in contrast to a "physicalist" (or "Laplacean") determinism that denies the existence of this level of action, or at least seeks to reduce it to a lower-level explanation.

25. The Hume-Mill thesis is what van Inwagen (1983) calls "the *Mind* argument"—because its classic formulation in the twentieth century came primarily in three papers published in *Mind* over two and a half decades, by Hobart (1934), Nowell-Smith (1948), and Smart (1961, 1984), in addition to Ayer (1954) and Schlick (1930/1939).

26. Dupré 2001, 178. The same statement about the Hume–Mill thesis can be found, e.g., in Ginet 1990, O'Connor 1995, and Russell 1995. Winkler (1998), §3, is one of the few scholars who recognizes Collins's anticipation of Hume. For more on Collins's "volitional determinism" see Wolfe 2007.

27. MacIntyre 1957, 35; cf. O'Connor 1995, 196.

28. I owe the latter formulation to an anonymous reviewer.

References

Ayer, A. J. 1954. Freedom and Necessity. In *Philosophical Essays*. London: Macmillan.

Borst, C. 1992. Leibniz and the Compatibilist Account of Free Will. *Studia Leibnitiana* 24:49–58.

Chappell, V. 1994. Locke on the Intellectual Basis of Sin. *Journal of the History of Philosophy* 32:197–207.

Chappell, V. 1998. Locke on the Freedom of the Will. In *Locke: Oxford Readings in Philosophy*, ed. V. Chappell. Oxford: Oxford University Press.

Churchland, P. S. 1986. *Neurophilosophy: Towards a Unified Science of the Mind/Brain*. Cambridge, MA: MIT Press.

Clarke, S. [1738] 1978. *Remarks on a book, entitled, A Philosophical Inquiry into Human Liberty*. In *The Works of Samuel Clarke*, vol. 4. New York: Garland.

Collins, A. 1717. *A Philosophical Inquiry Concerning Human Liberty*. London: Robinson.

Collins, A. 1976. *A Philosophical Inquiry Concerning Human Liberty*. In *Determinism and Freewill*, ed. J. O'Higgins. The Hague: Martinus Nijhoff.

Dretske, F. 1988. *Explaining Behavior: Reasons in a World of Causes*. Cambridge, MA: MIT Press.

Dupré, J. 2001. *Human Nature and the Limits of Science*. Oxford: Clarendon Press.

Ginet, C. 1990. *On Action*. Cambridge: Cambridge University Press.

Goldman, A. 1970. *A Theory of Human Action*. Princeton: Princeton University Press.

Hobart, R. E. 1934. Free Will as Involving Determinism and Inconceivable Without It. *Mind* 43:1–27.

Hobbes, T. 1839–1845. *English Works*, 12 vols. Ed. W. Molesworth. London: J. Bohn.

Hobbes, T. Chappell, V., ed. 1999. *Of Liberty and Necessity*. Cambridge: Cambridge University Press.

King, W. [1731] 1978. *An Essay on the Origin of Evil*. Trans. and ed. E. Law. New York: Garland.

Leibniz, G. W. 1982. *New Essays on Human Understanding*. Ed. P. Remnant and J. Bennett. Cambridge: Cambridge University Press.

Leibniz, G. W. 1989. *Philosophical Essays*. Trans. R. Ariew and D. Garber. Indianapolis: Hackett.

Locke, J. 1975. *An Essay Concerning Human Understanding*. 5th ed. Ed. P. Nidditch. Oxford: Oxford University Press.

Locke, J. 1976–1989. *Correspondence*. 8 vols. Ed. E. S. De Beer. Oxford: Clarendon Press.

Locke, J. Goldie, M., ed. 1997. *Political Essays*. Cambridge: Cambridge University Press.

MacIntyre, A. 1957. Determinism. *Mind* 66:28–41.

Nowell-Smith, P. H. 1948. Free Will and Moral Responsibility. *Mind* 57:45–61.

O'Connor, T. 1995. Agent Causation. In *Agents, Causes, and Events: Essays on Indeterminism and Free Will*, ed. T. O'Connor. New York: Oxford University Press.

Quine, W. V. O. 1995. Things and Their Place in Theories. In *Contemporary Materialism*, ed. P. K. Moser and J. D. Trout. London: Routledge.

Russell, P. 1995. *Freedom and Moral Sentiment. Hume's Way of Naturalizing Responsibility*. Oxford: Oxford University Press.

Schlick, M. 1939. When Is a Man Responsible? Trans. D. Rynin. In *Problems of Ethics*. New York: Prentice-Hall.

Sleigh, R., V. Chappell, and M. Della Rocca. 1998. Determinism and Human Freedom. In *Cambridge History of Seventeenth Century Philosophy*, vol. 2. Ed. D. Garber and M. Ayers. Cambridge: Cambridge University Press.

Smart, J. J. C. 1961. Free-Will, Praise and Blame. *Mind* 70:291–306.

Smart, J. J. C. 1984. "Ought," "Can," Free Will, and Responsibility. In *Ethics, Persuasion, and Truth*. London: Routledge & Kegan Paul.

Tully, J. 1988. Governing Conduct. In *Conscience and Casuistry in Early Modern Europe*, ed. E. Leites. Cambridge: Cambridge University Press.

Vailati, E. 1990. Leibniz on Locke on Weakness of Will. *Journal of the History of Philosophy* 28:213–228.

van Inwagen, P. 1983. *An Essay on Free Will*. Oxford: Clarendon Press.

Wegner, D. 2002. *The Illusion of Conscious Will*. Cambridge, MA: MIT Press.

Winkler, K. 1998. Anthony Collins. In *Routledge Encyclopedia of Philosophy*, vol. 2. London: Routledge.

Wolfe, C. T. 2007. Determinism/Spinozism in the Radical Enlightenment: the cases of Anthony Collins and Denis Diderot. In *Boundaries in the Eighteenth Century: International Review of Eighteenth-Century Studies (IRECS)*, vol. 1. ed. P. Ihalainen, J. Ilmakunnas, T. Kaitaro, P. Mehtonen, J. Nurmiainen, P. M. Pihlaja, J. Tunturi, and C. Wolff. Helsinki, Oxford: SIEDS/ISECS.

Yaffe, G. 2000. *Liberty Worth the Name: Locke on Free Agency*. Princeton: Princeton University Press.

Yaffe, G. 2001. Locke on Suspending, Refraining, and the Freedom to Will. *History of Philosophy Quarterly* 18:373–391.

7 The Fall of the *Mind* Argument and Some Lessons about Freedom

E. J. Coffman and Donald Smith

Libertarians believe that freedom exists but is incompatible with determinism, and so are committed to the compatibility of freedom and *in*determinism. Perhaps the most pressing objection to libertarianism is the so-called *Mind* argument for the incompatibility of freedom and indeterminism. This essay presents a new criticism of the *Mind* argument that is at once decisive and instructive. After some preliminaries, we introduce a plausible principle (γ) that places a requirement on one's having a choice about an event whose causal history includes only other *events*. We then argue for these three claims:

• The *Mind* argument presupposes that γ is true, a crucial point neglected by previous studies of the *Mind* argument.
• If γ is true, then (i) the *Mind* argument fails and (ii) the sole beneficiaries of this failure are *nonreductive* libertarians, libertarians who hold that *agents themselves* can contribute causally to events.
• If γ is false, then (a) the *Mind* argument fails and (b) the sole beneficiaries of this failure are *reductive* libertarians, libertarians who hold that—speaking strictly and literally—only *events* can contribute causally to events.

In short, we will argue that, depending on γ's truth-value, the *Mind* argument fails in such a way that one or the other of the two main species of libertarianism is the best approach to the metaphysics of freedom.

While our arguments for the three claims listed above constitute the heart of our project, we have another important goal in the sequel: We aim to build a case for the truth of γ, and so for nonreductive libertarianism. We make this case by emphasizing γ's *prima facie* plausibility, and by defending it from the best objections that have been brought to our attention. We thus hope that our argument from γ to nonreductive libertarianism, coupled with our defense of the former, will strike many as a strong case for the latter.

Some terminology and assumptions: Reductivism is the view that only *events* can contribute causally—or, be causally relevant—to an event. Nonreductivism, on the other hand, is the view that *agents themselves*—in addition to "agent-involving" events—can contribute causally to events, can themselves figure in an event's causal history. Nonreductive libertarianism is the conjunction of nonreductivism and libertarianism;[1] reductive libertarianism combines libertarianism with reductivism.[2] Reductive compatibilism, naturally enough, is the conjunction of reductivism and compatibilism (i.e., the view that freedom is compatible with determinism);[3] and nonreductive compatibilism combines compatibilism with nonreductivism.[4] These are the four main views of those who think that metaphysical freedom exists.[5]

For the sake of readability, we use the term "event" quite broadly so that it applies to *any* nonsubstance plausibly thought capable of standing in the *causal contribution* relation. On our usage, then, "event" applies not only to *changes*, but also to *processes*, *states*, and so on.[6]

Finally, we assume throughout this essay that some human agents are free. More fully, we assume that some human agent is such that there is an *earliest* or *first* event about which he had a choice.[7] This assumption—the *Freedom Assumption*—can be put more precisely as follows:

Some human agent, *S*, is such that there is an event, *e*, such that *S* had a choice about *e* but did not have a choice about any event prior to *e*.[8]

We take it that most parties to the current debate about the metaphysics of freedom accept this assumption, and so we reckon it quite uncontroversial (not to mention eminently plausible regardless of the contingent fact that it's widely accepted).

A brief overview of the essay: In section 1, we introduce γ, and provide some support for it. We then explain the two strongest versions of the *Mind* argument, those developed by Peter van Inwagen and Dana Nelkin. Here, we uncover a crucial fact overlooked by previous discussions of these arguments—namely, both presuppose that γ is true. Now, although van Inwagen's *Mind* argument is generally recognized to fail, Nelkin's more recent version has not yet faced decisive criticism. In sections 2–3, we develop our decisive and instructive objection to Nelkin's *Mind* argument. Finally, in section 4 we defend γ against the best objections that have been brought to our attention, thus bolstering a γ-based case for nonreductive libertarianism.

1   γ and the *Mind* Argument Explained

We begin with an example to introduce, and generate prima facie support for, γ. The example also serves to illustrate the familiar concept of *causal contribution*, which (following others) we leave unanalyzed.

A rock flies toward a window. A bystander, Jack, freely refrains from stopping the rock's flight. The rock then shatters the window. The window's shattering has a causal history: numerous events contributed causally to the window's shattering. Such events include the rock's travel-ing toward the window on a certain trajectory, and at a certain velocity; Jack's freely refraining from stopping the rock; and, of course, the rock's striking the window. Let it be that—speaking strictly and literally—only *events* were causally relevant to the shattering: by stipulation, no *nonevents* contributed causally to the shattering. Now, suppose that another person, Jill, did not have a choice about *any* of the events in the shattering's causal history. Our intuitive reaction to that last piece of information—one we invite readers to share—is that Jill *also* lacked a choice about the shattering itself. "In virtue of *what*," we want to ask, "could Jill have had a choice about the shattering, seeing as how she did not have a choice about *anything* causally relevant to it?" We are now ready to meet γ:

(γ)   Suppose an event, *e*, has only *events* in its causal history. Then an agent, *S*, has a choice about *e* only if there is an event in *e*'s causal history about which *S* has a choice (contrapositively: Then if *S* did not have a choice about anything in *e*'s causal history, then *S* did not have a choice about *e*).

We note two important facts about γ. First, γ nicely explains our intuition, concerning the Jack & Jill Example, that Jill did not have a choice about the window's shattering. By stipulation, Jill did not have a choice about anything in the shattering's causal history, which comprised only *events*. Then γ entails that Jill did not have a choice about the shattering, thus predicting and nicely explaining the aforementioned intuition. We submit that reflection on the Jack & Jill Example generates (at least) a fair amount of prima facie support for γ.

The second important—and heretofore unnoticed—fact about γ is that it is presupposed by the best versions of the *Mind* argument. We'll bring out this fact by explaining two versions of the *Mind* argument.[9] We start with Peter van Inwagen's version, then shift to a more recent formulation due to Dana Nelkin. (For aforementioned reasons, we'll focus mainly on Nelkin's version in subsequent sections, though everything we say there applies mutatis mutandis to van Inwagen's version of the *Mind* argument.)

We begin with the point that all recent presentations of the *Mind* argument share the following initial stage.[10] Consider a world in which agents' actions are indeterministic causal consequences of prior mental states (e.g., beliefs, desires, intentions, and so on). Suppose an inhabitant of this world, S, acts on some occasion. Let 'R' stand for the action performed by S, and let 'DB' stand for the mental state(s) causally relevant to R, and suppose R is an indeterministic causal consequence of DB. According to the *Mind* argument's proponent, these suppositions make it is plausible that (i) no one, including S, had a choice about the fact that R followed DB. Further, the proponent of the argument maintains that (ii) no one, including S, had a choice about the fact that DB occurred. And here is the standard justification offered for (ii), which was originally presented by van Inwagen and is simply echoed by every other recent presentation of the *Mind* argument:[11]

While we may sometimes have a choice about the inner states that precede our acts, very often we don't. For example, it is unlikely that [S] had any choice about whether DB occurred; *and even if he did, this could only be because he had a choice about some earlier states of affairs of which DB was a consequence* [our emphasis]; if so, the questions we are asking about DB could be asked about those earlier states of affairs. If someone maintained that *those* states of affairs, too, were states of affairs about which [S] had a choice, we could point out that they resulted from still earlier states of affairs, and this process could, in principle, be carried on till we reached [S's] "initial state" about which he certainly had no choice. So let us assume at the outset that [S] had no choice about whether DB occurred, for we should sooner or later have to make an assumption that would have the same philosophical consequences. (van Inwagen 1983, 146)

Consider the sentence we emphasized with italics. The claim there is that S could have had a choice about DB—a state whose causal history should be understood to comprise only other *events*—only if S had a choice about some event causally relevant to DB. Pretty clearly, this claim is just a less regimented statement of γ. If asked for a more formal rendering of the thought expressed by the claim in question, to what—besides γ—could the *Mind* argument's proponent possibly appeal? By our lights, γ is a suitably regimented and generalized statement of the italicized claim in question, which again is a key part of the standard justification for (ii). Hence, the *Mind* argument presupposes γ.

(Incidentally, we think the fact that the *Mind* argument presupposes γ also contributes to its prima facie plausibility. If γ failed to be initially plausible—or at least if it were initially *implausible*—it stands to reason that at least some of the aforementioned philosophers who have discussed the *Mind* argument would have noticed γ's role and considered it a potential weakness of the argument.)

We now focus briefly on van Inwagen's particular formulation of the *Mind* argument. Following van Inwagen, let 'Np' stand for 'p and no one has, or ever had, any choice about whether p'.[12] Van Inwagen's version of the *Mind* argument can then be put like this:

(1) N(DB)

(2) N(DB → R)

Therefore,

(3) N(R)

At this juncture, the following question naturally arises: what licenses the inference from (1) and (2) to (3)? The answer, according to van Inwagen (1983), is the (by now notorious) inference rule, Beta:

Beta: {Np & N(p → q)} implies Nq.

As it turns out, Beta underwrites not only van Inwagen's formalized version of the *Mind* argument, but also his formalized version of the Consequence argument for the incompatibility of freedom and determinism.[13] Alas, their mutual dependence on Beta undermines van Inwagen's *Mind* and Consequence arguments. For, when combined with certain obvious truths, Beta entails the following inference principle, which is vulnerable to clear counterexamples:

Agglomeration: (Np & Nq) implies N(p & q).[14]

Thus, were van Inwagen's the strongest version of the *Mind* argument, that argument would not pose much of a threat to libertarianism.

But van Inwagen's is *not* the most promising version of the *Mind* argument. For there is a more recent version due to Dana Nelkin (2001, 112–114) that depends not on the discredited Beta, but only on the following logically weaker principle (note that '□' here means 'it is broadly logically necessary that'):

Beta 2: {Np & □ (p → q)} implies Nq.[15]

(Essentially, Beta 2 says that one has no choice about the broadly logical consequences of truths one has no choice about.) Moreover, Nelkin's premises are as plausible as those in van Inwagen's earlier *Mind* argument; here is her version of the argument:

(1*)   N{DB & (DB → R)}

(2*)   □{(DB & (DB → R)) → R}

Therefore,

(3*)   N(R)

(2*) is a tautology, and (3*) follows from (1*) and (2*) by Beta 2. Pretty clearly, (1*) is this argument's weakest link; rejecting it seems to be the only prima facie viable escape route for libertarians. As even prominent libertarians concede, though, each of N(DB) and N(DB → R) is quite plausible,[16] and the conjunction of these claims seems to constitute a good reason for believing N{DB & (DB → R)}. Nelkin puts the point thus:

> We have no choice about either DB or (DB → R). Further, we cannot think of anything one could do to ensure the falsity of the conjunction of DB and (DB → R) itself, while lacking the ability to falsify the first conjunct and the ability to falsify the second conjunct. (2001, 113)

Granted, an important upshot of the recent literature is that the general inference principle one may be tempted to appeal to in inferring (1*) from N(DB) and N(DB→R)—namely, Agglomeration—is invalid. However, the fact that Agglomeration is invalid does not entail that it is possible for (1*) to be false while N(DB) and N(DB→R) are true. We're in agreement with Nelkin here: Anyone who accepts N(DB) and N(DB → R) should also accept (1*).

Though we concur with Nelkin's reasoning quoted above, we think she has overlooked an even stronger case for (1*). First, note the obvious point that a devotee of the *Mind* argument accepts that (i) no one had a choice about the proposition that *DB caused R*. Note also that (ii) the proposition that *DB caused R* entails the proposition expressed by '{DB & (DB → R)}'. (Any possible world in which *DB caused R* is also a world in which the proposition expressed by '{(DB & (DB → R)}' is true.) And from (i), (ii), and Beta 2, it follows that no one had a choice about the proposition expressed by '{(DB & (DB → R)}', that is, it follows that (1*) is true. At no point in this argument is there the faintest trace of an appeal to Agglomeration.

So, Nelkin's improved version of the *Mind* argument constitutes a serious challenge to libertarianism. We now turn in sections 2–3 to the heart of our project, our decisive and instructive objection to this improved version of the *Mind* argument.[17]

2   What If γ Is True?

Here, we argue that γ entails nonreductivism—the view that *agents themselves* (in addition to "agent-involving" events) can be causal contributors—and that this spells trouble for the *Mind* argument. Moreover, the indicated trouble does not also plague the strongest argument for incompatibilism about freedom and determinism.

To begin, recall γ:

(γ)   Suppose an event, *e*, has only *events* in its causal history. Then an agent, *S*, has a choice about *e* only if there is an event in *e*'s causal history about which *S* has a choice.

Assume γ for conditional proof. Suppose also, and for reductio, that reductivism is true, that—speaking strictly and literally—only *events* can be causal contributors. According to the Freedom Assumption, some human agent, *S*, is such that there is an event, *e*, such that *S* had a choice about *e* but did not have a choice about any event prior to *e*. It follows both that *S* had a choice about *e*, and that *e* had a causal history, *H*.[18] But, by reductivism, *H* comprises only other *events*. And by γ, there is a member of *H*—an event causally relevant to *e*—about which *S* had a choice. This, however, contradicts our assumption that *e* is the *earliest* or *first* event about which *S* had a choice; reductivism has thus landed us in a contradiction. Hence, if γ is true, then reductivism is false and *agents themselves* can contribute causally—or, be causally relevant—to events. Hence, γ entails nonreductivism.

We can now see why γ's truth spells trouble for the *Mind* argument. It does so because the *Mind* argument presupposes reductivism. To see this, recall that the *Mind* argument's sample indeterministically caused action, R, has only *events* in its causal history (most prominently, *S*'s prior mental state, DB). Of course, the *Mind* argument's conclusion—namely, incompatibilism about freedom and indeterminism—is a generalization covering *every* indeterministically caused action. Assuming that the *Mind* argument is valid, then, something prior to its conclusion must rule out the possibility of an indeterministically caused action having a causal history different in kind from R's, a causal history in which some *nonevents* figure. Put differently, given that the *Mind* argument is valid, something prior to its conclusion must entail that only *events* can contribute causally to actions. In sum, then, either the *Mind* argument is invalid or it presupposes reductivism. So, assuming (as we should) that the *Mind* argument is valid, one of its key presuppositions is false if γ is true. Accordingly, if γ is true, the *Mind* argument fails.

As we've seen, γ entails nonreductivism. We now argue that this benefits only nonreductive *libertarians*. Why think *that*? For the simple reason that, unlike the *Mind* argument, (what we deem) the best argument for incompatibilism about freedom and determinism *does not* presuppose reductivism. The argument we have in mind here is the recent version of the Consequence argument due to Finch and Warfield (1998), inspired of course by van Inwagen's (1983) version of the Consequence argument. Like Nelkin's *Mind* argument, Finch and Warfield's Consequence argument depends not on Beta, but only on Beta 2. This improved version of the Consequence argument runs as follows (see Finch and Warfield 1998, 521–522). Let F be any truth, P a proposition describing the complete state of the world at some time in the remote past, and L a conjunction of the laws of nature. Assume determinism for conditional proof. Then:

(1**) $\Box\{(P \& L) \to F\}$

Moreover, it is quite plausible that no one has a choice about the conjunction of P and L (what Finch and Warfield call the "broad past"):

(2**)   N(P & L)

By Beta 2, (1**) and (2**) entail that no one has a choice about any fact:

(3**)   N(F).

And from here, we can quickly generalize to the conclusion that if determinism is true, then no one is free.

Two points should be emphasized here. First, many (including us!) find this version of the Consequence argument cogent. Second, as we noted above, this version of the Consequence argument is perfectly consistent with γ and its entailing nonreductivism. This is because the Consequence argument does not presuppose reductivism; the argument is obviously and admirably *neutral* vis-à-vis the reductivism–nonreductivism debate. In short, then, if γ is true, the *Mind* argument fails in such a way that the Consequence argument is undisturbed.

We are also now in a position to make a significant point about the relation between the Consequence and *Mind* arguments. Much recent work on these arguments assumes that *if* the arguments depend on a common Beta-style inference principle, then the arguments stand or fall together.[19] But this common thought is mistaken. As we've seen, the *Mind* argument is burdened by the assumption of reductivism,[20] whereas the Consequence argument is neutral about the reductivism–nonreductivism debate. We speculate that widespread acceptance of reductivism explains previous failure to recognize that the *Mind* argument depends on stronger assumptions than does the Consequence argument.

This completes our argument from the supposition that γ is true. In the next section, we complete our critical evaluation of the *Mind* argument by arguing for the following claim: if γ is false, then (i) the standard justification for a certain premise of the *Mind* argument is undermined, and (moreover) there is good reason to think that the premise in question is false; (ii) *non*reductivism is untenable; and (iii) the Consequence argument again remains intact.

3   What if γ Is False?

Suppose γ is false. Then it is possible that an agent, *S*, has a choice about an event, *e*, the causal history of which includes only events, where *S* does not have a choice about any of the events in *e*'s causal history. We now argue that each of claims (i)–(iii) just listed follows from this supposition. To begin, recall (1*) of the *Mind* argument:

(1*)   N{DB & (DB → R)}

Obviously, one's having a choice about *either* DB *or* (DB → R) suffices for one's having a choice about {DB & (DB → R)}. Proponents of the *Mind* argument, then, should provide some reason to believe N(DB). And as we pointed out in section 1, the standard justification offered for N(DB) involves an appeal to γ. Since we are now supposing that γ is false, it immediately follows that the standard justification for N(DB) is undermined, thus undermining the standard justification for (1*).

Someone might reply by reminding us of this remark of van Inwagen's quoted earlier in section 1:

So let us assume at the outset that [*S*] had no choice about whether DB occurred, for we should sooner or later have to make an assumption that would have the same philosophical consequences. (van Inwagen 1983, 146)

One might go on to use this remark in an attempt to argue that γ is not an essential part of the justification of N(DB), and so, the standard justification of (1*) is not, *pace* our contention, undermined if γ is false.

This reply, though instructive, is ultimately mistaken. At *best*, it shows that γ need not be offered in direct support of the particular proposition that *S* had no choice about DB. The reply fails to show, however, that γ

does not play a critical role in justifying van Inwagen's claim that it's philosophically harmless to assume S had no choice about DB. Clearly, γ does play such a role. To see this, we remind the reader of what precedes van Inwagen's remark about why it's acceptable to assume that S had no choice about DB:

> For example, it is unlikely that [S] had any choice about whether DB occurred; *and even if he did, this could only be because he had a choice about some earlier states of affairs of which DB was a consequence* [our emphasis]; if so, the questions we are asking about DB could be asked about those earlier states of affairs. If someone maintained that *those* states of affairs, too, were states of affairs about which [S] had a choice, we could point out that they resulted from still earlier states of affairs, and this process could, in principle, be carried on till we reached [S's] "initial state" about which he certainly had no choice. (van Inwagen 1983, 146)

Observe that van Inwagen's reasoning to the "philosophical innocence" of assuming that S had no choice about DB employs the italicized claim, which (as we've said) is simply a less regimented statement of γ. In short, γ is what licenses van Inwagen's remark about the acceptability of assuming that S had no choice about DB. A proponent of the *Mind* argument, then, is entitled to assume that S had no choice about DB only if he antecedently assumes γ. Otherwise, there are no grounds for believing the claim that we could, in principle, "reason our way back" to mental states about which S plausibly lacked a choice.

So, we stand by our claim that the acceptability of N(DB) relies on the truth of γ. Accordingly, we stand by our claim that the falsity of γ undermines the standard justification for (1*). But there remains a more serious concern about (1*): given the falsity of γ, not only does (1*) fail to be well supported, but there is also good reason to believe that it is false. To begin to see this, recall that given γ's falsity, the following is possible: there is an event, e, the causal history of which includes only events; there is an agent, S, who has a choice about e; but S didn't have a choice about any event in e's causal history. For the sake of readability, we will call events like the one just described "non-γ events." We now argue that, assuming there could be non-γ events, there is good reason to deny (1*).

For the sake of argument, let the proponent of the *Mind* argument choose DB in such a way that N(DB) is acceptable. Still, as we've just argued, one must rely on γ in so choosing DB, in order to ensure that one can "reason one's way back" to some of S's mental states about which S plausibly lacked a choice. For the sake of concreteness, let us suppose there to be a mental state, φ, subsequent to DB but prior to R—for example, S's intending to R. Now, the proponent of the *Mind* argument thinks we can safely ignore φ—and any other intermediate mental event—because it is a consequence of DB and S could have had a choice about it only if he had a choice about his earlier state, DB. But again this reasoning presupposes γ, which we are now supposing to be *false*. We cannot then safely ignore φ—at least not for the reason given by the proponent of the *Mind* argument. In other words, since we are supposing γ to be false, for all we know, φ could be a non-γ event.

More importantly, φ (again, S's intending to R) looks to be as good a candidate as there could possibly be for being a non-γ event: *If* there could be such events, certainly φ could be one. But if S did have a choice about φ, then S would also have had a choice about *DB's causing R*, thereby falsifying 'N(DB → R)' and (1*) as well. Moreover, it is very plausible to believe (especially on the supposition that R is an action of S's) that there would be an event such as φ intermediate between DB and R. What follows is that given the falsity of γ, it is very plausible to think that there would be a non-γ event about which S had a choice such that S's having a choice about that event renders (1*) false.[21]

At this point, a proponent of the *Mind* argument might rightly point out that an event such as φ would need to be an *indeterministic* causal consequence of DB in order to be of use to a libertarian. We may then be invited to reflect carefully on the indeterministic causal connection between DB and φ, which amounts to reflecting on the proposition that φ could have failed to occur even if the laws of nature and the past just prior to φ (which would include DB) had been exactly the same. After reflecting on that proposition, we may then be invited to conclude that S could not have had a choice about φ. In reply, we record our failure to feel the force of this second invitation given the background supposition that γ is false. Perhaps we can bring out this failure of ours by considering our reactions to some other cognitive invitations.

First, suppose we are invited to imagine that we believe that an agent, S, had a choice about a non-γ event, say, e. Second, suppose we are invited to imagine coming to learn that e was an *indeterministic* causal consequence of the events in e's causal history—that is, we are invited to imagine coming to learn that it's possible for the laws of nature and e's causal history to have been exactly as they were and yet for e to not occur. Third, suppose we are then invited to consider how this new piece of information (and it alone) bears on our belief that S had a choice about e. After careful reflection, we are inclined to say that this new piece of information (all by itself) has no bearing on the acceptability of our belief that S had a choice about e. We do not, for instance, see any reason for thinking that coming to learn that e was indeterministically caused would provide us a reason for doubting our initial belief. After all, we already believe that S (somehow) had a choice about e without having a choice about anything that causally contributed to e. Why should merely learning that the causal contributors to e—each of which is an event S had no choice about—indeterministically contributed to e's occurrence provide us a reason for doubting that S did in fact have a choice about e? Note well: we are not saying that there is *nothing* we could learn that would constitute a reason for doubting our initial belief. If we were to learn, for instance, that e was the result of nefarious manipulation or some form of coercion, we would have a reason for doubting that S had a choice about e. But supposing e to be indeterministically caused does not require supposing it to be caused in such deviant ways. We cannot, obviously, speak for the general reader. All we can do is report our own intuitions (as we have done) about the lately discussed suppositions, invite you to carefully consider them, and hope that you too will conclude that given the falsity of γ, the mere appeal to φ's having been indeterministically caused does not constitute a good reason to think S could not have had a choice about φ.

So, the falsity of γ not only undermines the standard justification for (1*), but also provides good reason to deny it. The failure of the *Mind* argument is logically overdetermined by the supposition that γ is false. We now turn to the second advertised consequence of γ's falsity: the untenability of nonreductivism.

We grant the fairly widespread view that an *agent's* being nonderivatively causally relevant to an event is somewhat mysterious, obscure, or opaque in a way that an *event's* being so causally relevant is not. We are thus willing to grant that nonreductivism should be embraced only if there are *good reasons* to do so. Earlier, we argued that if γ is true, then there is indeed good reason to accept nonreductivism. We are now, however, supposing that γ is false, that it is possible for there to be non-γ events. It follows from this supposition that an agent can have a choice about an event even though that agent *does not* make a nonderivative causal contribution to the event. (Remember that non-γ events have only events as causal contributors.) Given the falsity of γ, then, having a choice about an event does not require nonderivative agent causal contribution. But again, nonreductivism should not be accepted in the absence of good reasons to do so. And outside of nonreductivism being required for our having a choice about an event—and why that's so—we can think of no good reason to accept it. For this reason, we conclude that if γ is false, then nonreductivism is untenable.

Now for the third and final consequence of the falsity of γ: the Consequence argument retains its probative force. To begin to see this, note that the falsity of γ provides no reason to doubt the Consequence argument's main premise, (2**)—N(P&L). There is no reason to doubt the independently plausible claim that no one has a choice about distant past events such as the big bang *simply because* γ is false. Likewise, the falsity of γ provides no reason to doubt the independently plausible claim that no one has a choice about the laws of nature.[22] Finally, γ's falsity provides no reason to doubt the validity of the highly plausible Beta 2. Informally, Beta 2 says that "one has no choice about the logical consequences of those truths one has no choice about" (Finch and Warfield 1998, 522). But it is consistent with this that one can have a choice about an event whose causal history is exhausted by events none of which one has a choice about, which is what γ informally says. We can see this point a little more formally by considering the following simplified example. Suppose e is an event and that the only causal contributors to e are the events d and f. Where x is an event, let 'Ox' abbreviate 'x occurs'. Consider the following argument:

A: N(Od & Of); $\Box\{(Od \ \& \ Of) \rightarrow Oe\}$; Therefore, N(O$e$).

Suppose we believe that A is valid on the grounds that Beta 2 is a valid inference rule. We could also consistently believe that an agent has a choice about e even though that agent has no choice about d and no choice about f, which of course implies that γ is false. The falsity of γ, then, does not call Beta 2 into question. So, even if γ were false, the Consequence argument would remain unscathed.

This section's argument and our case against Nelkin's improved *Mind* argument are now complete. Far from being detrimental to libertarianism, reflection on the *Mind* argument actually serves to advance the libertarian front.

We conclude by turning to our somewhat more tentative aim of strengthening the γ-based case for nonreductive libertarianism.

4 Defending γ

Let us begin by noting that the arguments of sections 2–3 provide a novel entry point into the debate between reductive and nonreductive libertarians. For if the arguments of those sections are sound, then the intramural dispute between nonreductive and reductive libertarians turns on γ's truth-value. In particular, a counterexample to γ will serve to establish reductive libertarianism. Obviously, the inability to provide a clear counterexample to γ does not *prove* that it is true; however, the lack of clear counterexamples should increase its initial plausibility, thereby strengthening the case for nonreductive libertarianism. The balance of this essay is devoted to defending γ against some alleged counterexamples.

First Example

Suppose at t_1, Ridley freely remains seated. At t_2, a baseball is shot toward a bottle, where this is a random occurrence, a matter of "ground-level chance." Suppose also that if Ridley had at t_1 stood, the indicated baseball would not have been shot toward the bottle at t_2. (Suppose Ridley's friend Brown would have pressed a button, thus disarming the device that randomly shoots baseballs, if Ridley had stood.) Finally, suppose the baseball shatters the bottle at t_3.[23]

Ridley has no choice about any event in the causal history of the bottle's shattering, since the baseball's being shot toward the bottle at t_2 is a random occurrence. Moreover, there is an unrealized chain of events the realization of which would have prevented the bottle shattering, namely, that chain of events that would have resulted if Ridley had refrained from sitting at t_1. Furthermore, Ridley was able to initiate that chain of events since he was free to stand at t_1. And so, Ridley had a choice about the shattering of the bottle at t_3 in spite of the fact that he had no choice about any event in the causal history of the shattering. Hence, γ is false.

Reply

A crucial claim in the example is that Ridley had a choice about the shattering *because* he was able to initiate a chain of events that would have prevented the bottle from shattering. But Ridley's being able to initiate a sequence of events that would have prevented the shattering implies that he was also able to initiate a sequence of events that would have prevented the baseball from being shot toward the bottle. The baseball's having been shot toward the bottle, however, was clearly causally relevant to the shattering. It follows that Ridley did have a choice about something in the causal history of the bottle shattering, and so the alleged counterexample fails.

One might try to get around this reply by modifying the first example in such a way that Ridley didn't have a choice about events prior to the shattering. Someone might suggest a modification along the following lines.

Second Example

Suppose a baseball is shot toward a bottle as described in the first example. Also suppose Ridley was stationed too far from the chain of events to intervene by, say, snatching the baseball mid-trajectory or grabbing the bottle before it was shattered. But suppose Ridley was within reach of a button the depression of which would have prevented the shattering in the following peculiar but perfectly coherent way: if the button had been depressed *just as* the baseball struck the bottle, then the bottle would have been instantaneously endowed with the power to resist the force of the strike; the bottle would have "stiffened up," so to speak, and wouldn't have shattered when struck. Depressing the button at any other time, however, would have done nothing to protect the bottle. In fact, Ridley doesn't press the button; having undergone relevant training, though, he was able to depress it at just the right time.

Ridley had no choice about any event in the causal history of the bottle's shattering. For, as is stipulated, he wasn't able to grab the baseball and he wasn't able to grab the bottle, and the like. So, he wasn't able to initiate a chain of events that would have prevented the baseball from being shot toward the bottle. ("But he can depress the button," you say. Yes, but having depressed the button before or after the baseball struck the bottle would have done nothing to protect the bottle.) Now, there's an unrealized chain of events that the bottle would have survived, namely, that chain of events which would have resulted if Ridley had depressed the button at just the right time. Furthermore, by hypothesis, Ridley was able to so depress the button and initiate this chain of events. So, Ridley had a choice about the bottle's shattering in spite of the fact that he had no choice about any event in the causal history of the shattering. Hence, γ is false.

Reply

The proponent of the second example is thinking along these lines: Ridley was able to do something about the shattering *only* at the moment at which the baseball struck the bottle; but by then, every event in the causal history of the shattering had occurred and he had no choice about any of those events.

We think the objector overlooks a pertinent event about which Ridley clearly had a choice. In the example, Ridley was able (by virtue of being able to depress the button at just the right time) to prevent the shattering of the bottle. Ridley, though, refrains from taking this action. It follows that Ridley *freely* refrains from depressing the button, that Ridley had a choice about refraining from depressing the button. Clearly, though, Ridley's refraining from depressing the button contributes causally to the shattering. Hence, Ridley did have a choice about something causally relevant to the shattering. The alleged counterexample fails.

Our suspicion is that other similar modifications of the first example will suffer from the same flaw as does the second example. In conversation, some have attempted to disabuse us of this suspicion with the following sort of example; it will be the final alleged counterexample we consider.

Third Example
Suppose Ridley's decision to freely remain seated was causally overdetermined by both *Ridley* and some combination of his beliefs and desires. More precisely, suppose the causal history of Ridley's decision can be partitioned into two distinct nonoverlapping but individually causally sufficient subhistories. One of these causal subhistories, call it 'the event-causal history', includes only events; it includes, for instance, Ridley's beliefs, desires, and presumably other events, as well. The other causal subhistory includes nonderivatively Ridley himself, that is, it includes Ridley himself as a nonderivative causal contributor. Plausibly, Ridley had a choice about his decision to remain seated since *he* nonderivatively causally contributed to that decision. However, (we can safely stipulate) that Ridley had no choice about any of the events in the event-causal history of his decision. (Perhaps Ridley's beliefs and desires are items in his initial complement of mental states, etc.) So, Ridley had a choice about his decision to remain seated *even though* he had no choice about any *event* in the causal history of that decision. Hence, γ is false.[24]

Reply
The first thing to note about this alleged counterexample is that it is obviously of no use to someone attempting to resist nonreductive libertarianism. This is because, as the case is described, Ridley strictly and literally figures in the causal history of his decision. Also, for this reason, the above case is not a counterexample to γ. For recall that γ is restricted to events the causal histories of which include *only other events*.

We can think of no other putative counterexamples that differ significantly from those considered above.[25] This could, of course, be a failure of imagination on our part. At any rate, we leave it as a challenge for the interested reader to construct her own potential counterexample that cannot be handled as we've handled those discussed above.

In light of the results of this section, it seems to us that the prima facie case for γ has strengthened. Accordingly, it seems to us that the main argument of section 2 constitutes a prima facie strong case for nonreductive libertarianism. We hasten to remind the reader, however, that regardless of γ's truth-value—and so regardless of how the dispute between reductive and nonreductive libertarians is to be adjudicated—the *Mind* argument (in its strongest form) fails, and does so in a way that has interesting ramifications for the metaphysics of freedom.

Acknowledgments

We are grateful to the following people for comments on and/or discussion of this essay: John Bishop, Thad Botham, Randolph Clarke, Chris Green, Jeff Green, John Hawthorne, Hud Hudson, Eddy Nahmias, Dana Nelkin, Michael Rea, Daniel Speak, Kevin Timpe, Neil Tognazzini, Peter van Inwagen, Ted Warfield, and some anonymous referees.

Notes

1. Proponents of this view include Chisholm (1983), O'Connor (2000), and Taylor (1966).

2. Proponents of this view include Nozick (1981), Kane (1996), and Ekstrom (2000).

3. Proponents of this view include Frankfurt (1983) and Watson (1983).

4. Though certainly the least popular of the four views countenanced here, nonreductive compatibilism is not an empty niche. See, e.g., Markosian 1999, and 2007.

5. For prominent arguments against the existence of freedom, see, e.g., Double 1991, 1996; Pereboom 2001; and Smilansky 2000.

6. We thank an anonymous referee for helpful comments that led us to clarify what we here mean by "event."

Incidentally, this broad use of "event" is by no means idiosyncratic. Our usage is, e.g., consonant with David Lewis's use of "event" in Lewis 1986.

7. See van Inwagen 1983, 67–68 and n. 31, 233–234, for the relevant understanding of "having a choice about" an event—or, more generally, a true proposition. Roughly, to have a choice about a truth, p, is to have it within one's power to ensure that p is false, to be able to act in such a way that p would be false were one to so act. Cf. Finch and Warfield 1998, 516.

8. Notably, all the arguments in which we use the Freedom Assumption would "go through" on a variety of slightly weaker assumptions—e.g., the assumption that

someone is such that there is a set of events, E, such that she had a choice about each of E's members but not about any prior events. We employ the Freedom Assumption mainly for the sake of simplicity and readability.

One reader worried that the Freedom Assumption might conflict with the plausible view that human beings gradually acquire capacities required to have a choice about events. But this worry is a wholly general one stemming from the perplexing philosophical problem of vagueness, not from the Freedom Assumption per se. We are confident that any particular theory of vagueness will allow for a plausible interpretation of the Freedom Assumption. A quick illustration of this point: Supervaluationists would say (roughly) that the Freedom Assumption is super-true (and so true *simpliciter*) because it is true on every admissible precisification of its vague terms; every admissible precisification of the Freedom Assumption locates, so to speak, a sharp cutoff for when a human being is able to have a choice about an event.

9. We should note that the label "the *Mind* argument" is somewhat misleading. There are really different kinds—and different versions of these respective kinds—of *Mind* arguments. Van Inwagen (1983, 126–150), for example, distinguishes three strands of the *Mind* argument. In what follows, we discuss what van Inwagen calls "the third strand." The distinctions among these strands noted, we will for stylistic reasons continue to speak of "the" *Mind* argument. For the record, we believe our arguments apply *mutatis mutandis* to the other two strands of the *Mind* argument distinguished by van Inwagen.

10. See, e.g., van Inwagen 1983; Finch and Warfield 1998; Nelkin 2001; and Clarke 2003.

11. See, e.g., Finch and Warfield 1998; Nelkin 2001; and Clarke 2003.

12. See note 5 for the relevant understanding of "having a choice about" a truth, p.

13. See chapter 3 of van Inwagen 1983.

14. See, e.g., McKay and Johnson 1996. Briefly, here is a representative counterexample to Agglomeration. Suppose you freely refrain from tossing a fair coin. Let p = *the coin does not land heads*, and let q = *the coin does not land tails*. We may safely assume that both $N(p)$ and $N(q)$ are true (no one had it within his power to ensure the falsity of p, and the same goes for q). $N(p \ \& \ q)$, though, is false: you, for one, had it within your power to ensure the falsity of ($p \ \& \ q$).

15. So far as we know, what we call Beta 2 was introduced by David Widerker in Widerker 1987. Finch and Warfield (1998) defend an improved version of the Consequence argument dependent on Beta 2 (which we discuss below), and go on to argue that Beta 2 cannot also be used to revitalize the *Mind* argument. As we are about to see, Nelkin (2001) shows the latter claim to be mistaken.

16. See, e.g., van Inwagen 1983, 146, 149–150; and Finch and Warfield 1998, 518.

17. Henceforth, unless we say otherwise, the reader should understand us to be concerned only with Nelkin's improved version of the *Mind* argument.

18. Presumably, an agent has a choice about an event only if that event has a causal history, or is such that something contributed causally to its occurrence. It is crucial to note that this is *not* tantamount to the claim that one has a choice only about *causally produced* events: an event that was not *causally produced* may nevertheless be such that something *contributed causally* to its occurrence. Thus, our assumption here is perfectly consistent with all the main approaches to the metaphysics of human agency, including views labeled "noncausalist." For noncausalists typically countenance events that contribute causally to ones about which an agent has a choice. Proponents of noncausalism include Ginet (1990) and Goetz (1997).

19. See, e.g., Finch and Warfield 1998, 519–520, and Nelkin 2001, 112.

20. We hasten to add that Finch and Warfield seem to display some awareness of this point when they say,

Introducing agent causation into the picture at this point in the discussion would *not* serve to show how [N(DB → R)] could be false. Rather, the successful introduction and defense of agent causation would show that the *Mind* argument is not relevant to human freedom. (1998, 519)

21. Perhaps you think we've taken an unnecessarily circuitous route here. Perhaps you think that once we suppose γ to be false, we can immediately see without considering an event such as φ that *DB's causing R* (and perhaps R itself) is an eminently plausible candidate for being a non-γ event. We are quite happy if you do think this, since you will then agree with us about γ's falsity implying the falsity of (1*). However, we think our admittedly less direct route is more satisfying. It seems to us more dialectically appropriate, and it offers an explanation for how *DB's causing R* could manage to be a non-γ event.

22. Recall our earlier discussion of newly acquired information that would constitute a reason to doubt our belief that *S* had a choice about *e*. We argued there that merely coming to learn that *e* was indeterministically caused would not constitute such a reason. However, we also pointed out that there may very well be some information we could acquire that would constitute a reason to doubt our belief—we considered there the possibility of coming to learn that *e* was the result of nefarious manipulation. We also think coming to learn that the distant past and the laws of nature entailed *e* would provide us good reason to doubt. For that new piece of information would entail the truth of '$\Box((P \& L) \to e$ occurs)'; N(P &L) is antecedently highly plausible; Beta 2 seems to us nearly unquestionable; and we would be in a position validly to infer that *S* did not have a choice about *e* from the conjunction of these claims.

23. Thanks to John Hawthorne and Hud Hudson for discussion of this kind of putative counterexample to γ.

24. This objection was inspired by conversation with Jeff Green.

25. Each alleged counterexample we have received in conversation with others is saliently similar to one of the above cases. Indeed, these cases are based on our best understanding of those alleged counterexamples.

References

Chisholm, R. 1983. Human Freedom and the Self. In *Free Will*, ed. G. Watson. Oxford: Oxford University Press.

Clarke, R. 2003. *Libertarian Accounts of Free Will*. New York: Oxford University Press.

Double, R. 1991. *The Non-Reality of Free Will*. New York: Oxford University Press.

Double, R. 1996. *Metaphilosophy and Free Will*. New York: Oxford University Press.

Ekstrom, L. 2000. *Free Will: A Philosophical Study*. Boulder, CO: Westview Press.

Finch, A., and T. Warfield. 1998. The *Mind* Argument and Libertarianism. *Mind* 107:515–528.

Frankfurt, H. 1983. Freedom of the Will and the Concept of a Person. In *Free Will*, ed. G. Watson. Oxford: Oxford University Press.

Ginet, C. 1990. *On Action*. Cambridge: Cambridge University Press.

Goetz, S. 1997. Libertarian Choice. *Faith and Philosophy* 14:195–211.

Kane, R. 1996. *The Significance of Free Will*. New York: Oxford University Press.

Lewis, D. 1986. Events. In *Philosophical Papers*, vol. II. New York: Oxford University Press.

Markosian, N. 1999. A Compatibilist Version of the Theory of Agent Causation. *Pacific Philosophical Quarterly* 80:257–277.

Markosian, N. 2007. Agent Causation as the Solution to All the Compatibilist's Problems. Manuscript.

McKay, T., and D. Johnson. 1996. A Reconsideration of an Argument against Incompatibilism. *Philosophical Topics* 24:113–122.

Nelkin, D. 2001. The Consequence Argument and the *Mind* Argument. *Analysis* 61:107–115.

Nozick, R. 1981. *Philosophical Explanations*. Cambridge, MA: Harvard University Press.

O'Connor, T. 2000. *Persons and Causes*. New York: Oxford University Press.

Pereboom, D. 2001. *Living without Free Will*. Cambridge: Cambridge University Press.

Smilansky, S. 2000. *Free Will and Illusion*. Oxford: Clarendon.

Taylor, R. 1966. *Action and Purpose*. Englewood Cliffs, NJ: Prentice-Hall.

van Inwagen, P. 1983. *An Essay on Free Will*. Oxford: Oxford University Press.

Watson, G. 1983. Free Agency. In *Free Will*, ed. G. Watson. Oxford: Oxford University Press.

Widerker, D. 1987. On an Argument for Incompatibilism. *Analysis* 47:37–41.

8 Selective Hard Compatibilism

Paul Russell

Compatibilism, Implantation, and Covert Control

Recent work in compatibilist theory has focused a considerable amount of attention on the question of the nature of the capacities required for freedom and moral responsibility. Compatibilists, obviously, reject the suggestion that these capacities involve an ability to act otherwise in the same circumstances. That is, these capacities do not provide for any sort of libertarian, categorical free will. The difficulty, therefore, is to describe some plausible alternative theory that is richer and more satisfying than the classical compatibilist view that freedom is simply a matter of being able to do as one pleases or act according to the determination of one's own will. Many of the most influential contemporary compatibilist theorists have placed emphasis on developing some account of "rational self-control" or "reasons-responsiveness."[1] The basic idea in theories of this kind is that free and responsible agents are capable of acting according to available reasons. Responsibility agency, therefore, is a function of a general ability to be guided by reasons or practical rationality. This is a view that has considerable attraction since it is able to account for intuitive and fundamental distinctions between humans and animals, adults and children, the sane and the insane, in respect of the issue of freedom and responsibility. This an area where the classical account plainly fails.

In general terms, rational self-control or reasons-responsive views have two key components. The first is that a rational agent must be able to *recognize* the reasons that are available or present to her situation. The second is that an agent must be able to "translate" those (recognized) reasons into decisions and choices that guide her conduct. In other words, the agent must not only be aware of what reasons there are, she must also be capable of being *moved* by them. This leaves, of course, a number of significant problems to be solved. For example, any adequate theory of this kind needs to be able to explain just how strict and demanding this standard of practical rationality is supposed to be. On the one hand, it is clearly too demanding to insist that agents must *always* be able to be guided by available reasons—otherwise an agent could never be held responsible for failing to be guided by the available reasons. On the other hand, more is required than that the agent is occasionally or intermittently guided by her reasons. An agent of this kind is not reliably and regularly rational to qualify as a free and responsible agent. So some set of conditions needs to be found that avoids both these extremes. This is not, however, the problem that I am now concerned with.[2]

Let us assume, with the proponents of compatibilist theories of rational self-control, that there is some account of these capacities that satisfies these various demands. We may call these the agent's RA capacities, as they provide for *rational agency*. This account still faces another important set of problems as presented by incompatibilist critics. One famous problem with classical compatibilist accounts of moral freedom ("doing as we please") is that agents of this kind could be *manipulated* and *covertly controlled* by other agents and yet, given the classical compatibilist account, still be judged free and responsible. This is, as the critics argue, plainly counterintuitive. Agents of this kind would be mere "puppets," "robots," or "zombies" who are "compelled" to obey the will of their covert controllers. Agents of this kind have no will of their own. They are not *real* or *genuine* agents. They only have the facade of being autonomous agents. When we discover the origins of their desires and willings—located with some other controlling agent—then our view of these (apparent) agents must change. The deeper problem with these (pseudo) agents, incompatibilists argue, is that although they may be "doing as they please" they have no control over their own will (i.e., they cannot shape or determine their own will). It is, therefore, an especially important question whether compatibilist accounts of rational self-control can deal effectively with objections of this kind.[3]

Rational self-control theories have two ways of approaching this problem. The first is to argue that what troubles us in situations of this kind, where manipulation and covert control is taking place, is that the agent's capacity for rational self-control is in some way being impaired or interfered with. The process of brainwashing, neurological engineering, or some other form of mind-control operates by way of damaging the agent's capacity to recognize and/or respond to the relevant reasons that are available.[4] The situation may, however, be more subtle and complicated than this. The manipulation or covert control, incompatibilists argue, can also work *without* impairing the agent's rational capacities but by controlling the way those capacities are actually *exercised* in particular circumstances. This sort of case is much more problematic for the compatibilist. Per hypothesis, the agent continues to operate with the relevant rational dispositions (recognition, reactivity, etc.). The way that this capacity is actually exercised in particular circumstances—that is, whether the agent's conduct succeeds or fails to track the available reasons—is not under the agent's control, as this would require libertarian free will to act otherwise in identical circumstances. In normal circumstances, the explanation for success or failure will rest with natural causes that involve no external controller or manipulation. The incompatibilist objection, however, is that there could be a situation whereby the agent is controlled in this way and the compatibilist has no *principled* reason for denying that the agent is free and responsible. It follows, therefore, that compatibilist accounts of rational self-control cannot provide an adequate account of conditions of free and responsible agency. Agents who are manipulated and covertly controlled are obviously not free and responsible despite the fact that they may possess a general capacity for rational self-control of the kind that compatibilists have described.

1   Libertarianism and the Implantation Standard

According to incompatibilists, the problem with manipulation and covert control is one that indicates a more fundamental and general weakness in the compatibilist position. Following some prominent compatibilist accounts, let us assume that our power of rational self-control presupposes that the agent possesses some relevant "mechanism" M, whereby the agent who possesses M is able to recognize and react to reasons.[5] Incompatibilists argue that cases of implantation highlight aspects of compatibilism in relation to the way that M is acquired and operates that is problematic even when manipulation and covert control is *absent* (i.e., in the "normal case"). Let us assume that M may be "implanted" by natural, normal causal processes that involve no manipulation or covert control by other agents. Implantation of M in these circumstances is "blind" and without any artificial interference of any kind. What still troubles us about these cases is that although the agent may be a rational self-controller, she nevertheless lacks any control over the way these capacities are actually *exercised* in specific circumstances. Whether M is such that in conditions C the agent will succeed or fail to track the available reasons is not something that depends on the agent. Even in these "normal" cases the agent is still subject to *luck* regarding the way M is actually exercised in C. In order to avoid this problem the agent must be able to choose or decide differently in the very same circumstances. An ability of this kind—let us call it *exercise control*—would require the falsity of determinism and some kind of libertarian free will. What ought to bother us about manipulation and covert control, therefore, is not simply that *some other agent* decides how the agent's will is exercised in conditions C, but that the agent herself lacks any such ability or power. It is a matter of luck how her powers of rational self-control are actually exercised. Clearly, then, the lack of exercise control is not a problem that arises only in (abnormal or deviant) cases of manipulation and covert control.

It may be argued that one way that compatibilists will be able to avoid this difficulty, without collapsing into libertarian metaphysics, is to give more thought to the problem of how M is *acquired* by the agent. That is to say, since the agent is held responsible for the upshots that issue from M (in particular circumstances), it surely must follow that the agent has some control over how M is acquired. Failing this, the agent will lack control not only over the particular way M operates in C, but also over the fact that it is this particular mechanism M that she is operating with. Another mechanism, $M\#$, may produce a different upshot in C. The agent, on the suggested compatibilist account, has control over none of this. What is need, therefore, in the absence of exercise control, is some control over mechanism acquisition. The incompatibilist will argue, however, that the compatibilist cannot provide any plausible account of how this could be possible.

Although we can make good sense of having control over our actions on the basis of possessing some reasons-responsive mechanism (M), it is not at all obvious what it *means* to say that an agent controls the process of acquiring such mechanisms. The mechanisms that we acquire generally develop through a process of (moral) education that begins at a very early stage of life. For this reason, responsibility for the kinds of mechanism that children acquire and develop rests more plausibly on the shoulders of the adults who have raised the child. Moreover, even at a later stage (e.g., adolescence) when a person becomes able to think critically about the way his own deliberative capacities actually operate, there is little or no question of the agent being able to radically modify or reform the mechanisms that he is (already) operating with. Control of this kind is not available even to mature adults, much less younger children.

Let us concede, nevertheless, that we can make some sense of the suggestion that the mature agent has control over mechanism acquisition.

This form of control must itself depend on the agent's ability to deliberate and decide about mechanism selection on the basis of some mechanism he already has. This situation presents compatibilist theory with a serious problem. The selection of some mechanism must be based on some mechanism that the agent currently operates with. This mechanism must be either chosen or given (i.e., through processes that the agent does not control). At some point, the mechanism involved in the process of mechanism acquisition must itself have been "unchosen" or presented to the agent through a process that he did not control (natural or artificial). Any choice concerning mechanism acquisition, therefore, must eventually depend on unchosen mechanisms—even on the optimistic assumption that mature agents are able to make choices of this kind.

It is evident that incompatibilist criticism of compatibilist theories of rational self-control reach well beyond narrow worries about manipulation and covert control. The deeper worries that situations of this kind bring to light is that rational self-control provides no (final) control over mechanism acquisition, nor over the way that these mechanisms are actually exercised in specific circumstances (i.e., success or failure to track reasons in particular conditions is not open for the agent to decide). Given these criticisms, it follows that agents who operate with rational capacities of these kinds are subject to luck about what specific mechanism (*M*) they acquire and operate with, as well as luck about the way the mechanism they operate with is actually exercised. Although these problems are certainly manifest in manipulation cases, they are by no means limited to them. On the contrary, these problems of limited control and luck are *systematic* to all circumstances in which agents operate on the compatibilist rational self-control model.[6]

Incompatibilist libertarians will be quick to contrast their own situation with respect to implantation and manipulation issues. Let us suppose that it is possible to artificially (intentionally) implant a mechanism of some kind that supports a libertarian capacity for free will. (Here again, the ontological basis of this mechanism is not our concern. There could be a biological basis for this or some soul-substance, and so on.) We may call a mechanism of this kind an *ML mechanism*. The fact that ML is implanted by another agent (God, a neurosurgeon, etc.) will not trouble the incompatibilist, because implantation as such will not compromise the agent's ability to operate with control over the way her rational capacities of deliberation and choice are actually exercised. Although the ML mechanism has been implanted by another agent, this does not make it possible to covertly control the implanted agent by means of this process. On the contrary, since the implanted agent possesses exercise control over the way this mechanism operates (i.e., controls the way reasons move her), the source or historical origins of ML is irrelevant to the way that the agent chooses to exercise her ML powers in specific circumstances. So long as the agent is capable of *exercise* control—then it is possible to set aside the issue of mechanism acquisition as irrelevant because there is no threat of manipulation or covert control.

It is true, of course, that libertarian agents who operate with ML mechanisms could not themselves control the process of ML acquisition unless they first possessed some ML mechanism. It follows from this that even libertarian agents of this kind do not control the process by which they become capable of libertarian free will (this must be a "gift of nature" or "God-given," etc.). Nevertheless, as I have explained, whether the implantation process in this case involves natural (blind) processes or artificial (other agent) involvement is irrelevant. The nature of the mechanism implanted precludes manipulation and covert control. More importantly, it ensures that the agent is not simply "lucky" or "unlucky" in relation to the way reasons actually move her. Because the agent possesses an ML mechanism her will is truly her own. Her will is truly her own because (per hypothesis) she has the power to determine when and how reasons guide her conduct. That is to say, her will is truly her own not because she chooses to be a ML agent but because being an ML agent allows her to determine her own will.

The immediate significance of this libertarian response is that it serves to provide an *alternative standard* by which compatibilist theories may be judged. That is to say, the libertarian may argue that in the case of libertarian ML capacities it is possible to implant them without compromising the agent's freedom and responsibility. This is a standard, the incompatibilist argues, that the compatibilist cannot meet. Compatibilists cannot meet this standard because the implantation of reasons-responsive or rational self-control capacities (M) is consistent with the possibility of manipulation and covert control. Even if compatibilists reject worries about "luck" in relation to the way that these capacities are actually exercised, surely no compatibilist can allow that an agent is free and responsible in circumstances where she is being manipulated and covertly controlled by some other agent by means of some (abnormal) implantation process.[7]

2   Soft Compatibilism and History

Critics of libertarianism argue, as we know, that all efforts to make sense of libertarian powers that could deliver on exercise control run into problems of intelligibility and/or nonexistence. Even if this is true, however, the compatibilist is still left with the problem of manipulation and covert control. More specifically, compatibilists who rely on accounts of rational self-control need to take a stand on whether or not the presence of covert control and manipulation will necessarily compromise an agent's freedom and responsibility when it is clear that the agent's general powers of rational self-control are not impaired or damaged by this process. There are two different approaches that compatibilist may take to this issue. The first is that of the "soft compatibilist" who holds that the presence of manipulation or covert control by means of mechanism implantation rules out freedom and responsibility.[8] The difficulty that soft compatibilists face is that, on the account provided, we could find ourselves with two agents (P and P^*) who have identical moral capacities and properties and deliberate, decide, and act in the very same way, and yet one is judged responsible and the other is not. The basis for this distinction rests entirely with the fact that one agent, P, has her deliberative mechanisms produced by natural (blind) causes, whereas the other agent, P^*, has her deliberative mechanisms produced by some other agent. Though we may concede that there is some residual intuitive worry about P^*'s circumstances, the question is on what *principled* basis can the soft compatibilist draw such an important distinction? It will not suffice for soft compatibilists to simply assume that the contrast in causal origins matters and then to construct an ad hoc set of principles to rule out manipulation and covert control cases. This leaves their position vulnerable to the criticism that they have failed to identify the real root difficulty in their position (i.e., that these agents lack exercise control).

The most convincing soft compatibilist reply to this problem that I know of is provided by John Fischer and Mark Ravizza.[9] What they argue is that reasons-responsiveness or powers of rational self-control will not suffice for moral responsibility. This is because it is also necessary that agents *own* the mechanism they are operating with. The problem of manipulation and covert control concerns the issue of ownership, not that of the agent's capacity for rational self-control. Briefly stated, an agent owns the deliberative mechanisms that issues in her conduct only if it has the right history or causal origins.[10] When a mechanism is implanted by some other agent, using artificial techniques of some kind, "ownership" is compromised. On the other hand, when the mechanism is produced by means of normal causal processes, ownership is not compromised. In the case of artificial implantation involving deviant causal processes, the problem is not that the agent's rational self-control is compromised but that the agent does not *own* the mechanism that issues in her conduct.

The question we now face is: does this appeal to ownership and history provide a secure basis for soft compatibilism? The first thing to be noted here is that there is no suggestion that ownership depends on control over mechanism acquisition or requires that the agent has somehow *consented* to the mechanism that she possesses and operates with. In fact, for reasons we have already considered, any requirement of this kind is highly problematic and will inevitably run into regress difficulties. Clearly, then, the distinction between acceptable and unacceptable processes of mechanism acquisition cannot depend on considerations of this kind. Nor is it obvious why one agent is said to own her own mechanism when it is naturally produced whereas the other does not because it has been artificially produced. In both cases the agents clearly *possess* these mechanisms and *operate* with them, and in neither case have they consented to or chosen their own mechanisms.[11]

These considerations suggest that it remains unclear why anyone should *care* about the different histories of mechanism acquisition when the "current time-slice" properties of both agents P and P^* are exactly the same. From the perspective of both the agent herself, as well as those she is engaged with in her moral community, there is *no difference* at all between P and P^*. There is no ability one has that the other does not also have, and both agents exercise these abilities in the exact same way. In other words, from both the internal and external perspective these two individuals are "interchangeable" in respect of all powers and abilities that matter (per the compatibilist hypothesis) to moral responsibility. In the absence of some further explanation for why "history" matters, therefore, the soft compatibilist way of dealing with manipulation and covert control cases seems arbitrary and ad hoc. Given that the soft compatibilist position depends on placing weight on historical considerations, we may conclude (for our present purposes) that the soft compatibilist strategy fails.

3   Should Hard Compatibilists Just "Bite the Bullet"?

Where do these observations about contemporary compatibilist strategies that rely on accounts of rational self-control leave us? I think it is clear that compatibilist accounts of this kind face the following dilemma. Either they must provide a more convincing account of why the history or causal origins of reasons-responsive mechanisms matters, *or* they must accept that, since history is irrelevant, some version of hard compatibilism is the right course to take. I have explained that there is some reason to be skeptical about the prospects of the first alternative, so let us take a brief look at the hard compatibilist alternative. Robert Kane has noted that hard compatibilists are willing to "bite the bullet" and so deny that the presence or theoretical possibility of covert control or manipulation in any way compromises an agent's freedom and responsibility.[12] This position certainly has some advantages when it comes to defending the compatibilist corner. One of these advantages is that it avoids a gap between libertarianism and compatibilism when it comes to the "implantation standard" that we considered above.

Recall that incompatibilist libertarians raised the following problem for compatibilist views. Compatibilist accounts of rational self-control exclude a power of exercise control, and because of this it is possible for the relevant mechanisms to be implanted in the agent by some artificial means that would permit manipulation and covert control. Granted that manipulation and covert control compromise an agent's freedom and responsibility, it follows that these compatibilist accounts fail to meet the implantation standard. In contrast with this, the implantation of libertarian deliberative mechanisms, which provide exercise control, will not leave any scope for manipulation or covert control by another agent. It is entirely irrelevant whether the libertarian mechanism is implanted by means of some natural, normal process or by some artificial intervention by another agent. Implantation in this case does not make possible manipulation or covert control. This opens up a significant gap between the two views—one that soft compatibilists have tried to close (unsuccessfully) by appealing to history.

The hard compatibilist response is to deny the (incompatibilist and soft compatibilist) assumption that manipulation or covert control necessarily compromises freedom and responsibility. Their claim is that, provided a suitably rich and robust account of moral capacity has been articulated and shown to be possible within compatibilist constraints (i.e., deterministic assumptions), then the mere fact that the agent may be covertly controlled or manipulated by this means is no more evidence that the agent is not free and responsible than it would be if natural, normal causal processes were at work and were the source of the agent's deliberative mechanisms. In other words, the hard compatibilist runs the argument in reverse. If we can provide a suitable account of rational self-control, where the relevant mechanism is *not* implanted by some other agent or a deviant causal process, it follows (since origins are irrelevant to the functioning of this mechanism) that, even if the mechanism has been implanted in a "deviant" manner that permits manipulation and covert control, there is no legitimate basis for denying that the agent is free and responsible. (E.g., if I discover later this evening that God, not nature, has implanted my deliberative mechanism and controls me through it, I still have no reason to change my fundamental conception of myself as a free and responsible agent. After all, I am unchanged and unaffected in all respects relating to my abilities, deliberations, and conduct. There is nothing I was able to do then that I cannot do after being informed about the causal history of my deliberative mechanism.) If we opt for compatibilism, therefore, we must accept the hard compatibilist implications that go with it. If we can't live with this, then we need to turn to incompatibilism and/or libertarian metaphysics to avoid these worries about manipulation and covert control.

My view is that this is the right general strategy *up to a point*. However, I want to suggest a significant amendment or qualification to this hard compatibilist alternative. Assuming that some suitably rich and robust account of moral capacity can be developed within compatibilist constraints, must we accept *unqualified* hard compatibilism? It is clear, I think, that there is something more to the basic intuition that covert control and manipulation compromise responsibility than the straight "bite the bullet" view allows for. It may be possible, however, to provide an alternative explanation for the *source* of our intuitive discomfort with this situation. We may begin by noting that the whole point of developing a theory of moral capacity is to describe the circumstances in which our moral sentiments of praise and blame, and the retributive practices associated with them, may be deemed appropriate or *fair*.[13] The basic idea here is that the agent who is held responsible is a legitimate target of the moral sentiments of other members of her moral community in virtue of possessing the relevant set of capacities and abilities (i.e., rational self-control). Consider now some different scenarios that may arise in circumstances where deviant implantation and covert control is present.

Consider, first, an agent A_m with relevant (reasons-responsive) moral capacity M. M is such that, bracketing off any worries about manipulation and covert control by others, it is reasonable and legitimate for another person B^1 to hold A_m responsible for the conduct that issues out of M. In other words, we assume some satisfactory compatibilist account of M, in circumstances where worries about manipulation by others do not arise. Now consider another scenario where agent $A_m{}^*$ has the very same (time-slice) moral capacity M and the very same conduct issues from M. In this case, however, $A_m{}^*$ is subject to manipulation and covert control by another agent B^2 who uses implantation processes of some deviant kind. What seems clear about this case is that $A_m{}^*$ cannot be legitimately *held* responsible by B^2, since B^2 is in fact covertly controlling $A_m{}^*$. If this situation was made transparent to $A_m{}^*$ or any third party, it would be correct to say that the demands and expectations that B^2 is making on $A_m{}^*$ are ones that B^2 decides will be met or violated. B^2 is, therefore, in *no position* to criticize, evaluate, or react to $A_m{}^*$ in these circumstances.[14] We might say that since B^2 controls $A_m{}^*$'s agency there is *insufficient causal distance* between them to sustain the reactive stance. Moral communication and responsiveness presupposes that agents are not related to each other as controller and controllee. When a controller takes up an evaluative/reactive stance toward an agent that he controls there is plainly an element of fraud or self-deception going on. The controller B^2 can only praise or blame *himself* for the way in which the agent $A_m{}^*$ succeeds or fails to be guided by available reasons.

These limitations do not apply to the relationship between $A_m{}^*$ and (noncontrolling) B^1. B^1 may be aware that there is some (deterministic) causal story to be told about how $A_m{}^*$ acquired the mechanism that she is operating with, but whatever it is (a natural or artificial process) all that matters is that $A_m{}^*$ is rationally competent and B^1 does not control her. The contrast in the relations between these individuals may be illustrated as shown in figure 8.1.

It is clear, per hypothesis, that A_m is responsible to B^1, and there is no responsibility-compromising relationship between them. Moreover, since $A_m{}^*$ possesses the same mechanism as A_m (i.e., M), and B_1 stands in the same (nonmanipulative) relation to $A_m{}^*$ as he does to A_m, there is no principled basis for B_1 treating A_m but not $A_m{}^*$ as responsible (i.e., since the causal origins of M do not alter or impair how A_m or $A_m{}^*$ deliberate and act, nor result in any relevant change in the relationship between B^1 and $A_m{}^*$). When we turn to the situation of B^2, however, there is a relevant difference in his relationship with A_m and $A_m{}^*$. Although B^2's situation in relation to A_m is no different from B^1's situation, his relation to $A_m{}^*$ is that of controller to controllee. Clearly, then, what is compromised in these circumstances is not the responsibility of $A_m{}^*$ as such (since *both* A_m and $A_m{}^*$ stand in the *same* relation to B^1); it is the stance that B^2 takes toward $A_m{}^*$ that is compromised by the relationship of manipulation and covert control.

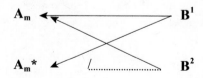

Figure 8.1
Agents, moral judges, and manipulators.

Putting this point in the familiar language of P. F. Strawson, we may say that when the relationship between two individuals is one involving covert control (e.g., through deviant implantation procedures of some kind) then the *participant stance* on the side of the *controller* is compromised. The controller is not *entitled* to take a participant stance in circumstances where he (e.g., B^2) decides when reasons, criticisms, and so on succeed or fail to move the agent (e.g., $A_m{}^*$). For the controller to retain some commitment to the participant stance in these circumstances would clearly be fraudulent or self-deceptive. However, in the absence of any relationship of this kind (e.g., as with B^1 to $A_m{}^*$) the participant stance is not compromised. Granted, therefore, that A_m and $A_m{}^*$ are identical in respect of their capacity for rational self-control, there is no reason to treat one as responsible and the other as not responsible, *unless* the stance being taken is compromised by a relation of covert control (e.g., as in the case of B^2 but not B^1). If the hard compatibilist strategy is to succeed then it must, I suggest, draw some relevant distinction along these general lines. A distinction of this kind will enable us to explain why manipulation and covert control is intuitively unsettling, without driving us away from the basic hard compatibilist stance.

The position that I have suggested that compatibilists should take in relation to manipulation examples and circumstances of covert control may be described as "*selective* hard compatibilism." Selective hard compatibilism accepts that there is some basis to our intuitive worries arising from circumstances of manipulation and covert control. Unlike soft compatibilism, however, the selective hard compatibilist does not concede that agents in these circumstances are not responsible because of the (deviant or abnormal) "history" involved in the way they acquired their reasons-responsive mechanisms. What is compromised in these cases is not the agent's responsibility, as such, but the legitimacy of the stance of *holding* an agent responsible *on the part of those who covertly control him* through the (deviant) implantation process. Assuming, however, that the agent's capacity for rational self-control is otherwise unimpaired by the process involved, the stance of those individuals who do not stand in the relation of controller to controllee is not affected or compromised by the agent's history of deviant implantation (i.e., in relation to others). Since the agent has all the time-slice properties and abilities of an agent who is fully responsible given a normal history (i.e., in the absence of manipulation and covert control) there is no relevant basis for refusing to take the participant stance toward an agent of this kind (e.g., $A_m{}^*$).

4   Modes of Manipulation: God, Walden Two, and Frankenstein

Having explained the general principles of selective hard compatibilism, it will be useful to consider a few further examples in order to test our intuitions about such cases. Perhaps the most obvious example—one that has an established place in the history of philosophy—is the theological case involving God as a cosmic covert controller, through the act of divine Creation. On one side, some compatibilists have taken the "hard" view that conditions of (divine) covert control or manipulation do not compromise (human) freedom and responsibility. They *deny*, therefore, that it is intuitively obvious that if God creates this world and ordains all human action, then we cannot be held accountable to him or anyone else.[15] On the other side, there are compatibilists who are clearly less than comfortable with this position. We find, for example, that Hume, in a well-known passage, considers the implications of his own necessitarian doctrine for Christian theology. In particular, he considers the objection that if the series of causes and effects can be traced back to God, then it follows that God and not humans are responsible for any crimes that occur.[16] Hume's reply to this objection oscillates between the suggestion that in these circumstances God *alone* is responsible for all that flows from his act of Creation (since he is their ultimate "author") and the distinct view that in these circumstances God must *share* responsibility with humans for any actions that we perform. Hume, in other words, oscillates between hard and soft compatibilist commitments on this issue.[17] The source of Hume's discomfort is that he cannot concede, consistent with his general compatibilist commitments, that (blind) *natural* causes of an agent's character and conduct would compromise freedom and responsibility. At the same time, there is something "absurd" about the suggestion that God holds humans accountable (in a future state) for events that he ordains. Clearly the unqualified hard ("bite the bullet") response is not one Hume is willing to accept in this case.[18]

Although I doubt that Hume was sincerely troubled by this issue, it should be clear that selective hard compatibilist principles provide a solution to this problem in a way that is consistent with Hume's *irreligious* intent on this topic. That is to say, the selective hard compatibilist view of this situation is that it is indeed illegitimate and inappropriate for *God* to hold humans accountable in these circumstances, insofar as God covertly controls us and all we do (as per the Creation hypothesis). On the other hand, this concession does nothing to compromise our basic (hard) compatibilist commitments. More specifically, it does not follow from the fact that God is in no position to hold us accountable that we are not (fully) accountable to our fellow *human beings* in these circumstances. Since we are not covertly controlled by other human beings, it is strictly irrelevant whether our conduct and character is ultimately determined by (blind) Nature or by (a personal) God. Nothing about our current abilities or our qualities of character and conduct is altered or affected either way. Therefore, to us (*qua* humans) this is not a consideration that fundamentally changes our relation with each other or compromises the participant stance that we take toward each other.

The incompatibilist and soft compatibilist critics may find this theological example less than convincing when we try to redescribe it in terms of purely human circumstances and conditions. For example, suppose that instead of God serving as a "global manipulator" we imagine a world like Walden Two, where individuals are "engineered" by the methods of implantation or some related technique adopted by the state for its "utopian" ends.[19] How will the principles of selective hard compatibilism fare in this situation?

In cases like Walden Two, selective hard compatibilism draws the following distinction. Insofar as *within* human society there are covert controllers and those who are controlled by them, the former are not in any position to hold the latter responsible or take a participant stance toward them. Given their relationship, the participant stance is not appropriate, since it is the state controllers who are determining how their subjects deliberate, decide, and act (e.g., through controlled implantation procedures). Any stance of evaluation and criticism is, for them (the controllers), not in order.[20] However, on the assumption that the subjects of Walden Two are not related to each other in this way (i.e., they play no role in the process of implantation and covert control), and still possess unimpaired powers of rational self-control, no restriction of this kind applies. These individuals have every reason to continue to view themselves as free and responsible agents (as they would if they were created through the processes of blind nature) and to take the participant stance toward each other. In this way, and to this extent, *within* Walden Two conditions of freedom and responsibility will survive.

As in the theological case of divine Creation, the subjects of Walden Two could wake up one morning and be told, by the relevant authorities, that they are all covertly controlled. Though they may well be surprised by this, they have no more reason to suddenly regard themselves as standing in fundamentally different relations *with each other* in respect of their status as responsible agents than their theologically conditioned counter-parts (or, indeed, than they would if they were informed that they are all determined products of blind, natural processes). In neither case do these agents find that their abilities or qualities have been altered or changed. There is nothing that they were able to do yesterday that they cannot do today. What has changed is that these individuals will no longer view themselves as appropriate targets of moral sentiments in relation to the state authorities who control and condition them—since there is evidently something "absurd" about the authorities criticizing and condemning agents whom they are covertly controlling.

The incompatibilist and soft compatibilist may remain unconvinced and argue that the chosen examples continue to obscure the real problems here. In both the divine Creation and Walden Two examples we are pre-sented with circumstances of *global* manipulation, whereby all agents (i.e., "normal" or "ordinary" agents) are being covertly controlled. However, if we consider an isolated individual case of covert control, our intuitions may change. Viewed from this perspective, the case of an artificially designed agent who is covertly controlled by his creator is obviously prob-lematic. Let us call cases of this sort "Frankenstein-type examples," in order to highlight this familiar and "troubling" theme in both literature and film.[21] Cases of this kind, it may be argued, make clear that something "abnormal" and "disturbing" is taking place. Surely, our critic continues, no one will claim that Frankenstein-type agents, as described, can be viewed as free and responsible.

"Biting the bullet" in cases of this kind is an act of philosophical despair—or at least a sign of an inability or unwillingness to think imagi-natively about cases of this kind.

The first thing we must do, in order to get clear about the significance of these Frankenstein-type examples, is to eliminate features of the example that are strictly irrelevant or misleading.[22] In the first place, it is important to note that the moral qualities of the *covert controller* may vary—they may be good, evil, or mixed. (The same is true in cases of global manipulation, as described above: e.g., either God or the Devil may rule the world.) The case, as described, leaves this issue open. Second, the literature concerned with examples of this kind often suggest not only the shadow of *evil* manipulators operating in the background, they also typically conjure up the image of a "monster" or "freak" who serves as the agent involved (e.g., as in *Frankenstein*). However, cases of this kind are strictly irrelevant since, per hypothesis, we are concerned with individuals who have time-slice properties that are entirely "normal" and present them as otherwise fully functioning and complete agents (i.e., in the absence of any worries about manipulation and covert control). With these distortions removed, we are now in a better position to test our intuitions about such cases and the intuitive force of the principles of selective hard compatibilism.

Clearly, selective hard compatibilism does not license any unqualified hard compatibilist approach to these cases. The individual who covertly controls the agent is in no position to take up the participant stance toward this individual—no matter how "complex" or "robust" the capacities and qualities of the (created) agent may be. Having said this, similar constraints and limitations do not apply to other individuals who stand in a relevantly different relation to the agent ("Frankenstein"). Given that the agent is not in any way impaired in his powers of rational self-control (i.e., he is not "abnormal" or "monstrous" in time-slice terms), and he is not covertly controlled by these other individuals, then the agent remains an appropriate target of *their* reactive attitudes. For these individuals, therefore, the participant stance is not ruled out or compromised simply on the ground that some other individual covertly controls him. From the perspective on other noncontrolling individuals, it is immaterial whether the agent's mechanism M is blindly implanted by Nature or implanted by a covert controller. How the agent functions, and how he relates to those of us who do not covertly control him, is entirely unaffected. Indeed, the case for selective hard compatibilism may be put in stronger terms. Any policy that *demands* that this agent be treated with a systematic "objective" attitude, simply on the basis of the *origins* of his (artificially implanted) mechanism, is itself intuitively *unfair*. Such a policy fails to recognize and acknowledge the agent *as an agent* and treats this individual as if he lacks capacities that he clearly possesses (and as such constitutes a form of *discrimination*).[23]

Our critic may persist that the relevant points have still not been covered. Consider, for example, discovering that *you* are a creation of Dr. Frankenstein and that he has implanted *you* with some mechanism M and thereby covertly controls you. Even if you do not assume that Dr. Frankenstein is evil, and you accept that this discovery in no way implies that you have suddenly been transformed into a "monster" of some kind (i.e., as judged by time-slice criteria), surely there remains something *deeply* disturbing about this discovery from the point of view of *the agent*? More specifically, what we find disturbing about this situation has nothing to do with the stance of the people who may or may not hold the agent responsible; it has everything to do with how the agent must regard *himself*.

If there is something about the discovery that we find disturbing, from the agent's point of view, it must be judged in relation to cases where the mechanism M has been blindly implanted by natural processes and there is no possibility of covert control. So the relevant question we should be asking in this situation is: what does the agent have to worry or care about in these circumstances? The agent may well find the discovery of a history of *artificial* implantation and covert control disturbing on the ground that the *moral* qualities of the covert controller will indeed matter to the way that he functions and operates as an agent. In respect of this issue, the agent may be lucky or unlucky. Naturally, in these circumstances the agent would want to be created and controlled by a benevolent and good creator (just as in the parallel theological situation we would prefer that God and not the Devil is arranging the order of things). In general, if we are being covertly controlled the best we can hope for is a controller who directs our reasons-responsive capacities in some desirable way, as judged from our own point of view and that of those other individuals who must deal with us. Notice, however, that an agent who is *blindly* implanted through *natural* processes, without any possibility of covert control, will also have a parallel worry about whether he has been lucky or unlucky in the way these (blind) forces of nature shape his character and conduct. He will want to discover what these forces are and he will hope that they are benign and not malevolent in their outcomes (i.e., as judged from his own point of view and that of the people he is dealing with).[24]

It is clear, then, that the agent's discovery that he has been implanted and is covertly controlled will raise some distinct issues for him—concerns that do not arise in the "normal" case. However, it is by no means obvious that this discovery must lead the agent to cease viewing himself as a free and responsible agent. On the contrary, if he thinks carefully about his situation he will see that his (time-slice) capacities are not changed or impaired in any way. Moreover, any worries he may have about the (artificial) causal factor that conditions and directs the process of mechanism acquisition have clear counterparts in the case of agents who are subject to a process of blind, natural implantation—such as he took himself to be until the moment of discovery. Finally, the agent in question may also recognize that his situation does not *necessarily* leave him worse off than his "normal" counterpart who is not covertly controlled. It may well be that the "normal" agent is (deeply) unlucky in the natural causes that shape the process of mechanism acquisition, whereas it remains an open question whether the agent who is implanted and covertly controlled is lucky or unlucky. Nothing about the agent's circumstances, as described, determine *this* issue, and it is this issue that the agent has most reason to care about.

These observations suggest that when Frankenstein-type scenarios are accurately described, they are not disturbing in any way that implies that the agent involved must lose all sense of himself as a free and responsible individual (i.e., not unless he has similar reason for this worry based on *blind* implantation processes). Faced with these observations, the critic may try one last maneuver. If we turn to our perspective as *observers* in these circumstances—where we are neither controller nor controllee—we may find the principles of selective hard compatibilism are unconvincing. According to this position, the critic continues, conditions of covert control are relevant only to the individual who actually covertly controls the agent. More specifically, this situation is otherwise irrelevant to all third party observers, since they can continue to take up the participant stance unconcerned about the circumstances of convert control. Surely the knowledge that an agent has been artificially implanted by another individual, who covertly controls him on this basis, cannot be dismissed as *irrelevant* to our attitude and (third-party) perspective on this agent. Once this relationship becomes transparent it will matter to us—in our capacity as *observers*.

Once again, this line of objection is mistaken. For reasons made clear in my earlier replies, it may be important for us to know that an agent is *artificially* implanted and covertly controlled, given that the *moral nature* of the *controller* (e.g., the aims and purposes involved) will indeed matter to us—just as this will also matter to the agent. The covert control may be benign and benevolent, or it may not. We certainly have reason to care about *that*. At the same time, however, even if no artificial implantation or covert control is present, we have good reason to care about and investigate the blind, natural causes that may condition and shape the agent's powers of rational self-control. The nature of these causal origins, and the character of the upshots that they bring about, will matter to us *either way*. It is, therefore, a mistake to think that because we have reason to care (and worry) about whether an agent is being covertly controlled, and what the character and purposes of his covert controller may be, it follows that we cannot view this individual as a responsible agent. No such conclusion is implied, any more than it follows that because we care about the nature of the blind causal forces that may shape and condition an agent's mechanism we must cease to view him as a free and responsible individual. The observer or third-party interest in both cases is similar. Whether the process involved is artificial or natural—whether it leaves open the possibility of covert control or not—the agent continues to enjoy the same capacities and abilities either way. Nor is our own relationship with the agent changed or altered in any relevant way by this discovery. We have, therefore, no relevant grounds for abandoning the participant stance toward this individual simply on the ground of the history of artificial implantation and covert control (i.e., unless we also entertain some *further* skeptical doubts about the implications of *any* process of implantation, be it blind or covertly controlled). In these circumstances all that has changed is our specific understanding of the *particular history* involved in the agent's mechanism acquisition—something that is of interest and importance to us (and the agent) whether covert control is involved or not.

The examples that we have considered in this section make clear that selective hard compatibilism involves a distinct set of commitments from those of either soft or hard compatibilism. Unlike hard compatibilism, selective principles acknowledge that circumstances of implantation and covert control have implications that *are* relevant to issues of responsibility. The way that it *interprets* these issues is, however, very different from the soft compatibilist approach. Whereas the soft compatibilist follows the incompatibilist in holding that responsibility in these circumstances is *systematically* undermined, the selective hard compatibilist maintains that what is compromised is not the agent's responsibility as such, but the legitimacy of the *stance* of holding the agent responsible *on the part of those who covertly control him*. Beyond this, however, there is no general failure of responsible agency. It follows from this that compatibilist accounts of rational self-control cannot be said to fail simply on the ground that they permit covert control (i.e., just as orthodox hard compatibilists have maintained). In this way, selective hard compatibilism blocks the fundamental conclusion that incompatibilists are anxious to establish—a conclusion that motivates soft compatibilist attempts to add historical requirements to conditions of responsible agency.

5 Nothing Too Hard to Swallow—Some Final Thoughts

Let us now review the argument of this essay. We began with a discussion of the problems that contemporary compatibilist theories of rational self-control face when presented with cases of implantation and covert control by another agent. One way of trying to deal with this problem is to embrace soft compatibilism and accept that situations of this kind do indeed compromise the agent's freedom and responsibility. The soft compatibilist claims that what this shows is that we must also care about the "history" involved in the way that we have *acquired* our reasons-responsive dispositions. Considerations of this kind, they suggest, will allow us to draw the relevant distinctions we need to make in this area. I have expressed skepticism about this approach on the ground that it remains unclear why, on this account, we should *care* about the agent's history when it makes no difference to the way that the agent actually deliberates, decides, and acts. Having the "right" history does not provide any form of "enhanced freedom," nor will it satisfy incompatibilist worries about having effective control over the process of mechanism acquisition (i.e., given regress problems, etc.).[25]

Granted that the strategy of soft compatibilism based on history fails, we must choose between incompatibilism and some form of hard compatibilism. The hard compatibilist accepts the "implantation standard": any adequate account of the capacities associated with freedom and moral responsibility must be such that they could be implanted by either natural or artificial processes without compromising the agent's standing as free and responsible (this being a standard that libertarians claim they are able to satisfy). The obvious difficulty for the hard compatibilist, however, is that this seems to open up the door to covert control and manipulation. I have argued that it will not do for hard compatibilists to *simply* "bite the bullet" on this issue. Something more plausible must be said about the basis of our intuitive discomfort with this situation and why we resist this suggestion.

The strategy I have defended involves drawing a distinction between those who can and cannot legitimately hold an agent responsible in circumstances when the agent is being covertly controlled (e.g., through implantation processes). What is intuitively unacceptable, I maintain, is that an agent should be held responsible or subject to reactive attitudes that come from another agent who is covertly controlling or manipulating him. This places some limits on who is *entitled to take up the participant stance* in relation to agents who are rational self-controllers but are nevertheless subject to covert control.[26] In this way, what is compromised by conditions of covert control is not the responsibility of the agent as such. It is, rather, the participant stance of those other agents who covertly control him. Clearly it is possible to establish *these specific limits* on who can *hold* these agents responsible without denying that the agents themselves remain free and responsible. When we take this approach we will find that we are no longer faced with an unattractive choice between simply "biting the bullet" or having to "spit it out." All we need to do is chew carefully, until there is nothing left that we find too hard to swallow.

Acknowledgments

I am grateful to audiences at the Fifth European Congress for Analytic Philosophy (Lisbon, 2005); the Inland Northwest Philosophy Conference (Moscow, Idaho, and Pullman, Washington, 2006); University of British Columbia, McGill University, and Queen's University at Kingston, for their helpful comments and discussion relating to this essay. For further discussion and correspondence I would also like to thank Joe Campbell, John Fischer, Arash Farzam-kia, Ish Haji, Josh Knobe, Rahul Kumar, Alistair Macleod, Storrs McCall, Michael McKenna, Alfred Mele, Jeff Pelletier, Saul Smilansky, and Kip Werking.

Notes

1. See, e.g., Dennett 1984; Wolf 1990; Wallace 1994; and Fischer and Ravizza 1998. For a critical discussion of these theories (and others) see Russell 2002a.

2. See Fischer and Ravizza 1998, which aims to provide an acceptable answer to this problem.

3. In relation to this problem, see Dennett's well-known discussion of the "nefarious neuro-surgeon" (Dennett 1984, 8). See the related discussion in Fischer and Ravizza 1998, 196–201.

4. In these circumstances the agent is no longer sensitive or capable of being guided by any consideration other than the implanted desire. For example, a hypnotized agent may start to act in some arbitrary or random manner when some relevant psychological "trigger" is pulled. This way of dealing with problems of manipulation and behavior control is discussed in Wallace 1994, 176ff., 197ff.

5. This terminology comes from Fischer and Ravizza (1998, 38): "although we employ the term 'mechanism', we do *not* mean to point to anything over and above the process that leads to the relevant upshot. . . ." In a note to this passage, Fischer and Ravizza go on to say that they "are not committed to any sort of 'reification' of the mechanism; that is, we are not envisaging a mechanism as like a mechanical object of any sort. The mechanism leading to an action is, intuitively, the way the action comes about; and, clearly, actions can come about in importantly *different ways*" (emphasis in original).

6. For a more detailed discussion of this point, see Russell 2002b, esp. sect. v.

7. Philosophers of quite different views and commitments accept that it is simply intuitively obvious that a manipulated agent cannot be responsible. See, e.g., Kane 1996, 65ff.; Pereboom 2001, 112ff.; Fischer and Ravizza 1998, 194–202, 230–239; and Haji and Cuypers 2004.

8. Kane 1996, 67–69. This terminology is Kane's.

9. Fischer and Ravizza 1998, ch. 8. Fischer and Ravizza defend their "historicist" views against a number of critics in Fischer and Ravizza 2004. For an earlier "historicist" (or "externalist") account of the conditions of responsible agency see, e.g., Christman 1991. See also Mele 1995, esp. ch. 9.

10. Fischer and Ravizza (1998) describe this required history in terms of a process of "taking responsibility." There are, they maintain, three required conditions for this process. The first begins with a child's moral education, as she comes to see herself "as an agent" (1998, 208, 210–211, 238). At this stage the child sees that certain upshots in the world are a result of her choices and actions. When this condition is satisfied, the child is then in a position to see herself as "a fair target for the reactive attitudes as a result of how [she] exercises this agency in certain contexts" (211). Finally, Fischer and Ravizza also require that "the cluster of beliefs specified by the first two conditions must be based, in an appropriate way, on the evidence" (238). As I explain, my general doubt about a historicist approach of this kind is that it fails to show that the agent has any (final) control over the process of mechanism acquisition—and to this extent it fails to answer incompatibilist objections. I discuss these issues in more detail in Russell 2002b.

11. The account of "ownership" that Fischer and Ravizza (1998) provide is one that leans on the analogy of Nozick's (Lockean) historical entitlement conception of justice (see Fischer and Ravizza 1998, ch. 7; cf. Nozick 1970, esp. ch. 7). The general idea, in both cases, is that ownership of something (e.g., a "mechanism") depends on the historical process involved (as opposed to "current time-slice" considerations). That is to say, what matters to *ownership* is the *way* something was acquired. The difficulty with this analogy, as it relates to Fischer and Ravizza's "soft compatibilism," is that on a Nozickean/Lockean theory of property, individuals may (legitimately) come to own property through processes that do not necessarily involve their own activities or consent (e.g., gift, inheritance, etc.). In these circumstances ownership is possible even though the person concerned did not choose the property or select the mechanism—and so may view what is owned as *imposed* upon him. In general, from the point of view of the analogy with Nozickean/Lockean property theory, mechanism ownership is entirely consistent with a lack of control over acquisition.

12. Kane 1996, 67. Among the more recent and valuable defenses of "hard compatibilism are Watson 2004 and McKenna 2004. For two other interesting compatibilist counterarguments to the incompatibilist "global control" examples, see Vargas 2006 and also Berofsky 2006.

13. See, e.g., Wallace 1994, 5–6, 15–16, 93–95.

14. In the language of P. F. Strawson, we may say that B^2 must take an "objective," not a "reactive," stance to $A_m{}^*$ (cf. Strawson 2003, esp. sect. iv). Since B^2 is manipu-

lating $A_m{}^*$ by deciding when and which reasons will or will not move $A_m{}^*$, it would be *fraudulent* or *self-deceptive* for B^2 to adopt a reactive stance. B^1 is not, however, constrained in these ways.

15. For a classical statement of this ("hard compatibilist") view, see Hobbes 1839–1845, IV, 248ff.

16. Cf. Hume 1999, 8.33–8.36.

17. See my discussion of this point in Russell 1995, 160–163.

18. Hume's strategy was to show that this dilemma reveals the *absurdity* of the "religious hypothesis." To this extent his apparent worry about this problem is insincere.

19. Skinner 1962. See also Kane's illuminating discussion of the significance of Walden Two from an incompatibilist perspective: Kane 1996, 65–69.

20. A similar situation may be imagined when an author enters into a dialogue with one of his own (fictional) characters. Should the author adopt a critical, reactive stance toward such characters, *we* might suggest to the author: "If you don't like this character, why criticize him—just *change* him." (It is true, of course, that the author may take up the reactive stance insofar as he *pretends*, to himself and others, that he is *not* the creator and controller of this character—then his reactive stance may seem more appropriate.)

21. What I have described as "Franken*stein*-type examples" should not, of course, be confused with widely discussed "Frank*furt*-type examples," as associated with Harry Frankfurt's influential paper, "Alternate Possibilities and Moral Responsibility," reprinted as Frankfurt 2003. Frankenstein-type scenarios have more in common with cases like the "nefarious neuro-surgeon" referred to in note 3.

22. Cf. Dennett 1984, 7–10, which is especially effective in identifying the (incompatibilist) misuse of "bogeymen" in cases of this general kind.

23. Keep in mind here that, per hypothesis, if the mechanism M were *blindly* implanted by natural processes the agent would be regarded as *fully* responsible and a fit target of reactive attitudes.

24. Related to this, consider how we may be lucky or unlucky in the parents we have, insofar as they may greatly influence the process of mechanism M acquisition. Evidently we *care* about this—and we all hope to have had good parents (and, more generally, we want to be "lucky" in respect of the way we have been brought up).

25. I take this observation to apply not just to the particular historicist approach that Fischer and Ravizza (1998) defend, but also to a number of other historicist approaches that I have not directly discussed. This includes, for example, the approaches of Christman (1991); Mele (1995), esp. chs. 9 and 10; and Haji and Cuypers (2004). These "historicist" (or "externalist") approaches vary in significant

and interesting ways, and each deserves consideration in its own right. Nevertheless, my primary concern in this essay is not to provide a series of refutations of these various historicist/externalist strategies but rather to sketch an *alternative* compatibilist approach that avoids the need for any historicist/externalist commitments (and also avoids simply "biting the bullet").

26. Josh Knobe has suggested to me (in correspondence) that this general conclusion of "selective hard compatibilism" receives some significant support from experimental data. More specifically, the data concerned show that people who stand in different relationships to the agent have different views about whether or not the agent is morally responsible. One way of reading this is that they just disagree with each other about whether or not the agent really is responsible. However, another way of interpreting the data is that although everyone agrees about the agent's moral status, they also believe that the agent may be held morally responsible by some but not by others (i.e., depending on their relationship). For more on this see Knobe and Doris forthcoming.

References

Berofsky, B. 2006. Global Control and Freedom. *Philosophical Studies* 87:419–445.

Christman, J. 1991. Autonomy and Personal History. *Canadian Journal of Philosophy* 21:1–24.

Dennett, D. 1984. *Elbow Room: The Varieties of Free Will Worth Wanting*. Cambridge, MA: MIT Press.

Fischer, J. M., and M. Ravizza. 1998. *Responsibility and Control: A Theory of Moral Responsibility*. Cambridge: Cambridge University Press.

Fischer, J. M., and M. Ravizza. 2004. Responsibility and Manipulation. *Journal of Ethics* 8:145–177.

Frankfurt, H. 2003. Alternate Possibilities and Moral Responsibility. In *Free Will*, 2nd ed., ed. G. Watson. Oxford: Oxford University Press.

Haji, I., and S. Cuypers. 2004. Moral Responsibility and the Problem of Manipulation Reconsidered. *International Journal of Philosophical Studies* 12:439–464.

Hobbes, T. 1839–1845. Of Liberty and Necessity. In *The English Works of Thomas Hobbes*, 11 vols. Ed. W. Molesworth. London: John Bohn.

Hume, D. 1999. *An Enquiry Concerning Human Understanding*. Ed. T. Beauchamp. Oxford: Oxford University Press.

Kane, R. 1996. *The Significance of Free Will*. Oxford: Oxford University Press.

Knobe, J., and J. M. Doris. Forthcoming. Strawsonian Variations: Folk Morality and the Search for a Unified Theory. In *The Oxford Handbook of Moral Psychology*, ed.

J. Doris, G. Harman, S. Nichols, J. Prinz, W. Sinnott-Armstrong, and S. Stich. Oxford: Oxford University Press.

McKenna, M. 2004. Responsibility and Globally Manipulated Agents. *Philosophical Topics* 32:169–192.

Mele, A. R. 1995. *Autonomous Agents: From Self-Control to Autonomy*. Oxford: Oxford University Press.

Nozick, R. 1970. *Anarchy, State, and Utopia*. New York: Basic Books.

Pereboom, D. 2001. *Living without Free Will*. Cambridge: Cambridge University Press.

Russell, P. 1995. *Freedom and Moral Sentiment*. Oxford: Oxford University Press.

Russell, P. 2002a. Pessimists, Pollyannas, and the New Compatibilism. In *The Oxford Handbook of Free Will*, ed. R. Kane. Oxford: Oxford University Press.

Russell, P. 2002b. Critical Notice of John M. Fischer and Mark Ravizza, *Responsibility and Control*. *Canadian Journal of Philosophy* 32:587–606.

Skinner, B. F. 1962. *Walden Two*. New York: Macmillan.

Strawson, P. F. 2003. Freedom and Resentment. In *Free Will*, 2nd ed., ed. G. Watson. Oxford: Oxford University Press.

Vargas, M. 2006. On the Importance of History for Responsible Agency. *Philosophical Studies* 87:351–382.

Wallace, R. J. 1994. *Responsibility and the Moral Sentiments*. Cambridge, MA: Harvard University Press.

Watson, G. 2004. Soft Libertarianism and Hard Compatibilism. In *Agency and Answerability: Selected Essays*. Oxford: Clarendon Press.

Wolf, S. 1990. *Freedom Within Reason*. Oxford: Oxford University Press.

9 Manipulation and Guidance Control: A Reply to Long

John Martin Fischer

1 Introduction

With my coauthor, Mark Ravizza, I have sought to sketch an overall frame-work for moral responsibility. Part of this framework involves the presentation of an account of a distinctive sort of control, *guidance control*; on our view, guidance control is the freedom-relevant condition necessary and sufficient for moral responsibility. (I distinguish guidance control from *regulative control*, according to which an agent must have genuine metaphysical access to alternative possibilities, and I contend that guidance control, and not regulative control, is properly associated with moral responsibility. See Fischer and Ravizza 1998.)

On this account, there are two chief components of guidance control: mechanism ownership and moderate reasons-responsiveness. More specifically, I contend that an agent displays guidance control of behavior (a choice, an action, an omission, and so forth) just in case the behavior issues from his own, moderately reasons-responsive mechanism.

A key feature of this approach to control (and moral responsibility) is that it is in a certain sense "subjective"—an agent acquires control by taking control, and he does so by taking responsibility. Further, taking responsibility is defined in terms of certain beliefs of the agent; this is the subjective component. When acting from the relevant mechanism, the agent must (a) see himself as the source of his behavior, (b) believe that he is an apt candidate for Strawson's "reactive attitudes" as a result of how he exercises his agency in certain contexts, and (c) have the complex of beliefs in (a) and (b) as a result of his evidence (in an appropriate way) (Fischer and Ravizza 1998, 210–214).

I (and my coauthor) have argued that, on this sort of approach, moral responsibility is arguably compatible with causal determinism. Thus, the approach I favor is consistent with the traditional compatibilist insistence that not all causal chains are to be considered equally threatening to freedom. According to a compatibilist, not all causal chains are created equal. I would contend that some deterministic causal chains contain instances of guidance control (whereas others do not). Of course, a traditional challenge for the compatibilist is to distinguish those deterministic causal chains that threaten or eliminate freedom from those that do not; my account of guidance control is my attempt to do just this.

2 Long's Critique

There is a set or range of scenarios that is puzzling and difficult for *any* account of moral responsibility; these scenarios involve various kinds of "manipulation" or "induction" of mental states. The scenarios are diverse, multifaceted, and perplexing, It is evident that one must be judicious with respect to one's considered judgments about the cases in these sorts of scenarios and also the application of one's theory to such cases. It should not be surprising that a fairly reasonable and plausible general theory of moral responsibility might not apply straightforwardly to all such scenarios, or might give indeterminate or even somewhat unexpected results in some cases. Also, it would not be a good idea to suppose that all manipulation examples should be treated in the same way by a theory of moral responsibility (or that, upon careful consideration, one would have the same view about the moral responsibility of the individuals in such scenarios).

It is nevertheless entirely fair to press worries about how my account of guidance control (and moral responsibility) would handle certain conceivable kinds of manipulation or artificial induction of mental states. Various philosophers have explored these issues helpfully and have pressed legitimate concerns.[1] In this essay I wish to focus primarily (but not exclusively) on a thoughtful and probing challenge presented by Long (2004). Here is Long's story:

Schmidt is a high-ranking official in the German government just prior to Hitler's rise to dictatorial power. Having been raised by parents with a deep inner moral sense and resolve, Schmidt learned from an early age the difference between right and wrong. As he developed, so did his moral wisdom. Suffice it to say that Schmidt developed into a man of impeccable moral judgment.

Owing to Schmidt's high rank in the German government, he is a member of a secret group that will decide by vote whether or not Hitler is to be given supreme power. Schmidt has known Hitler for many years. The two became friends when each was a budding young politician. During those early years, they shared with each other their dreams and ideas about how to build a better Germany. Schmidt was impressed with both the ingenuity of Hitler's ideas and the deep moral sense that those ideas displayed. From the things that Hitler said to Schmidt during those early years, Schmidt had very good reasons to think that Hitler would be an honest, forthright, and morally upstanding asset to Germany's future. However, several years before the vote is to take place, Schmidt begins to hear disturbing stories about Hitler. From reliable sources, he hears that Hitler has intentions of building up a master race of pure-blooded Aryans, driving non-Aryans out of the country, and perhaps killing those who do not leave. Schmidt develops deep doubts about Hitler's moral character.

Schmidt's role in the decision is to cast the deciding vote, should the voting members reach a deadlock. The members do reach a deadlock, so Schmidt is called upon to cast the deciding vote. Schmidt deliberates. Waiting in the wings is Block, a malevolent being with extraordinary causal and predictive powers. Should it become clear to him that Schmidt is going to vote against Hitler, Block will take effective steps to ensure that Schmidt votes *for* Hitler. Otherwise, Block will do nothing. So, whatever Schmidt's initial preferences and inclinations, Block will have his way. (Long 2004, 157–158)

Now Long considers two possibilities. In the first, Schmidt would deliberate and vote for Hitler on his own. This would involve Schmidt's freely acting out of character, and Long points out that it is plausible that here Schmidt would be both morally responsible and blameworthy for his choice and behavior. Long also notes that the Fischer–Ravizza approach can accommodate these views.

Long goes on to consider the second basic possibility, characterized by Schmidt's having a certain disposition: here it is true that Schmidt is such that, were Block not to intervene, Schmidt would vote against Hitler. Long divides the second basic possibility into three scenarios. In the first, a minute before Schmidt casts his vote, Block realizes that Schmidt is about to vote against Hitler (in the absence of Block's intervention), and Block manipulates Schmidt in such a way as to ensure that Schmidt votes for Hitler. We can here imagine that Block does something directly to Schmidt's central nervous system; the intervention "bypasses" Schmidt's normal deliberative voting mechanism (Long 2004, 158). Long observes that the Fischer–Ravizza approach would correctly imply that Schmidt is not morally responsible for his choice and behavior here insofar as Schmidt's behavior does not issue from his own, moderately reasons-responsive mechanism. Presumably, the mechanism in question would neither be Schmidt's own nor suitably reasons-responsive.

Here is Long's description of the second scenario:

A minute before Schmidt casts his vote, Block becomes convinced that Schmidt is going to vote against Hitler. Block goes into action: he *adds* new inputs into the *very same mechanism* that is operant in the actual sequence. Suppose that these new inputs come in the form of *reasons* for voting for Hitler. Block directly feeds into Schmidt's deliberative voting mechanism enough reasons, or reasons powerful enough, to ensure that Schmidt will vote for Hitler. (Ibid., 159)

Long contends that simply adding inputs to a deliberative mechanism should not "change the mechanism." So he initially says that this case "appears" to be a counterexample to the Fischer–Ravizza contention that guidance control is the freedom-relevant condition sufficient for moral responsibility (ibid., 160). Long gives a similar analysis of his third scenario, which is like the second except that instead of adding an input, Block *removes* inputs from what is putatively *the very same mechanism*; these inputs are Schmidt's own reasons for voting against Hitler (ibid., 160–161). Since I believe the issues raised by scenarios 2 and 3 under the second "basic possibility" are the same, I shall, for simplicity's sake, focus on scenario 2.

As I said above, Long initially says that this case appears to be a counterexample to the Fischer–Ravizza theory. Later in the paper, however, Long returns to the second scenario, and this time he argues that the initial appearance that such a case provides a counterexample to the Fischer–Ravizza approach is mistaken. He says:

[In the second scenario] not only did Schmidt meet the conditions of [moderate reasons-responsiveness], but he also intuitively did the morally responsible thing, given the evidence he had to go on. And if we knew the relevant facts about each case, we might even praise him for his action, even as we deeply regret or deplore the trick Block played on him and the consequences that followed. . . . The moral is that we are morally responsible for our actions when they are consonant with our reasons in an appropriate way . . ., but whether we are praiseworthy or blameworthy for our actions depends on additional facts about the cases. (Ibid., 164)

Given the distinction between moral responsibility and praiseworthiness–blameworthiness, then, Long is willing to accept that Schmidt is morally responsible for his choice in scenario two. He says, "After doing this ground clearing, we are in a position to see that [Fischer and Ravizza's] theory *does* get the cases right" (ibid.).

On the occasion of Long's presentation of the main criticism contained in his paper at the Inland Northwest Philosophy Conference, I said that it was my intuition that Schmidt is not responsible in scenario 2. I further suggested that the Fischer–Ravizza account would have this result, since the installation of inputs by Block would seem to render the mechanism a different one—not Schmidt's own deliberative mechanism. Long says:

Fischer himself has responded to my examples by saying that intuitively Schmidt is not morally responsible in [scenario 2]. Fischer infers from this intuition that the manipulation of the inputs makes the mechanism in those cases a different mechanism from the one operant in the actual-sequence [the first basic possibility]. I find this response disappointing, for Fischer concedes that he has no principled way to distinguish the mechanisms in question. (Ibid.)

I wish to note that I did not intend to infer straightforwardly from my intuitive judgment about the case to the conclusion that the mechanism is different from the one operant in the actual sequence. That would be circular in a troubling way. I do, however, grant that the methodological issues here are complex; I have sought to address them elsewhere (Fischer 2004). Additionally, I have sought to explain the role of mechanism-individuation in my overall approach. Like Long and others, I also find it somewhat disappointing that I do not have a general and completely reductive account of mechanism individuation; but I do not judge this to be a decisive reason to reject my overall approach. Further, I would have thought that the fundamental reason for disappointment on Long's part would be that my reply disagrees with his more reflective judgment about the case.

In defending this judgment, Long says:

Nothing about Block's manipulation prevents Schmidt from meeting [the conditions for "taking responsibility" posited by Fischer and Ravizza]. To think that Schmidt fails to satisfy those conditions is to suppose that Schmidt would have to be responsible both for his prior evidence (or beliefs) and for the way in which he acquired that evidence (or those beliefs). But, surely this is to add too much to the notion of taking responsibility. Evidence (and reasons) supporting beliefs come to us from various directions and in many different ways. Some of it we are quite aware of, and some of it were are less aware of. Earlier I mentioned that nobody would balk at the suggestion that Schmidt could have been convinced to vote for Hitler by more ordinary external means (news reports, personal testimony, etc.). What is the relevant difference between manipulating the inputs in those ways and manipulating the inputs directly?

Consider a case in which a group of conniving folk manipulate the inputs of someone's deliberative mechanism by affecting the information that person gets. Suppose a group of Young Republicans who work at a news press manipulate the inputs that Karen's deliberative voting mechanism receives by changing the text of Karen's newspaper every time something good is said in print about being a Democratic candidate. Would this prevent Karen from being morally responsible for her voting? If you are inclined to answer "yes," then you owe us an explanation of why any of us are morally responsible for our acts of voting. After all, very few of us control the political reports or the political opinions that are propounded in our newspapers and other media; thus, most of us do not control the inputs our deliberative voting mechanisms receive. . . . On what basis should we judge ourselves as morally responsible for our voting but deny that Karen is morally responsible for her voting? (Long 2004, 165)

Long summarizes his critique by stating that although the Fischer–Ravizza account of guidance control wants and needs it to be the case that a certain fixed mechanism can operate on various different inputs, "the only way to make sense of Fischer's response to my examples is to think that Schmidt would have to be responsible for his input acquisition as well as for the mechanism itself. This amounts to building the inputs into the mechanism" (ibid., 166). As Long notes, this would be fatal to the Fischer–Ravizza approach.

3 Reply

As I said above, cases involving manipulation or (putative) artificial induction of mental states are complex and difficult to sort through. I also suggested that there are importantly different kinds of such manipulation and that these differences may make significant differences in how we analyze and evaluate the cases. These considerations apply to the scenarios presented in sketchy form by Long. Consider again the way in which he describes scenario 2:

A minute before Schmidt casts his vote, Block becomes convinced that Schmidt is going to vote against Hitler. Block goes into action: he *adds* new inputs into the *very same mechanism* that is operant in the actual sequence. Suppose that these new inputs come in the form of *reasons* for voting for Hitler. Block directly feeds into Schmidt's deliberative voting mechanism enough reasons, or reasons powerful enough, to ensure that Schmidt will vote for Hitler. (Ibid., 159)

Note that Long begins by saying that Block swings into action "a minute before Schmidt casts his vote." This suggests something important—or perhaps subtly frames the description in such a way that it would naturally suggest that "something" to the reader. The suggestion in question is that the implantation or manipulative induction of "reasons" is done immediately prior to the choice and subsequent behavior, and that there is thus no reasonable or fair opportunity for Schmidt to reflect on or critically evaluate the new input in light of his standing dispositions, values, preferences, and so forth.

I contend that when "inputs" are implanted in a way that does not allow for a reasonable or fair opportunity for the agent to subject those inputs to critical scrutiny in light of his or her normative orientation, then such manipulation does indeed remove moral responsibility. Such manipulation typically "changes the mechanism." On the other hand, if an "input" is artificially implanted in such a way as to leave it open to the agent (in a reasonable and fair way) to critically scrutinize and reflect on the new input, then this sort of manipulative induction of inputs *may well be* compatible with moral responsibility for the choice and subsequent behavior. Such manipulation could leave the ordinary mechanism of practical reasoning intact.[2]

Long's examples are underdescribed in precisely this way—he does not make it explicit whether Schmidt has a reasonable and fair opportunity to evaluate the mysteriously appearing inputs in light of his overall normative orientation—his other values, preferences, and so forth. As I pointed out above, his description *suggests* that Schmidt would not have such an opportunity, and thus it is plausible (in my view) that such manipulation would rule out moral responsibility.[3] Perhaps then it is not surprising that Long himself seems to exhibit a certain sort of ambivalence about the scenario—at first suggesting that it appears that Schmidt is not morally responsible, and then subsequently claiming that, upon reflection, Schmidt is responsible. The ambivalence may reflect the underdescription of the case; filled in one way, we are inclined to deny responsibility, but filled in another way, we are inclined to affirm responsibility. Either way, the Fischer–Ravizza approach yields exactly the correct results.

Recall Long's statement that I "infer" from my intuition that Schmidt is not morally responsible in scenario 2 (interpreted in the way I have explained) the conclusion that the alternative sequence would involve a *different* kind of mechanism (from the mechanism in the actual sequence). This of course would be an uncomfortably tight circle. One wants at least some sort of story by reference to which it is independently plausible that we have a different mechanism in the alternative sequence; I would like to sketch some elements of such a story.[4]

Ordinarily, when we have some new "input" to our practical reasoning, or we simply find ourselves with some new mental state—a new desire or a desire with a new intensity or urgency—or perhaps a new tendency to recognize or weigh reasons in a certain way, we can pause to reflect on this new element of our mental economy or normative orientation. We can then filter it through our practical reasoning in the sense that we can bring to bear *other* (presumably, nonmanipulatively induced) elements of our character or standing dispositions; we can typically affect the new element in light of standing features. This may involve affecting the intensity or even "direction" of a desire, or affecting the way one identifies or gives weight to reasons. What is crucial is that we have a fair and reasonable opportunity to filter new elements of our mental economy through our character as a whole.

Typically, of course, we do not have control over what the world presents us in terms of factors that correspond to or generate reasons, or even evidence for certain judgments. I agree with Long that it would be implausible to demand that, in order to be morally responsible, I must somehow be responsible for or in control of all the inputs to my mechanism of practical reasoning. But what *is* plausible is to demand that I have a reasonable and fair opportunity to filter a new input through my character and practical reasoning. Given that I have certain information from newspapers and political candidates, and stipulating that I have little if any control over much of what comes to me through these media, I can critically scrutinize and evaluate it. Similarly, if a desire or other "input" suddenly and mysteriously presents itself to me, I can typically subject it to critical scrutiny and filter it through my practical reasoning (employing the other elements of my normative orientation). Even if the input is implanted via clandestine manipulation or induction, I could in certain instances then subject it to critical evaluation and filter it through my practical reasoning. In these instances I could be morally responsible for my choices and behavior. But if I do not have this sort of reasonable and fair opportunity, then my character as a whole and my practical reasoning has been "bypassed" (Mele 1995, 144–176).

This, then, suggests a natural way to respond to Long's basic critique presented in his summary. There he states that my way of responding to cases such as the second scenario force the input into the mechanism, as it were; Long is certainly correct that this would be a fatal result for the Fischer–Ravizza approach, which presupposes that one can give the same mechanism different inputs (and thus have in certain cases different outputs). My response should now be clear. In a case in which there is a reasonable and fair opportunity to filter the inputs through one's deliberative mechanism, there is no problem with changing the inputs while maintaining the same mechanism. In those cases where one's deliberations or practical reasoning or, more generally, normative orientation is bypassed, then such manipulation does indeed change the mechanism; we no longer would have the ordinary human mechanism of unimpaired practical reasoning.

As practical reasoners and normative agents, we identify and weigh (or "process") reasons in certain distinctive ways. This way of identifying and weighting reasons could be physically implemented in the brain in various different ways, and by different physical parts; it would still be the same unimpaired human mechanism of practical reasoning. This mechanism of practical reasoning involves the reasonable and fair opportunity to subject to critical scrutiny any emergent or newly presenting desire, or any new tendency to identify or weigh reasons in a certain way. Although the specific way in which the more abstract processing is physically implemented can change compatibly with having the same mechanism, one cannot change crucial features of the processing of reasons, such as the capacity for evaluating new inputs in light of one's standing normative orientation (without thereby changing the mechanism). Thus, anything that disrupts the typical relationship between the agent's existing normative orientation and a new element—sequestering the new element and rendering it immune from the causal interaction with the preexisting elements— cannot be the ordinary mechanism of human practical reasoning.[5]

4 Conclusion

Manipulation scenarios are diverse and resistant to simple, one-size-fits-all analysis. I have argued that Long's scenario 2 is underdescribed. When the description is filled in suitably, we can see that he has not produced a counterexample to the Fischer–Ravizza account of guidance control and moral responsibility. I note that we have here explored cases that might be called "local manipulation," in which one input is manipulatively implanted but the other elements of one's character or normative orientation are not tampered with. A more comprehensive treatment would seek to address global manipulation cases of various sorts.[6]

A final thought. Some philosophers (some of whom are compatibilists) have an easier time with manipulation scenarios; they simply banish them. That is, they assert that for conceptual or perhaps scientific reasons they are skeptical of even the possibility of the artificial implantation of mental states. Sometimes these philosophers invoke their considerable knowledge of neuroscience, and sometimes they invoke their impressive analytic skills; they like to make fun of "armchair philosophers" who believe in the coherence of thought experiments involving "nefarious neurosurgeons" and their ilk.

Oh, how easy it would be not to have to address the range of manipulation cases! If it turns out that the skeptics are correct (for whatever reason), then it will be that much easier to defend compatibilism, as one would not have to work so hard to distinguish responsibility-conferring causally deterministic paths from those causally deterministic paths that rule out moral responsibility; more carefully, one would not have to worry about this subclass of causally deterministic paths (involving putative artificial induction of mental states via direct electronic stimulation of the brain).

But I have always thought that one can make the best case for the compatibility of causal determinism and moral responsibility only by being maximally charitable to the opponent—the incompatibilist. I have felt that it is only by taking incompatibilism seriously and fully engaging the incompatibilist that one can get the best argument for compatibilism. It has never seemed promising simply to dismiss the Consequence Argument (as so many compatibilists seem to do); nor has it seemed promising simply to dismiss the possibility of manipulation. It has always seemed better to take these worries seriously and to seek to address them head on.[7]

Acknowledgments

I am deeply grateful to generous, gracious, and thoughtful comments by Todd Long delivered at the Inland Northwest Philosophy Conference, March 2006. I have also benefited from questions and comments by other participants in the conference, including Randolph Clarke and Manuel Vargas.

Notes

1. See, e.g., Stump 2002; Pereboom 2001, 110–126; Shabo 2005; and Judisch 2005. There are preliminary responses in Fischer 2004 and 2005a.

2. I favor an "actual-sequence" account of moral responsibility, according to which moral responsibility does not require that the agent have genuine metaphysical access to alternative possibilities. Although I speak in the text of this essay in terms of (say) Schmidt's having a reasonable and fair opportunity to evaluate a new input, this is solely for simplicity's sake; I wish to interpret such statements in terms of the properties of the actual-sequence mechanism. So, slightly more carefully, I would contend that the actual-sequence mechanism must exhibit the general power or capacity to evaluate the new input in relevant ways.

3. I wish to emphasize that I am not contending that the timing in itself makes a difference. Rather, what is important is that the actual-sequence mechanism exhibit the appropriate capacity to evaluate the new input. One could in principle have this capacity even with very little time between the induction of the input and the

decision point, and one could lack this capacity, even with plenty of time between the induction and the decision point. What ultimately matters is the capacity in question, not the timing; but certain ways of presenting hypothetical examples, especially where there is little or no time after the induction and prior to the need to make a decision, *suggest* the absence of the relevant capacity.

Note that presumably we sometimes have "go-permissions" (to employ a term suggested to me by Manuel Vargas) as part of our total normative orientation at a given point in time; thus, on the basis of these go-permissions (fixed antecedently), we can instantaneously (as it were) react to new inputs in circumstances that require this.

4. See also Fischer 2005a.

5. This sort of sequestration gives one instance of what Mele must have in mind when he invokes his important notion of "bypassing" the agent's practical reasoning (Mele 1995, 144–176).

6. See Fischer and Ravizza 1998, 230–236, and Fischer 2004.

7. Daniel Dennett is an example of a compatibilist who is inclined to brush aside both the Consequence argument and the range of manipulation scenarios. See Dennett 1984 and 2003. For a critical discussion of some of these points, see Fischer 2005b; Dennett seeks to respond in Dennett 2005, esp. 451–454.

I do not wish to suggest that there are no perfectly reasonable worries—both conceptual and scientific—about the possibility of artificial induction of mental states. These worries are deep and significant, and I do not in any way mean to dismiss their importance. I simply point out that if they are decisive, my form of compatibilism is that much easier to defend; for the sake of the argument, I am willing to put aside worries about induction and still attempt to defend my form of compatibilism. Despite what some philosophers appear to believe, I am in no way committed to the coherence of thought experiments involving artificial induction of motivational states; if anything, they make my (philosophical) life more challenging.

References

Dennett, D. 1984. *Elbow Room: The Varieties of Free Will Worth Wanting.* Cambridge, MA: MIT Press.

Dennett, D. 2003. *Freedom Evolves.* New York: Viking.

Dennett, D. 2005. Natural Freedom. *Metaphilosophy* 36:449–459.

Fischer, J. M. 2004. Responsibility and Manipulation. *Journal of Ethics* 8:145–177.

Fischer, J. M. 2005a. Reply: The Free Will Revolution. *Philosophical Explorations* 8:145–156.

Fischer, J. M. 2005b. Dennett on the Basic Argument. *Metaphilosophy* 36:427–435.

Fischer, J. M., and M. Ravizza. 1998. *Responsibility and Control: A Theory of Moral Responsibility*. Cambridge: Cambridge University Press.

Judisch, N. 2005. Responsibility, Manipulation, and Ownership: Reflections on the Fischer/Ravizza Program. *Philosophical Explorations* 8:115–130.

Long, T. R. 2004. Moderate Reasons-Responsiveness, Moral Responsibility, and Manipulation. In *Freedom and Determinism*, ed. J. K. Campbell, M. O'Rourke, and D. Shier. Cambridge, MA: MIT Press.

Mele, A. R. 1995. *Autonomous Agents: From Self-Control to Autonomy*. New York: Oxford University Press.

Pereboom, D. 2001. *Living without Free Will*. Cambridge: Cambridge University Press.

Shabo, S. 2005. Fischer and Ravizza on History and Ownership. *Philosophical Explorations* 8:103–114.

Stump, E. 2002. Control and Causal Determinism. In *Contours of Agency: Essays on Themes from Harry Frankfurt*, ed. S. Buss and L. Overton. Cambridge, MA: MIT Press.

10 Free Will: Some Bad News

Saul Smilansky

1 Preliminaries

I believe that if we reflect more on the free will debate, and on ourselves as participants in it, we shall do better in tackling the free will problem. More specifically, I will argue here that the free will debate is characterized by an effort to see the bright side of things. This feature is striking, and it is shared by almost all participants, irrespective of their disagreements. We are not critical enough about this (natural) tendency. And I do include myself here. There is some good news, even if we lack libertarian free will (LFW). But all in all, and in different ways, the free will issue is very bad news. I will first sketch the way I see the free will debate, and thereby explain why, if I am correct, this means that we need to work on ourselves in order to tackle it more successfully. Second, I will illustrate why the free will problem is "bad news," and briefly discuss what this implies. This is a metaphilosophical overview of the free will problem and debate, from a particular angle, which does not aim to capture all that is valuable in contemporary work on our topic. I have also refrained from referencing many of works that I will touch upon (except for the few publications that I refer to by name). The bibliographical materials of the people I refer to are easy to discover and I wish to avoid cumbersome details. Throughout, I have sought to maintain the conversational tone of my talk.

In my work on the free will problem I have made two radical claims. The first is that we must aim to systematically integrate the partial but crucial insights both of compatibilism and of hard determinism, and become that unfamiliar beast, a compatibilist hard determinist. My diagnosis of the debate has been that both sides on the compatibility question seem to take for granted what I call the "Assumption of Monism," whereby (if there is no LFW) we must be either compatibilists or hard determinists. Once we are free of this assumption, we can address the business of exploring when, how, and how much of each side we can integrate with the other. I point this out not only in order to signal where in the debate I am coming from, but because the issue of "either–or" on the compatibility question also has a strong psychological basis, for people are naturally inclined one way or the other. Now that some of the debate is beginning to be more open to the sort of "compatibility dualism" or "pluralism" that I have been advocating, we can reflect more easily on why this harmful dichotomy has existed for so many years.

The second radical idea is that illusion plays a central role in the free will problem, and that, moreover, this role is mostly positive. My diagnosis of the debate on this level has been that we are mostly blind to the centrality of illusion. I will not repeat too much of this previous work in this essay, but I will both end and begin with illusion—end, for it is an implication of my claim that the free will problem is "bad news"; and begin, because I think that to deal with the free will problem adequately we must be sensitive to the temptations of deluding ourselves, temptations that exist regarding this problem more than any other. Put differently, our difficulties with this problem are not only cognitive, for we are smart enough to tame it; our difficulties are in large measure psychological.

2   Apologia

Before I jump into these murky waters, I would like to spend a brief while saying something self-reflective here, which is, after all, what I have just said that we should all do more of. In this essay I shall be critical of a central tendency within the free will debate, and not only of specific positions within it. This stance is unpleasant for me. I think that here we might do well to follow Sidgwick's advice in *The Methods of Ethics*: "I have thought that the predominance in the minds of moralists of a desire to edify has impeded the real progress of ethical science: and that this would be benefited by an application to it of the same disinterested curiosity to which we chiefly owe the great discoveries of physics" (Sidgwick 1963, viii). Though we are still interested in edifying, I think that if Sidgwick were here today he would see the major problem as a desire to comfort ourselves. This is a natural extension of the dominant general human bias toward views (primarily of ourselves) that make us feel good. Sidgwick's example is important because he is widely recognized as having been a very pleasant and decent person. Despite being pleasant and decent—or perhaps because of this—when he took a dispassionate attitude, he was able to contemplate fairly unpleasant proposals (such as a deceitful "Government-house utilitarianism," in Bernard Williams's phrase).

We must be on guard lest we find ourselves talking about the debate in ways, or indeed recommending certain ways of dealing with the free will problem, that are psychologically motivated by our needs to comfort ourselves, rather than "going with the issues." However, we also need to remind ourselves that dispassion itself may be dubiously psychologically motivated; and similarly for urges for simplification, or for seeming radical. In any case, in order to "purify" our thoughts we must become more aware of the various ways in which our fears and hopes are entangled with them. We must make room for looking at the free will problem, at the debate, and at ourselves, in a cold-blooded fashion.

There might seem to be a particular danger to this "psychological turn": that, as the saying goes, "everyone falls in love with his own compromises." It is enough, we might think, that people find it difficult to enter into other people's philosophical perspectives, without adding an attempt to connect those positions to psychology. I think that there are clear dangers here; nevertheless, we should spend some of our time on such navel gazing. I certainly spend more of my time reflecting on my own motivations than I do on those of others. And I have enormous respect for the labors and achievements of many philosophers working on the free will problem. But as I mentioned already, I think that the long shadow cast by the free will problem affects the way in which we approach it, and makes this problem particularly demanding emotionally, and particularly requiring of self-awareness and self-reflection, as correctives. The proof of what I am proposing is in the pudding, and I would like now to proceed to say something about how I perceive the free will debate, and then to argue that matters are far grimmer than that debate brings out. Or, in active mode—far grimmer than we have allowed ourselves to realize, internalize, and declare.

3   A Reinterpretation of the Free Will Debate

A common perception of the free will debate goes something like this. It is a combination of a number of distinct questions, on each of which many philosophers hold contrary positions. The classical questions are the "libertarianism question," whether there is universal determinism or, irrespective of determinism, the possibility of the sort of transcendent freedom we know as libertarian free will. Then comes the second question, the "compatibility question," which asks if we can have moral responsibility even if determinism (or an absence of LFW) is the case. Compatibilists say "yes"; hard determinists say "no." This was largely the way the debate looked for some two thousand years, until quite recently. Today, of course, we know that the issues are more subtle: do we really need the "ability to do otherwise" in order to be free, or responsible? Would it be bad if we did not have moral responsibility? Do we at all need to worry about the continuation of common attitudes and practices, or are they self-perpetuating? There is (rightly) a sense of satisfaction within the debate about the great philosophical progress that has been made in the last two generations. And the common perception is that the variety has only brought more things to disagree about. I think that most readers will find this picture familiar.

Now I will briefly sketch out a different interpretation of the free will debate. It is necessarily rough, as I do not have the space to go into details, but I believe that you will find it also, perhaps reluctantly, familiar. Here there is a progression from idea to idea, with every pessimistic reply generating a new possibility—sometimes a new question, sometimes a new answer. Occasionally, indeed, old skeletons pay a return visit. The common denominator is that *every time a door closes, a new one opens*. We never really confront the feeling that a door has been shut in our face, and we are at a loss. Determinism threatens, so perhaps quantum mechanics will help us. Quantum mechanics is unable to give us control, so perhaps, as Robert Kane suggests, we do not need the sort of control we thought we did. For those libertarians for whom this sort of compatibilism-with-randomness hardly seems worthwhile, maybe there is a new form of causality, "agent-causality," available especially for us. And if nothing seems to be plausible, maybe (as Peter van Inwagen claims) LFW still evidentially exists, but as a mystery. Let's now go beyond LFW, and I will be assuming in the rest of the discussion that we do not have it (for any of a number of reasons, namely, because determinism dominates human life, or because indeterminism cannot give us much, or because in any case the very notion of LFW does not make sense).

At this stage we used to get the compatibilist reply that what matters is simply doing what you want—which we typically surely can do, even in a deterministic world. Or, a bit differently, 'can', it was explained, simply *is* 'would, if she wanted to'. It was countered that all this will hardly do, for surely we are often rightly worried about the *sources* of our desires. Moreover, perhaps we are not free just because we cannot want to *X*, even if we would X if (counterfactually) we could have wanted to. In response, compatibilists moved on, with scarcely a heartbeat, to other explications. My point is not that these compatibilist, or Fischerian semicompatibilist, explications are not valuable—they are, and as a partial compatibilist I share some of them. I also think that they are shallow, in that they do not address the chief worry, that even under ideal compatibilist conditions all our blameworthy or praiseworthy actions are ultimately beyond our control, merely the unfolding of who we happen to be; the unfolding of the given. But the present point is that no major conscious sense of crisis appeared, but only rather quick solutions. I do not think, for instance, that we can really understand the full attractiveness of "Frankfurt-type examples" and the bypassing of the "ability to do otherwise" if we cannot see, and feel, how similar they are in *function* to quantum mechanics— namely, a way to "change the subject" and overcome the increasing sense that traditional compatibilist accounts of the "ability to do otherwise" are beginning to seem less and less convincing. I will not be able to enter into a detailed discussion of the subtleties of state-of-the-art compatibilism and its varieties, and in any case there is no reason to think that my own view carries particular weight here; the present point is to see the pattern of the debate.

Similarly, consider some more out-of-the-way versions of compatibilism, or views that at least support compatibilist-like conclusions. First, P. F. Strawson's classic "Freedom and Resentment" (Strawson 2003). This is one of the greatest and most salient philosophical papers of the twentieth century.[1] But can we really not see that it *means* something, that we have this unusually influential paper, which basically says, "Don't worry"? Strawson rejects the libertarian metaphysics, which he considers "panicky," and he thinks that LFW is incoherent. He also does not seem to put great store by traditional compatibilist stands. All this, however, does not matter, for except in the drawing rooms of philosophers no one will or, indeed, needs to take the difficulty seriously, he claims. This position has also confronted strong objections: substantively, even if certain reactions are unavoidable, this is still far from saying that they are justified (say, that resentment is deserved). And pragmatically, the threats of a loss of moral confidence by people, if hard determinist views become more prevalent, and of the temptations of handling people through social means that do not respect innocence, and do not track responsibility, show that Strawson was much too complacent. But as with previous views, I have not attempted to do justice to his position here, merely to help us to see how, for all the differences, it is the same *sort* of thing: a strong affirmation of the positive, at the very instant when all the attempts to give it a basis, until that point, have been given up.

From neo-Humeanism to neo-Kantianism: Christine Korsgaard and Hilary Bok are not convinced by P. F. Strawson's justification for the "don't worry" attitude, but they also think that there is hardly anything to worry about: after all, a competent moral agent surely can think that he can do the right thing when acting, and that is all that we need. One problem with this view is that it avoids the issue of what people may come to think when reflecting on the past. Surely anticipations of such "retrospective excuses" can affect us in the present, when acting. I will say a bit more about this in the second half of my essay, when I give direct examples of "bad news."

It is interesting to note that almost all these positive views have remained more or less within the common, broadly Kantian, paradigm, which puts desert at the center, requiring control for responsibility, and responsibility for desert. (Arguably this is the case even with the Strawsonian view, which is why Jay Wallace was able to fuse Kant and P. F. Strawson.) Here is a quick proof of my claim for the dominance of deontological desert-based views: although Thomas Scanlon is one of the most influential contemporary moral philosophers, and he has also written on the free will problem, almost no one has followed him within the free will debate, in his attempt to offer an alternative contractualist basis for the discussion. Similarly, although utilitarianism has been central in ethics for over a century, it has hardly been allowed into the free will debate. For example, J. J. C. Smart's utilitarian reinterpretation of blame is, if considered at all, typically presented as proof of the crudity of utilitarianism. Similarly for Dennett's work. Now, again, I don't so much disagree with the charge of crudity made, in the free will context, against utilitarianism or Dennett, as seek to map things so that we become *amazed* at the nature of our debate. Like the defenders of some medieval fort, again and again we see our walls come tumbling down and, without a blink, we manage to retreat a bit, and miraculously set up completely new walls. One way of doing so, apparently, is to assure ourselves that little has changed, and that we don't even need to make use of radical or different materials, but rather can rebuild our cozy philosophical castle in familiar deontological form, by using the old ruins.

It is not, of course, the case that everyone is optimistic about everything: typically each one thinks that the solutions offered by others will not work. But he or she still offers his or her own solutions, and those *will* do the trick. It seems that on the metaphilosophical level we are all students of that great philosopher and football coach Vince Lombardi: for us, failure is not an option.

The last position we need to consider is hard determinism. Here, surely, pessimism will triumph at last: if the ghost of LFW is long given up, and *any* of the numerous palliatives concocted by scores of capable compatibilists are also scorned, then we can finally confront disappointing reality and, surely, descend into the called-for depression. But *no*! Like Spinoza and B. F. Skinner in the past, our contemporaries Waller and Pereboom (and some new younger philosophers such as Sommers and Werking) are full of optimism and joy at giving up the old order, and at the new dawn awaiting us when, please notice—in terms of the traditional debate—all is lost.

Have you ever heard of a hardier bunch of men and women than us free will philosophers? Pollyanna herself should be sent to us for classes on positive thinking. I am reminded of that cheerful knight in the sketch in Monty Python's *Holy Grail* movie, who has one limb cut off, then another, and so on, but still calls on his enemies to continue fighting, taunting them, while they are carving off more of him with every blow, with cries of "Chicken, eh, chicken!"

Finally, a striking illustration of the nature of the contemporary debate is the book *Four Views on Free Will* that has recently come out (Fischer et al. 2007). The four philosophers are very diverse: Robert Kane is a libertarian, John Martin Fischer and Manuel Vargas are compatibilists of different sorts, and Derk Pereboom is a hard determinist. Yet the book could nevertheless be accurately subtitled "Four Optimists." This, I hasten to add, is not criticism: these are excellent philosophers and good choices for such a book that aims to survey the debate. But that is exactly my point: the book is representative, yet all four are clearly optimists on the free will problem, if each for very different reasons (and each rejecting the optimism of the others).

4   Why the Free Will Problem Is Bad News: A Few Illustrations

It is time for me to get down to some more conventional philosophical work. I will not be able to say much within the present scope, and those of you who are into negativity, pessimism, and depression can pursue them in my book, *Free Will and Illusion* (Smilansky 2000), or in the more recent papers such as "Free Will and Respect for Persons" (Smilansky 2005). I am assuming that we do not have LFW. In that case, I think we should sleep much less well at night.

Injustice

No sustainable systematic way has been found, so far, of constraining criminal behavior except through a system of punishment and incarceration. Even the humane and daringly experimental Dutch, who have been willing to permit doctors to intentionally bump off the ill and the old, and have legalized drug use in coffee shops, have not found a way to avoid punishments and prisons. I suspect that we would prefer serving time in a Dutch prison to the pleasures of doing so in most other countries, but still, serving a twenty-year sentence in any prison is a *terrible* experience. Now, on the assumption that we shall continue to put people in prison, consider what an awful thing this is, and what it means about injustice in life. Again, this does not mean that we should not, by and large, follow compatibilist guidelines: we should establish and maintain what I have called the Community of Responsibility, in which punishment will track responsibility based on intentional action, and the common excuses will prevail. Even in a determinist world, not all thieves are kleptomaniacs, just as we are not all alcoholics, and this matters. Taking these distinctions (however shallow they are) seriously is, as I have argued, a condition for respect for persons and for any civilized form of human interaction. That is why the compatibilist has a case. But even if we grant the compatibilist everything that she wants, people will still spend twenty years in prison, when (as nonbelievers in LFW) we must say that in fact there is no *other* way in which their lives could have unfolded and which was within their control. No way, that is, in which they would not have committed the crimes for which they are being (compatibilistically justly) punished. The criminals have willingly done awful things, but their being such people, who want to do awful things to others (or are at least indifferent about the harm they do when they do what they want to do), was not ultimately up to them. When they are punished they are, in an important sense, victims of the circumstances that have constituted them, making them what they are, with their particular set of motivations and sensibilities. Compatibilism of the sort that follows the responsibility paradigm (which I have called "control compatibilism") is, morally, the "best game in town," but the results it affirms are nevertheless horrible. Their being horrible does not mean that some mistake has been made, and that we can do better, but it is what it is. Similarly for countless other spheres where injustice prevails, even under ideal compatibilist conditions.

The Risks of Change

There seem to be two very different approaches to change. Consider the issue from a hard determinist perspective. Assume that we have lost belief in free will and moral responsibility. According to the moderate approach, this will only help us to get rid of some of the extremes of our common views—help us not to feel excessive guilt, or not to be unduly judgmental— but all that is good will remain. I find this incredible. How will change "know" that it is supposed to limit itself in such ways? Why would having a strong sense of self-worth, based on one's freely chosen achievements, not be at risk as well? Or, similarly, many of the forms of social motivation connected to the idea of praiseworthiness? The second, extreme approach embraces change, but sees the brave new world as welcome. Again, this seems to me to be incredible—why think that we could do just as well if major supporters for our best moral and personal beliefs and practices were being given up?

This is not to say that I myself have any certain way of knowing what will happen with a given scope of change. First, I might have got certain descriptive matters wrong, about what many people believe, and about how they base those beliefs. The work that experimentally minded philosophers have done on the free will problem in recent years should make everyone pause before they pontificate. But for my present point I do not need to have much of a positive view about where we are, let alone where we will end up if we undergo this or that change: all I require is a measure of skepticism about, one, our capacity of controlling any significant changes, and two, the belief that all will turn out wonderfully well. And those two forms of skepticism seem to me to be very compelling.

Or consider the more compatibilistically inclined. Let us take some quick snapshots of some things that seem to matter a great deal. Constraints on how people are dealt with are one example. There is surely a constant temptation to get things done, to use people, to achieve good social results at the expense of individuals, in short, to bypass "respect for persons," particularly if interpreted in an individualistic and liberal manner. History is full of examples. Whether in the form of bigotry that cares nothing for choice and responsibility, or in the form of the dominance of the need to manage things and the call for efficiency, which bypasses them, the temptation is always present. But constraining such natural social and political tendencies is no mean feat. And traditional free will–related beliefs have played a major role here. For example, the idea of the *sanctity of innocence*: the thought that the innocent must not be harmed, whereas those who freely chose to do bad may be harmed, at least if this would produce good results. This, of course, connects directly to a robust sense of desert—which must exist to enable negative sanctions, and which is the ground for positive reactions and rewards. Now, all these very important matters can have some limited, local justification through broadly compatibilist forms of thought. But surely, the libertarian story grounds them in a much *stronger* way. This is related to my previous point, about injustice: if we become aware of how deeply unjust even our best practices (under ideal compatibilist conditions) can be, would this not make us *care* less about those standards and constraints, and opt more for pragmatic compromises and considerations? So how can we rest assured, with P. F. Strawson, that no big changes can occur? Or with more conventional compatibilists, that the significantly watered-down senses of compatibilist possibility, or comparative innocence, or desert, will *suffice*? Or, with those who hope to build on contractualist or utilitarian justifications, that those will carry sufficient weight with people to lift the required load, something that was done for two millennia by distinct belief in libertarian free will and in the crucial importance of respecting it?

Quick Thoughts about Heroism

Think about the firefighters who rushed into the collapsing, burning buildings in 9/11. Envisage a situation in which a few of them who survived, after losing most of their mates, and perhaps being physically harmed themselves, are sitting around and talking about things. Assume that a hard determinist philosopher comes in and tells them that fundamentally they are not better than any common thief or rapist, explaining that ultimately everyone is what he is as an inevitable outcome of forces beyond his control. Do you think that they would welcome this philosopher? Or that, if one or two of them were to listen to him, and begin to understand and internalize what he was saying, that those people would not feel that something very unpleasant and deeply threatening was being said? Then another philosopher, a compatibilist, joins the conversation, and offers his opinion that what matters is only that they did what they wanted, guiding their own actions and being responsive to reasons in the right way. But he too will, reluctantly, admit that there isn't really an actually possible world in which they would not have done exactly what they did do, since they were simply built to choose as they have done. Do you think that the compatibilist would be found to be significantly comforting?

Or think about a case in which there was more time to reflect about the dangers and risks, about the majority of people who decide to do nothing, about one's life and what one will think about oneself—depending on what one does—if one survives. Consider, for example, European non-Jews risking their lives to hide Jews who were personally unknown to them during the Nazi occupation. In Eastern Europe, the price of a Jew was frequently a bottle of vodka—this is what you would get from the Germans if you turned him or her in. So, should a non-Jew risk his own life and that of his family (even if they were innocent: the Nazis were no respecters of innocence), for something whose market price is a bottle of vodka? That is not easy to do. Studies have shown that such exceptional people had a particularly strong sense of their individual autonomy and responsibility. Do we not think that their (at least tacit) beliefs about free will mattered?

We might also think about the murderers, and those who handed human beings over to them in return for the promise of a bottle of vodka, and what taking the free will problem seriously might mean for what we could then say about them (and what this, in turn, would mean for survivors, or the victims). But things are depressing as they are, and let us return to reflection on positive people.

Think about someone on the eve of a mission that he knows is more likely than not to cost him his life: say, being parachuted into al Qaeda territory in Afghanistan, or being sent to infiltrate the Mafia. Do we not think that such a person is affected by what he thinks others will think and feel about his or her actions? That he will be honored by his colleagues, or respected by the public, or even forever hero-worshipped by his young nephew, in a real, robust way? A robust way assumes that it was, in fact, in a strong sense up to him to do this or not, and that hence he is deserving of our appreciation (not only because to do so makes good utilitarian sense), and has through his choice acquired high moral value.

Heroism, if in less dramatic ways, is much more common than we usually think, for many people regularly risk their lives for us, and many people regularly make decisions that go against their self-interest, in order to take care of sick or elderly relatives for many years, for instance. For such people the free will problem (again, assuming we don't have LFW) is bad news. And since we need such people, awareness of this problem may be bad news for us all in a further way. Moreover, the same sort of beliefs and emotions that I have sketched in the context of heroism make up the stuff of our daily tribulations, expectations, and hopes, even if less dramatically.

What Do I Want in Life?

Think about some aspects of what it means to be a person. I have purposefully phrased this in the first person, for I would not want to speak much for others. There is a danger of saying what "we" want, when speaking about one's own idiosyncratic preferences. There is also a danger of caricaturing what is implied by positions one disagrees with: it might come out of some presentation, say, that anyone who is unperturbed by hard determinism thinks that human life is only about gluttony and fornication, and that's certainly not the case. So I'll just talk a little bit about my grandfather and his son, my father, and myself; hopefully some of this will resonate with you as well.

My grandparents on my father's side immigrated to Israel from Russia in 1925 because they were Zionists. This turned out to be a very good idea: my grandfather's elder brother decided to stay on a bit, as in the "New Economic Policy" (instigated by the Communists to forestall economic collapse) things seemed to be getting a bit better. The brother ended up being sent to Siberia during Stalin's reign for most of the rest of his life. My mother's family had lived in the Ukraine for generations, and almost all of her many relatives (who did not immigrate to Israel) were murdered by their neighbors even before the Nazis arrived, neighbors who then took their property. My wife's grandfather was sent by the Germans up the chimney at Auschwitz. It was not a good idea to be Jewish and European just then. So, coming over proved in hindsight to be a smart move, but it was done out of idealism. And this idea, that it was important to do things for idealistic reasons, was emphasized even when the striking thing was how smart the move was pragmatically.

At first my grandfather did quite well, in the book-publishing business, but then—as a result of some deceit by his partners, the story was never fully revealed to me—he and the whole family ended up poor for some years. That was a trauma in my father's life. My grandfather then got back on his feet, and, significantly, in time became a very high public servant in the Ministry of Trade, supervising the allocation of scarce goods in those post–World War II days of severe shortages. Significantly—because this completes the story that began with the poverty he had suffered "because he was too honest"—here he was chosen because of his manifest honesty, and triumphed. Being honest was central to my grandfather, and to my own father's image of his father. I have not had a similar trauma, but my father's honesty also matters to me. With my father there were other scenarios that shaped his life, and his perception of himself. For example, he joined an underground cell of the anti-British resistance when he was thirteen and then, when he was less than twenty years old, organized a group of young men and women (including his sister, and my mother), to help out in a beleaguered kibbutz in the north of the country. As my father used to point out, although there is a prevailing tale of idealization about those times, only four out of his high school class of over sixty joined the underground, and very few went on risky volunteering missions such as he did.

Now, I am not telling these stories in order to familiarize you with the Zionist narrative, but because I expect that on a deeper human level they will be familiar. Your grandparents also immigrated from somewhere, or were cheated, or triumphed although—or because—they were honest, or volunteered, or went to war, or made sacrifices for the sake of their children, or were poor or handicapped, or had to deal with mentally ill or alcoholic relatives, and so on. To confront such situations and to do such things is central in the lives of human beings. But I have no doubt—whatever the experimentalists might tell us—that my grandfather, and my father in his turn, did believe, when reflecting on their actions, that they *had* real choices. So did others, when thinking about them. And the fact that they chose as they did—to leave home for a distant and risky place, to remain honest even if it meant becoming poor, to enlist in an illegal underground organization, or to sacrifice years of hard work for the sake of their children, *while others chose otherwise*, is what gives their story, nay, their lives, in their own eyes, dignity, and integrity. They felt that they can say *"we did the best we could,"* where this is not tautological (as it is under determinism, for, whatever one does, it is the only thing that strictly speaking one could have done). It was not trivial to do one's best, while others did not. Hence they could respect themselves and feel that they are worthy of appreciation. All this is of great importance: to my grandfather and father and, I feel, to the meaning and memory of their lives. If they had been told that all this was not so, they would strongly object, and if they were to begin to see things as determinists want them to (even compatibilists)—they would feel cheated, perhaps even that they were suckers, and in any case deflated and depressed. To use a big word, their sense of meaning in their lives, their sense of achievement of meaning, crucially depends on a free will–related story. Being musical, or tall, or even intelligent, are much less central, and even when they matter, it is in a different way. There are things that it is very useful to have, or even to be, but there are things that one cannot be without and maintain one's self-respect.

So we do not need to think about heroes in order to see why the paradigm of real libertarian choice, as a basis of real responsibility, and real desert, and a real sense of acquiring value, is very significant. I do not want to talk much about myself. But with all of the years I've spent on the free will problem, and although I am convinced that LFW is nonsense, I can still feel the loss, and want to fool myself. Do I want my daughter to feel that *I* had real choices? Would it *matter* to me if she saw my efforts on her behalf as, well, just the way I was built, as ultimately beyond my control? Of course!

5   Conclusion

I have discussed here issues telegraphically, and yet I feel that I have merely touched upon few of the topics that need to be taken up. I took up injustice, and the basis for taking moral constraints seriously, the unpredictability of change, heroes, and finally, expectations we have from ourselves, and our expectations from others to respond in the right way to the way we have chosen to fulfill our own and their expectations. Similar things can be said about moral depth, and about the way accountability can be undermined, about responsibility and betrayal, about what happens to excuses when they become universal, and about many of the other ways in which we acquire a sense of value in life.

There is one further question: what now? My reply is not simple, but if I need to put it in simple terms, then I say "Illusion." The most important fact about the free will issue, and one of the most important facts about human beings, in my view, is that we have at least tacit libertarian beliefs. And the more someone is sensitive and morally sophisticated, the more she will see the need for that, for without it morality, and human life, are very crude indeed. Illusion, and the need for illusion, is the human predicament.

We need to make various distinctions and elaborations here. Partly we need illusion for pragmatic reasons, because of the danger of overreaction, the danger that things that do make sense on the compatibilist level will nevertheless not be taken sufficiently seriously without the invisible support of the tacit assumption of LFW. Partly we need it because in the end the story is so grim that we had better continue to fool ourselves on free will. Of course, there are factors that call us to resist making use of illusion: the value of knowledge, and of honesty, and what all this means for the role of philosophy, and the attractions of the possibility for what I have called UMIs (Unillusioned Moral Individuals). I cannot discuss all this here. But my own views about the various questions that make up the free will problem are not the focus of this essay. My hope is that you will be more inclined to see how large the change that would be implied by awareness of the absence of libertarian free will, and that we have strong reasons to fear that sort of change. Such ideas play hardly any role in the free will debate. This is implausible. As philosophers, I urge you to look the bad news in the face, and explore it and its implications.

Acknowledgments

This essay was presented as a talk at the Ninth Annual Inland Northwest Philosophy Conference. I am grateful for the invitation to the conference, as well as for the acceptance of my essay for this collection. I am also grateful to respondents to my talk, and to Iddo Landau, Michael O'Rourke, and Daniel Statman for comments on drafts of this essay.

Note

1. McKenna and Russell 2008 is a large collection of articles devoted solely to this paper.

References

Fischer, J. M., R. Kane, D. Pereboom, and M. Vargas. 2007. *Four Views on Free Will.* Malden, MA: Blackwell.

McKenna, M., and P. Russell, eds. 2008. *Free Will and Reactive Attitudes: Perspectives on P. F. Strawson's "Freedom and Resentment."* Aldershot: Ashgate.

Sidgwick, H. 1963. *The Methods of Ethics*, 7th ed. London: Macmillan.

Smilansky, S. 2000. *Free Will and Illusion.* Oxford: Oxford University Press.

Smilansky, S. 2005. Free Will and Respect for Persons. *Midwest Studies in Philosophy* 29:248–261.

Strawson, P. F. 2003. Freedom and Resentment. In *Free Will*, ed. G. Watson. Oxford: Oxford University Press.

11 Responsibility and Practical Reason

George Sher

In the *Nicomachean Ethics*, Aristotle observed that agents are responsible only for what they do voluntarily—that "[a]cts that are voluntary receive praise and blame, whereas those that are involuntary receive pardon and sometimes pity too" (Aristotle 1955, 111). Aristotle also observed that "[a] ctions are regarded as involuntary when they are performed under compulsion or through ignorance" (ibid.). Following Aristotle, most subsequent philosophers have agreed that responsibility has two distinct necessary conditions, one pertaining to the will, the other to knowledge.[1]

Although these conditions seem equally important, they have not received equal amounts of attention. Because philosophers are preoccupied by determinism, and because determinism threatens freedom more directly than it threatens knowledge, most of what philosophers have said about responsibility has focused on its freedom-related condition. In recent years, they have lavished attention on the question of whether responsibility requires a form of freedom that involves genuine alternative possibilities, and if not what else might distinguish free from unfree acts. By contrast, philosophers have had far less to say about what responsibility requires in the way of knowledge. As a result, a certain familiar way of understanding the knowledge requirement has not received the scrutiny it deserves. My aims in this essay are, first, to make this understanding explicit, and, second, to raise some doubts about whether it can be defended.

According to the interpretation of the knowledge requirement that I have in mind, an agent's responsibility extends only as far as his awareness of what he is doing. He is responsible only for those acts he consciously chooses to perform, only for those omissions he consciously chooses to allow, and only for those outcomes he consciously chooses to bring about. Because each act has many different properties—here I presuppose a coarse-grained approach to act-individuation[2]—there is an obvious question about which aspects of a given act, omission, or outcome an agent must be aware of in order to be responsible for it. However, to this obvious question, there is an equally obvious answer: namely, what the agent is responsible for is not his act or omission *simpliciter*, but only those aspects of it and its outcomes of which he *is* aware. Because the aspects of a person's acts, omissions, and outcomes that raise questions about his responsibility are precisely those that are morally or prudentially significant, this answer implies that it rarely matters whether an agent is aware that his act involves the contraction of certain muscles or will disturb a fly, but that it often does matter whether he is aware that that act is a lie, that it will hurt someone's feelings, or that it will endanger his own career prospects. The answer also implies that it often matters whether the agent is aware of the range of alternative actions he might perform, of the different outcomes that each action might have, and of the rough likelihoods that the different possible outcomes will eventuate.

Given the many limitations on what we can know, it is impossible for any agent to be aware of every morally and prudentially relevant fact about every act that he might perform. Thus, if being fully responsible requires being aware of all such facts, then no agent is ever fully responsible for what he does. Still, because agents vary widely in the sorts of things of which they are aware, there remains ample room for the view that how much responsibility any given agent has for what he has done is a direct function of the range of relevant facts of which he was aware. This is the view that I want to discuss.

If we accept this view, then we will regard the possibility that an agent might choose among a set of options all of whose morally and prudentially relevant features are fully apparent to him as a kind of limiting case. If, unrealistically, an agent were to make a free choice under these conditions, then the clarity of his vision would guarantee that he was fully responsible both for his act itself and for any good or bad consequences that might flow from it. By contrast, in the more realistic case in which the searchlight of an agent's consciousness does not reach as far as some possible outcome of some available act, the fact that the agent cannot consciously choose either to produce or not to produce that outcome will imply that he cannot be responsible for doing either. Analogously, if the beam of the searchlight is too narrow to illuminate the possibility of performing a certain act, then the fact that the agent cannot consciously choose either to perform or to refrain from performing that act will imply that he cannot be responsible for doing either. Analogously again, if the searchlight's beam is too dim to illuminate some feature that a given act would have, then the fact that the agent cannot consciously choose either to perform or to refrain from performing an act with that feature will similarly excuse him from the responsibility for doing either.

Because this view is organized around the metaphor of consciousness as a kind of searchlight, I will from now on refer to it as *the searchlight view*. In adopting this locution, I do not mean to imply that the searchlight view restricts an agent's responsibility to those features of his acts of which he is actively thinking when he performs them. Just as we do not focus our attention on everything that a searchlight illuminates, so too do we not focus it on everything of which we are aware. A driver who is concentrating on not missing his exit may at the same time be aware that a car is approaching on his left, that he is hovering just over the speed limit, that his passenger is telling an anecdote, and of much else. This distinction between active focus and mere awareness is important because the situations in which we make our decisions are generally too complex to enable us to focus simultaneously on each of their morally relevant features. Thus, in its most plausible form, the searchlight view says not that we are responsible only for those features of our acts to which we are actively paying attention, but rather that we are responsible only for those features of which we are at least passively aware.

Even with this refinement, my description of the searchlight view is incomplete in various respects. To give just one example, the description does not distinguish between a version of the searchlight view that requires only that an agent be aware of whichever features of his choice situation *are in fact* morally and prudentially relevant and a version that also requires that the agent be aware *that* those features are relevant. This distinction is important because the alternative we select will determine exactly how much an agent must be aware of before the searchlight view will count him as responsible for a particular act, omission, or outcome. However, because such refinements will tell us only which version of the searchlight view is most plausible, the need to provide them seems less pressing than the need to ascertain whether that view is defensible in principle. If it is, we can always fill in the details later.

1

Is the searchlight view defensible? This is not an easy question to answer; for although that view is implicit in much that philosophers say, it has received strikingly little direct attention. Thus, to evaluate the case for accepting it, I will have to engage in some imaginative reconstruction.

Let us begin by asking why anyone should find the view attractive. It owes its appeal, I think, to the fact that the limits of what it takes each agent to be responsible for are a precise match with what each of us sees as the limits of his own choice situation when he confronts the world *as* an agent. When we engage with the world in this way—when we ask ourselves what we should do, weigh the reasons for and against the acts we see as available, make our decisions on the basis of our assessment of these reasons, and so on—the process as we encounter it is at every stage fully conscious. We can only deliberate about the possibilities as we see them, can only weigh the significance of the facts as we know them, and can only base our decisions on our reasons as we understand them. Because deliberation is conscious through and through, anyone who engages in it—that is, each of us, all the time—must encounter himself simply as a (volitionally effective) center of consciousness. Even if we are aware that we hold many beliefs of which we are not aware, we must view those beliefs as inaccessible to us and hence as irrelevant to the question we are trying to answer.

Taken by itself, this is not an argument for the searchlight view. It is one thing to invoke the deliberative perspective to account for the searchlight view's attractiveness and quite another to invoke the deliberative perspective to *justify* the searchlight view. Still, if the searchlight view can in fact be justified, it will be surprising if its rationale does not bear some close relation to the main source of its appeal. Thus, in what follows, I will adopt as my working hypothesis the assumption that the best defense of the searchlight view is likely to involve some premise that makes essential mention of the deliberative perspective.

What form, exactly, might such a defense take? I can envision two main possibilities, only one of which can be discussed here. For completeness, I will briefly summarize both arguments before I proceed to my main discussion.

The first argument—the one I will not discuss—takes as its point of departure the widely held principle that it is unfair to hold someone responsible for what he cannot (and could not in the past) control. Although this principle is uncontroversial when it is expressed abstractly, it becomes controversial as soon as we specify any particular interpretation of control. Thus, before the principle can be brought to bear in favor of the searchlight view, it must be backed by a demonstration that the relevant form of control is one that involves conscious awareness. The obvious way to defend this interpretation is to argue that if an agent is unaware that a given act would have a certain feature, then it is unfair to demand that he consider that feature when he deliberates about what he should do. Because requiring the agent even to consider the relevant feature does not seem fair, it seems a fortiori to be unfair to hold him responsible if he goes on to perform an act that has that feature. This, therefore, is one way in which a premise about the deliberative perspective may be part of a defense of the searchlight view. Having criticized this argument in another place (Sher 2005), I will not discuss it further here.

By contrast, the second way of invoking the deliberative perspective to support the searchlight view—the one that I *will* discuss—takes as its point of departure the claim that responsibility itself is a practical rather than a theoretical concept. Following a line of thought inspired by Kant, at least two contemporary philosophers have advanced well-known arguments to the effect that the concept of responsibility has its origins, or is somehow implicit, in the very stance that we occupy when we try to decide what we should do. If anything like this is true, then the conditions for the concept's application may reflect its practical origins. Thus, although neither philosopher has endorsed the searchlight view, it is natural to wonder whether their view that responsibility is a practical concept can provide a bridge from the premise that deliberation takes place at the conscious level to the conclusion that agents are only responsible for those features of their acts of which they were consciously aware.

2

The claim that responsibility is a concept of practical rather than theoretical reason has been advanced by both Christine Korsgaard and Hilary Bok. In her influential essay "Creating the Kingdom of Ends," Korsgaard has written that

[o]n Kant's view, we first encounter the idea of freedom when we are deciding what to do. We encounter it in the necessity of acting under the idea of freedom, and in the commands of the moral law. At the moment of decision, you must regard yourself as the author of your action, and so you inevitably hold yourself responsible for what you do. (Korsgaard 1996, 206)

And, along similar lines, Bok writes that

I have argued that when we engage in practical reasoning we must regard ourselves not as caused to choose by antecedent events but as determining our conduct for ourselves. . . . And I have argued that this gives us reason to regard ourselves as responsible for our conduct in a sense that transcends causal responsibility. (Bok 1998, 162)

Although the details of their accounts differ, Korsgaard and Bok both deny that the point of regarding someone as responsible is either to describe him or to explain what he has done. In Korsgaard's words, we should not "think that it is a fact about a person that she is responsible for a particular action" (Korsgaard 1996, 197).[3] Instead, both philosophers construe our attributions of responsibility as ineliminable components of our attempts to decide what we have reason to do.

This way of thinking about responsibility offers some definite advantages. For one thing, by taking the concept to originate in the requirements of practical reason, we would locate it squarely within the larger family of moral concepts (right, wrong, ought, etc.), each other member of which is also action-guiding. Conversely, by denying that responsibility is a property that an agent can either have or lack, we would open up the possibility of circumventing the seemingly endless dispute about whether the conditions for having the relevant property include not having been caused to act. However, for present purposes, the crucial fact about the practical approach is neither that it promises to simplify moral theory nor that it offers a fresh perspective on the free will problem, but rather that introducing it puts us in a position to formulate a simple argument for the searchlight view—one that I suspect has exerted a good deal of covert influence. Here, in brief, is how that argument runs.

When we deliberate, we are attempting to decide not what is true, but rather what we should do. Because what we should do depends on the strength of the reasons for and against various possible acts, we cannot deliberate without asking ourselves whether, and if so how strongly, the different features of the acts that are available to us tell for or against their performance. However, in order to ask ourselves this question about any feature of any act, we must be thinking both about the act itself and about the feature of it that is in question. We can only think about the act if we are aware that it is among our options, and we can only think about the feature if we are aware that the act would have it. Thus, from the claim that "our reasons for using [the concept of responsibility] are derived from its role in our deliberation" (Bok 1998, 146), it may indeed seem to follow that we can be responsible only for those features of our acts of which we are antecedently aware.

In calling attention to this argument for the searchlight view, I do not mean to suggest that it is one that either Korsgaard or Bok has actually advanced. As we will see, there are indications that Korsgaard would not accept the searchlight view, while Bok's views on the matter are simply unclear. Still, if we identify our ordinary concept of responsibility with the one that we apply when we deliberate—an identification that Korsgaard and Bok both seem to endorse—then we will be hard pressed to resist the argument's force. Thus, to assess the argument's strength, we will have to look more carefully at that identification.

Despite its initial appeal, I think the claim that our ordinary concept of responsibility is practical is deeply problematic. Put most simply, the central problem is that whereas it is logically impossible to deliberate about anything except one's own future actions, our ordinary concept of responsibility is neither oriented to the future nor restricted to the first person. That our ordinary concept of responsibility is not oriented to the future is evident from the fact that the reactions that presuppose that agents are responsible—most saliently, praise, blame, punishment, and reward—are thought to be appropriate only when the acts that occasion them are already completed and thus in the past. That our ordinary concept of responsibility is not restricted to the first person is evident from the fact that the reactions that presuppose its applicability are usually not reflexive—that our praise, blame, and the rest are most often directed not at ourselves but at other people. Because our ordinary concept of responsibility appears so different from the one that is implicit in our deliberations, the claim that these concepts are the same is implausible on its face.

This, of course, is hardly the end of the story. Although Korsgaard is happy enough to downplay the connections between responsibility and praise and blame—"[t]here is," she writes, "something obviously unattractive about taking the assessment of others as the starting point in moral philosophy" (Korsgaard 1996, 189)—both she and Bok are well aware that those connections exist and therefore must somehow be accounted for. Moreover, each in her own way attempts to do just that. Thus, before we can assess the prospects for grounding the searchlight view in the claim that responsibility is a practical concept, we will have to examine the ways in which Korsgaard and Bok have tried to show that a practical concept of responsibility can apply not only to our own future acts, but also to (a) acts that we have already performed and (b) the acts of others.

3

If practical reason is exclusively future oriented, then how can the concept of responsibility to which it gives rise apply to past as well as future acts? Although Korsgaard and Bok agree that the concept of responsibility is practical, they appeal to very different features of practical reason to show that the concept's sphere of application encompasses past acts. Here, in brief, is what each has said.

Where Korsgaard is concerned, the crucial feature of practical reason is its mutual or reciprocal quality, and the reason this feature is crucial is that genuine mutuality can obtain only among temporally enduring agents. That this is Korsgaard's position is suggested by the combination of her well-known insistence that "the only reasons that are possible are the reasons we can share" (Korsgaard 1996, 301) and her contention that "you cannot enter into *any* reciprocal relations . . . if you do not take responsibility for your own actions at other times, since relationships after all are enduring things" (ibid., 207; emphasis in the original). It is suggested, more concretely, by her illustrative treatment of Parfit's Russian nobleman example. In that example, a young socialist who intends to distribute his inheritance to the poor when he receives it, but who fears that he may become conservative and change his mind before then, attempts to preempt the change by asking his wife to hold him to his current promise to redistribute. By thus dissociating himself from the decisions of his future self, Korsgaard argues, the young nobleman is both disavowing his own future agency and, in so doing, depriving his wife of the sort of temporally extended partner that genuine collaborative decision making requires. As Korsgaard herself puts it,

[t]he young nobleman's attitude toward his own future attitudes is essentially a *predictive* and theoretical one, and, because it is so, he abdicates the kind of responsibility that is necessary for reciprocity: the kind of responsibility that enables people to act in concert. (Ibid., 207; emphasis in the original)

Although the example as cited concerns only the nobleman's refusal to take responsibility for his own *future* actions, Korsgaard presumably views her argument as bidirectional. She would presumably maintain that in order to be the sorts of agents with whom others can act in concert, we must be willing to take responsibility for what we have done no less than for what we expect to do.

Korsgaard's argument that our practical concept of responsibility applies to what we have already done is part of her larger interpersonal theory of practical reason. By contrast, Bok's argument for the same thesis is much more narrowly focused. In her view, the practical considerations that compel us to view ourselves as responsible for what we have done pertain not to our ability to deliberate in concert with others but only to the adequacy of our own future decisions.

According to Bok, the way our past acts bear on our future decisions is by disclosing enduring features of our characters that are likely to *influence* those decisions. For example, if I have acted cruelly or dishonestly in the past, then the cruel or dishonest streak that I then manifested may well lead me to act cruelly or dishonestly again in the future. Thus, if I accept a set of practical principles that forbid cruelty and dishonesty, then the reasons these principles give me not to act in these ways are also reasons to change these aspects of my character. Moreover, since I cannot know whether I have reason to alter my character without knowing whether my past acts *have* violated my practical principles, the same principles also give me reason to reflect on my past acts and omissions (including those that caused or allowed my character to develop as it did) with an eye to discovering what I should have done differently. Thus, insofar as we occupy the practical stance, Bok concludes that each of us has "reason to define and to use a conception of responsibility according to which we are responsible for those actions that reveal the quality of our character and our will" (Bok 1998, 139).

Given the complexity of these arguments, we obviously cannot evaluate either philosopher's position without addressing various further questions. To assess Korsgaard's account, we would have to ask how practical reason can be essentially interpersonal if its core question—what should I do?—is one that each individual must answer for himself. We would also have to ask exactly how Korsgaard's remarks about the Russian nobleman can be applied to his past as opposed to his future choices. To assess Bok's account, we would have to ask, among other things, whether our attempts to identify and alter the character flaws that our past acts manifested are either backward-looking enough or focused enough on the acts themselves to qualify as taking responsibility for those acts. Although I have addressed some of these issues elsewhere,[4] any full treatment would obviously take us too far afield.

But, fortunately, no such treatment is needed here. Put most simply, the reason we can afford to sidestep a closer examination of Korsgaard's and Bok's accounts is that even if both philosophers have succeeded in showing that a practical concept of responsibility must apply to past as well as future acts,[5] the premises on which they base this conclusion are not ones that can be pressed into service to support an omnitemporal version of the searchlight view. We were able to derive a forward-looking version of the searchlight view from the premise that we must regard ourselves as responsible when we deliberate because we can only deliberate about those features of the available acts of which we are currently aware. However, when we think of those same acts afterward, we often recognize facts about them of which we were *not* antecedently aware. Moreover, when Korsgaard and Bok argue that practical reason also compels us to take responsibility for our actions after we perform them, the aspects of practical reason to which they appeal provide no reason to disregard these newly appreciated facts. If the reason we must take responsibility for what we have done is either to sustain relations of mutuality with our interlocutors or to avoid future betrayals of our own principles, then the limits of what we must take responsibility for appear to be set not by what we realized when we acted but rather by what we realize now. Thus, even if Korsgaard and Bok are correct in maintaining that we must regard ourselves as responsible in retrospect as well as in prospect, their arguments do not appear to show that the features of our actions for which we must take retrospective responsibility are restricted to those of which we were prospectively aware.

To bring this point into sharper focus, let me briefly elaborate it as it applies to each philosopher's reasoning. Where Korsgaard is concerned, the argument was that practical reason requires a form of mutuality that can exist only among temporally extended agents, and that therefore compels us to take responsibility for our past as well as our future acts. At least offhand, there is nothing in this mutuality requirement that restricts the features of our past acts for which we must take responsibility to features of which we were antecedently aware. Indeed, if anything, the prospects for mutuality are actually enhanced when we take responsibility for a more extensive range of features of our past acts. Suppose, for example, that when the Russian nobleman was young, he was so obsessed with social justice that he was blind to the need to hold onto some of his money to provide for his children. If this is how things were, then the nobleman and his wife will obviously be in a better position to weigh the relevant considerations together if he subsequently recognizes and takes responsibility for his earlier omissions. Thus, if taking responsibility for what one has done is a prerequisite for codeliberation, then the features of one's past acts for which one must take responsibility cannot be restricted to those of which one was antecedently aware.

An analogous point can be made about Bok's argument. Even if we accept her claim that anyone who accepts a set of practical principles must scrutinize his previous actions for evidence of character defects that might prevent him from acting on those principles in the future, there is nothing in this requirement that restricts anyone's investigation to those features of his past acts of which he was antecedently aware. Indeed, if anything, our ability to minimize future violations of our principles seems again to be enhanced by our willingness to own up to the bad features of our acts of which we were previously *un*aware. Thus, to stick with our amended nobleman example, if in his youth the Russian nobleman was insufficiently attentive to the needs of his children, then the obvious first step toward improving both his character and his conduct is precisely to take responsibility for the failures to consider his children's needs that he did not previously recognize as wrong. Thus, if taking responsibility for what one has done is called for as a way of minimizing future violations of one's principles, then the features of one's past acts for which one must take responsibility are again not restricted to those of which one was antecedently aware.

4

So far, we have seen that there are more and less expansive versions of the claim that practical reason gives rise to a concept of responsibility. In its least expansive version, which derives the concept exclusively from the demands of the deliberative perspective, the claim does seem to imply that we are responsible only for those features of our acts of which we are antecedently aware, but it does so at the cost of restricting our responsibility to acts that we have not yet performed. By contrast, in its more expansive versions, each of which relies on some richer notion of practical reason, the claim does *not* restrict our responsibility to acts that we have not yet performed, but it also does not preserve the implication that we are responsible only for those features of our acts of which we are antecedently aware. Because we have found no version of the practical approach that yields a concept of responsibility that is both backward- as well as forward-looking and restricted to the features of our acts of which we are antecedently aware, we have also found no version that supports the claim that our ordinary concept of responsibility (which undeniably *is* backward- as well as forward-looking) presupposes searchlight control.

Even by itself, this objection seems strong enough to discredit the inference from the premise that our ordinary concept of responsibility is practical to the conclusion that that concept presupposes the searchlight view. However, that inference becomes still more problematic when we shift our focus from the claim that practical reason yields a concept of responsibility that applies to our own past acts to the claim that practical reason yields a concept of responsibility that applies to the acts of others. Because the exact nature of the problem will vary with the reasons for thinking that a practical concept of responsibility must apply to the acts of others, and because Korsgaard and Bok defend this claim in very different ways, I will again discuss their arguments separately.

In Korsgaard's view, the way in which practical reason compels us to view others as responsible for their acts is by compelling us to enter into relations of reciprocity with them. Reciprocity, which Korsgaard takes to lie at the heart of both moral and personal relationships, requires both that we view other people's ends as reasons because they seek them and that we expect those others to view our own ends as reasons because *we* seek them. These requirements give us reason to regard other people as just as capable of weighing reasons, and hence as just as responsible for any ensuing decisions, as we ourselves are:

The relations of reciprocity . . . call for mutual responsibility for two important reasons. In order to make the ends and reasons of another your own, you must regard her as a source of value, someone whose choices confer worth upon their objects, and who has a right to decide on her own actions. In order to entrust your own ends and reasons to another's care, you must suppose that she regards you that way, and is prepared to act accordingly. . . . Reciprocity is the sharing of reasons, and you will enter into it only with someone you expect to deal with reasons in a rational way. In this sense, reciprocity requires that you hold the other responsible. (Korsgaard 1996, 196)

Because practical reason requires a form of reciprocity that can exist only among beings each of whom views himself as only one rational agent among others, any practical concept of responsibility will have to be intersubjective as well as transtemporal.

Like Korsgaard's argument that the practical concept of responsibility must apply to past as well as future acts, her argument that it must apply to others as well as ourselves gives rise to many further questions. They are, indeed, many of the same questions. However, also as with Korsgaard's previous argument, we need not answer these questions to see that the current argument for extending the practical concept of responsibility to others does not preserve the implication that those others are responsible only for those features of their acts for which they were antecedently aware.

Put most simply, the reason the current argument does not preserve this implication is that it treats responsibility only as a general capacity. What it says is only that in order to enter into relations of reciprocity with others, we must regard them as responsible in the sense of having the capacity to deliberate about what they have reason to do, and of having the further capacity to take our own deliberative capacity into account when they do so. Because regarding someone as responsible in this sense has no implications at all about what we must regard him as responsible *for*, this argument goes no distance toward showing that we must view others as responsible only for those features of their acts of which they are antecedently aware. It is, of course, true that other people cannot regard *themselves* as responsible for any features of any available acts of which *they* are unaware; but the crucial question is precisely whether we have reason to import this limitation on the others' awareness, which is internal to *their* (part of our shared) deliberative perspective, into our own quite different point of view. Because Korsgaard's reciprocity argument gives us no such reason, it appears to be fully consistent with the view that agents can be held responsible even for those features of their acts of which they are not antecedently aware.

Indeed, there are indications that Korsgaard herself would accept this view. For one thing, she clearly thinks we have considerable discretion about when we do and do not hold others responsible. She writes, for example, that "while of course facts about the agent and about her condition at the time of the action *guide* your decision about whether to hold her responsible, they do not fully *determine* it" (ibid., 198). Although she mainly emphasizes the contexts in which charity or kindness decrees that we not hold others responsible even though we might, her view also leaves us a good deal of leeway in the other direction. In addition, she explicitly acknowledges that

we may well blame people for involuntary attitudes or expressions, because we blame people for lack of control itself. If you cannot repress a victorious grin on learning that your rival has met with a gruesome accident, you ought to be blamed, precisely on that account. (Ibid., 198–199)

Given her evident willingness to hold agents responsible for reactions that are not voluntary, it is hard to see on what basis Korsgaard could rule out holding them responsible for features of their acts over which they lack searchlight control.

Unlike Korsgaard, who bases her extension of the practical concept of responsibility to others on her views about the intersubjectivity of practical reasons, Bok bases her version of the extension on the simpler premise that we have good reason to regard others, in the relevant ways, as just like us. Bok argues, in particular, that each of us has good reason to regard others as "persons who are capable of governing their lives through practical reasoning" and that "[w]hen we regard others as persons, we must both extend to them a view we would otherwise take of ourselves and allow ourselves to enter into their view of themselves" (Bok 1998, 188). From these premises, together with her previous conclusion that practical reason compels us to view ourselves as responsible (and the further premise that each other person's practical reason can be seen to impose the same demands on him), Bok concludes that we are indeed compelled to extend our practical concept of responsibility to others as well as ourselves.

We have already seen that Bok's (and Korsgaard's) reasons for extending the practical concept of responsibility from our own future acts to our own past acts do not preserve the implication that we are responsible only for the features of those acts of which we were antecedently aware. Thus, even if Bok's current argument succeeds in showing that we must view other people as responsible for their own past acts in exactly the same sense in which we are responsible for ours, it will not support the conclusion that we must view those others as responsible only for those features of their own past acts of which they were antecedently aware. However, we have also seen that it does seem plausible to say that we can only view ourselves as responsible for those features of our own *future* acts of which we are now aware. Thus, the question that remains is whether Bok's current argument can at least support the conclusion that we are similarly restricted to viewing others as responsible only for those features of *their* future acts of which they are now aware.

When we deliberate, the reason we cannot view ourselves as responsible for any features of our own potential acts of which we are unaware is, trivially, that we are not aware of those features. Thus, to mount a parallel argument that we also cannot view others as responsible for any features of their potential acts of which *they* are unaware, we would have to show that this restriction, too, follows trivially from someone's lack of awareness of those features. But from whose lack of awareness could the restriction follow trivially? It clearly cannot be a trivial consequence of *the others'* lack of awareness that the acts available to them would have the relevant features, since the only thing that follows trivially from this is a restriction on what the others can regard *themselves* as responsible for. It also cannot be a trivial consequence of *our own* lack of awareness that the acts available to the others would have the relevant features, since we, unlike them, may indeed be aware of this. Of course, we would not be aware of it if "allow[ing] ourselves to enter into [the others'] view of themselves" involved rendering ourselves unaware of everything of which they are not also aware. However, although it is indeed possible for us to *discount* some of the things of which we but not the others are aware, the actual excision of these items from our consciousness is clearly impossible. Because this is so, and because nothing less than their actual excision can support the proposed extension of our earlier argument, we may safely dismiss the suggestion that the same reasoning that previously established that we cannot view ourselves as responsible for those features of our own potential acts of which we are unaware will now support a similar restriction on our attributions of responsibility to others.

5

In this essay I have tried to raise some doubts about the searchlight view by arguing against one apparently promising attempt to ground that view in the demands of the deliberative perspective. Given the failure of this attempt, it is natural to wonder, first, whether any other defense of the searchlight view might do better, and, second, whether any other interpretation of the epistemic requirement for responsibility is any more defensible. My own answers to these questions are, respectively, "no" and "yes." However, my reasons for giving these answers are part of a much longer story whose telling must await another occasion.[6]

Notes

1. Thus, for example, in the introduction to their influential anthology on the topic, John Martin Fischer and Mark Ravizza have written that

[t]he first condition, which may be termed a "cognitive condition," corresponds to the excuse of ignorance. It captures the intuition that an agent is responsible only if she both knows (or can reasonably be expected to know) the particular facts surrounding her action, and also acts with the proper sorts of beliefs and intentions. The second condition, which may be termed a "freedom-relative condition," corresponds to the excuse of force. It captures the sense that an agent is responsible only if his action is unforced, that is, only if he acts freely. (Fischer and Ravizza 1993, 8)

2. This approach is taken by Anscombe (1958) and by Davidson (1963, 1967). For an influential version of the contrasting fine-grained approach, see Goldman 1970.

3. Compare Bok: "I do not see the distinction between the theoretical and practical points of view as a distinction between two standpoints that allow us to describe the world in different idioms" (Bok 1998, 59).

4. For an extended discussion of the relation between a bad act and the character of the person who performs it, see chapters 2 and 3 of Sher 2006.

5. They can both succeed in showing this because their arguments are different but not incompatible.

6. Since this essay was written, that longer story has in fact been told. See Sher 2009.

References

Anscombe, G. E. M. 1958. *Intention*. Ithaca, NY: Cornell University Press.

Aristotle. 1955. *The Ethics of Aristotle: The Nicomachean Ethics*. Trans. J. A. K. Thomson. Harmondsworth: Penguin.

Bok, H. 1998. *Freedom and Responsibility*. Princeton: Princeton University Press.

Davidson, D. 1963. Actions, Reasons, and Causes. *Journal of Philosophy* 60: 685–700.

Davidson, D. 1967. The Logical Form of Action Sentences. In *The Logic of Decision and Action*, ed. N. Rescher. Pittsburgh: University of Pittsburgh Press.

Fischer, J. M., and M. Ravizza, eds. 1993. *Perspectives on Moral Responsibility*. Ithaca, NY: Cornell University Press.

Goldman, A. 1970. *A Theory of Human Action*. Englewood Cliffs, NJ: Prentice-Hall.

Korsgaard, C. 1996. *Creating the Kingdom of Ends*. Cambridge: Cambridge University Press.

Sher, G. 2005. Kantian Fairness. *Philosophical Issues* 15:179–192.

Sher, G. 2006. *In Praise of Blame*. New York: Oxford University Press.

Sher, G. 2009. *Who Knew? Responsibility without Awareness*. New York: Oxford University Press.

12 The Metaphysics of Collective Agency

Todd Jones

1 Introduction

In both scholarly and everyday discussions of responsibility, the ways in which *collectives* like corporations or governments have responsibilities remains a contentious issue (see Kutz 2000; French 1995; May and Hoffman 1991). In such discussions, one comparatively neglected area of focus is the precise metaphysical underpinnings of collective agenthood. We continually speak about collections of people believing, desiring, or being responsible for something (e.g., "Exxon fears that Venezuela is trying make other Latin countries rethink capitalism"). But we seldom think much about exactly how it is possible for a collection of people to do anything like "believe" or "want" in the way that an individual can. It's possible, of course, that when we speak this way we are only using rough metaphors. It's also possible that there are instrumental reasons for talking about corporate actions or responsibilities without really thinking that groups are intentional *agents* in the way that individual human beings are. Presumably, however, there are stronger reasons for using the vocabulary of individual agency for talking about the beliefs, desires, and responsibilities of collections, if collections can literally have things like intentional states. In this essay, I discuss how collective agency might be possible in a literal, nonmetaphorical way. To be a moral agent, something must first be a type of intentional agent. If I can show how groups can be intentional agents, we will be well along the way to better understanding whether and how they can be moral agents with certain responsibilities.

2 Choosing a Theory of Intentionality

In order to examine whether a group can have beliefs and desires and the like, we need to start off with some account of what it is to have beliefs and desires. This is problematic, since the relevant literature contains a large number of different accounts of what it is to have a belief. (See Haugeland 1990 and Lyons 1995 for good surveys.) If anyone successfully shows that by this or that account of belief, groups can have them (or can't have them), he or she will invariably face opposition from proponents of other accounts of intentionality. These critics will say that groups only counted or failed to count as having beliefs because the criteria used to decide were too loose or too stringent. (Claims about animal belief face the same problem.) At that point the defender of claims about group belief could do two things. She could try to persuade people that her own favored theory of intentionality is, indeed, the correct one, with the rival theories being too loose or too stringent. Alternatively, she could *stipulate* that she will be using a certain notion of belief. She could then show that groups could (or couldn't) have beliefs in *that* sense of the term. Proponents of each rival theory could then acknowledge that groups had (or failed to have) beliefs in that sense, and then say what additional (or fewer) criteria groups would have to have to qualify as having beliefs on *their* accounts.

In this essay, space dictates I follow the latter course. I will proceed, then, by outlining one theory of intentionality, and then examining whether groups could qualify as having intentional states on that view. Even though I will be stipulating, I will have to describe the view at some length, since the question of whether groups have beliefs will be largely decided on the basis of what a theory of intentionality says intentional states are. I hope that others will find the view of intentionality I describe to be a plausible one.

Note that in what follows, I am less interested in the question of whether groups specifically have "belief" states than in whether they have intentional states of any sort. It might turn out that "belief" is a complex hybrid intentional state, perhaps even conceptually linked with the human mind (see Stich 1983). Below, then, I'll more often focus on whether groups can have the more broad "representation" and "goal" states than the more narrow "belief" and "desire" states. Looking at whether more fine-grained distinctions can be made concerning, say, whether a particular "goal" state counts as a "desire" state is a project I'll leave to others.

3   An Account of Intentionality

3.1   Goals

What does it mean for a creature to have intentionality? Let's begin with the bare bones of our commonsense "folk" theory of the subject. Jonathan

Bennett describes the core idea of our common sense view this way: an intentional system is one which *"does* what it *thinks* will bring about what it *wants"* (Bennett 1990, 176). What does this mean? How does any system do this? Let's take these terms one at a time. I find it most useful to begin understanding what intentionality is by getting clear about what it is for a creature to want something, or to have a goal.

The intuitively central characteristic of a system said to have a goal is that the system is one with a robust disposition to produce a similar range of end states ("a goal") in a variety of environments. (Having a robust disposition, of course, need not mean the system always produces the goal. It is only necessary that it typically makes the movements that *would* produce that end state if conditions were (a) the way they usually are, or (b) the way they were in the system's [or system's ancestors'] past.) However else one would describe a person who picks up a variety of litter from an area and puts it in a trash can, we say that that person has the goal of putting litter in the trash can. A frog that flicks its tongue and moves various small dark objects to its stomach is said to have the goal of eating them (or to "want" to eat them, or to be "trying" to eat them). The early MIT robot that roamed the rooms and halls, scanning them for electric sockets and plugging itself in, is often described as having the goal of charging its batteries.

A second central feature of all systems said to have goals is that such systems tend to employ a number of different mechanisms in producing the end state. If we didn't require this additional feature, we would say that raindrops had the goal of reaching the ground or that salt wanted to dissolve in water. The term "goal" seems to be prototypically used to describe systems that use a number of *different* tricks to get to similar end states. We would be hesitant to say that a mouse trap that guillotined rats (and everything else) that poked their heads in had a mouse-killing goal. John Haugeland (1990) points out, however, that we'd feel little hesitation in using goal language to describe a "supertrap" that used numerous different mechanisms for killing mice in different circumstances. If a battery-charging robot that did not locate an outlet began moving furniture and scanning behind it, or finally drilling holes and tapping electric lines, we'd be even more inclined to talk about its behavior in teleological terms. In general, the more ways a system has of producing a certain end state from a variety of initial states, the more comfortable we are of speaking of the system's "goals" and "wants" (see Bennett 1990 for a similar account of goals).

How do such systems, readily describable in teleological terms but difficult to describe in mechanical terms, come to develop in nature? The basic story of how nature builds these sorts of entities is the familiar one from evolutionary biology: during the course of its history, some entity or entity cluster randomly undergoes a change that makes it behave in a manner that helps prevent it from being destroyed—or helps it recreate a replica of itself. The persistence of the entity or its replicas helps ensure that the source of the helpful behavioral disposition also survives. Eventually, the entities that exist at a given time are the ones that are there because they have come to acquire a number of such mechanisms, which help them in various ways. If the number of mechanisms is large enough, and if they are different enough in different circumstances, we begin to speak of an "organism" with a "goal" of survival.

The set of mechanisms that help an organism survive are likely to be ones that enable it to engage in, as the old joke goes, the four F activities: feeding, fleeing, fighting, and reproducing. Each of these activities achieves certain end states via mechanisms that lead to some or other *portion* of that end state, or via mechanisms that create an *intermediate-*state launching pad for reaching that end state. Each portion or intermediate stage is subjected to the same evolutionary pressures as the organism itself. Over time, through "trial and error," the organism can come to be structured such that the attainment of these portions or intermediate stages can themselves come about via a number of different mechanisms. When this happens we begin speaking of each of these "subsystem" mechanism sets as having its own goals, or alternatively, about the organism having a "subgoal." An organism that eludes predators in a number of ways is said to have not merely the goal of survival, but a subgoal of eluding predators. An organism that develops a number of means of hiding comes to have what we'd call a subgoal of hiding. An organism that develops a number of ways of locating and identifying rocks to hide behind has a subgoal of finding rocks. This process can continue indefinitely. Over millennia, there emerge complicated machines, best described as organisms with the overall goal of survival, and with numerous subgoals, and sub-subgoals. Pursuing these goals normally helps (or helped) ensure the organism's successful interaction with, and survival in, its environment.

Our world, then, is structured such that through trial-and-error processes an entity can come to acquire complicated clusters of dispositions to make movements that usually enable it to achieve certain ends, or, as we say, "to try to achieve certain goals." This, then, is how certain entities in the world have the capacity to want certain things.

3.2 Representation

Our intuitive notion is that a creature possesses intentionality when "it does what it *thinks* will bring about what it *wants.*" I have claimed that talk of wants or goals is a way of describing a state of having numerous dispositions that usually bring about a certain end state. I submit that we speak of "representations" when we want to give *further* information about the more *fine-grained* subgoals that a creature has developed by becoming "tuned" to certain environments in a way that enables it to succeed in its goals and subgoals.

Presumably, the evolutionary and learning processes that we described above can get more and more sophisticated, enabling the organism to overcome an inordinate amount of different types of obstacles that stand between it and the end-state goals (or subgoals) that it's disposed to try to achieve. It can do so by developing a large number of nested "if–then" dispositional mechanisms. These can emerge in this way: through trial and error (in evolution or learning), mechanisms for registering different kinds of energy signals from the external environment develop. (For example, an organism can come to have carbon-atom arrangements called rhodopsin molecules, which react to the presence of certain colors by absorbing light at longer wavelengths.) Through trial and error, it can also develop different kinds of behavioral responses, such as moving various appendages to produce movements. Though feedback mechanisms, which may involve pleasure and pain, pathways develops that *coordinate* certain input signals with certain responses that are appropriate for achieving goals. Over time, organisms develop regular sensorimotor repertoires such as this one: if a light occlusion occurs above (a likely predator), move your tail muscles in a way that gets you away from the occlusion, unless it is a very small occlusion (likely prey), in which case, move your tail muscles to travel in the direction of the occlusion, and move your jaw muscles in a way that enables you to ingest its source (see Churchland 1980). Creatures may also learn that the best thing to do at a given time is nothing, save to be in a state of "readiness" to make particular movements, when, in the near or distant future, certain conditions arise.

Now, how can we describe the set of conditional dispositional mechanisms an organism has developed? The most elaborate description would be to actually name the sets of physical mechanisms. We could, for example, describe the entire physiological process that enables, say, a fish, to detect, track, and ingest its prey. A very minimalistic way of describing these conditionals, on the other hand, is to simply refer to them as mechanisms an organism uses to get its goals. Giving a minimalistic description saves us time, of course, but it gives us little information about the exact ways in which the organism will be interacting with the world or calculating its interactions. The middle way is to give people a fair amount of information about the internal mechanisms indirectly *by describing the sort of world* with which the creatures are set up to make appropriate interactions. We call being set up to interact effectively with that kind of world "having a representation" of that world. When a thirsty creature has mechanisms that enable it to push a rock, gauge how far it has moved, dig under it, stick its tongue there, and move its throat muscles in a certain way, we describe this by saying that the creature believes or has the representation "water is under the rock."

We can describe the *internal* state of the creature indirectly through describing some *external* world because, over time, the creature's internal states come to be set up to interact with the nooks and crannies of that world in a way that enables it to fulfill its goals and subgoals. The inner organization is "tuned" to interacting with a particular external world. In general, the more subgoals a creature has come to be able to regularly achieve in a given realm via its sensors and responses, the richer we say its representation of that realm is. If we know a creature's goals (which we often do), and we know about the shape of the world that it is disposed to navigate properly, then we can infer a good deal about the types of inner states that the creature must have developed to guide its actions. Note that it needn't be the case that the world a creature has come to be "tuned to" matches the world it's currently in. It can be prone to dig for water under a rock because that's where water has been in the past, even if there is no water there now. In these cases we are still often inclined to say it "believes" there is water under a rock. Indeed, the term "belief" seems to be used more often to describe situations in which the real world *doesn't* match a creature's tunings. The "internal" aspect of a belief is highlighted to a greater extent in these cases.

Why do we not describe a creature's inner guiding mechanisms directly, instead of giving information about them indirectly by describing the world they are "tuned to"? First, when talking about a creature's internal guidance system, we seldom have any interest in communicating much detail about these mechanisms. Saying "it thinks a bug is at the end of the line" usually gives us all the information we need about how the various sensory, tail-moving, and jaw-opening mechanisms will guide a fish to interact with a hook. Second, because we directly see the external world (or at least seem to), we have readily available vocabularies for describing it. We are far less likely to have readily available vocabularies for describing internal mechanisms at either a high or low level unless we have done extensive studies of them. Consequently it's much easier to describe mental mechanisms by describing the external worlds that these mechanisms are mechanisms *for* interacting with.

Over time, then, along with developing goals, creatures come to have fine-grained internal dispositions that guide them through particular worlds in order to reach their goals. When we want to describe these internal systems, we call them the system's "representations" and describe them quickly and indirectly by describing the sort of world the creature is wired up to navigate through. The labels we use to describe a given representational state are chosen for their usefulness. But the representational states themselves, on this view, are real, existing psychological states, controlling an organism's movements through the world.

4   The Possibility of Group Belief

We now have a theory of how something could be an intentional system and how such systems could have developed in the natural world. Could groups of people come to be intentional systems, according to this theory? I don't see any obstacles, in principle. A cluster of individuals could come, through various processes, to be arranged so that it has a robust disposition to produce a particular end state. It could come to be able to produce this end state in a large number of different ways. If it did so, it would be implementing the same sort of system that we'd be inclined to call "an entity with a goal," when such a system is constructed out of smaller, less cognizant units. I see no reason why we should not refer to, say, an army equipped to destroy an enemy through a large number of different means as a group *with the goal* of destroying the enemy.

The people comprising a system can also act in ways so that a *portion* of the end state, or an *intermediate* state required for bringing about the end state, also tends to be produced in a large number of different ways. When systems made of smaller parts are disposed to produce an intermediate state in a large number of ways, we recognize this to be a system with subgoals. In a parallel manner, we can say that a subunit of the army that tries to knock out the enemy's artillery through a number of different means is a group with the subgoal of knocking out the artillery.

If the intentional theory described above is adequate, then one can see how groups of individuals can come to have representations as well. A representation, on this account, consists of numbers of fine-grained subgoals that specify how to appropriately interact with the world in order to succeed at goals and subgoals. We describe this set of subgoals by describing the world they are "tuned" to. A portion of the army that has plans to enter the palace, go down the secret passageways, seal off the exits, engage the guards in certain types of combat, and capture the king, can be said to *represent* the king's whereabouts and the ways in which he might try to avoid capture.

If the theory of intentionality I have given above is correct, then certain groups don't merely behave "as if" they have goals and representations. Certain groups actually realize the functional criteria determining the identity conditions for counting as an intentional agent. I see no reason, then, not to use terms like "goal" and "representation" to describe the dispositions of groups whose activities parallel those of systems with simpler parts. I think one of the main reasons we hesitate in giving such a designation to a large system is that we already use terms like "goal" and "representation" to describe the thinking and behavior of the component *parts* of that system. Each of the people involved in these group goals has goals and representations of their own—representations at a grain size that is quite familiar to us. It's tempting when we hear talk about group goals or representations, then, to think in terms of the goals and representations of the people within the groups. It's even possible that the goals of some of the people in the group happen to be the same as the goals that our theory of intentionality would lead us to identify as the group's goals. But the point is that they *need not* be the same. On the theory of intentionality given above, it's perfectly possible for a group to have a goal or representation that none of the people in that group has. We can see that the group's goals need not be identified with those of any of the people in it when we realize that we would still be inclined toward giving descriptions like "that unit is trying to knock out the enemy artillery," even if every soldier and commander were gradually replaced by ones with somewhat different beliefs and desires, as long as overall activities remain highly similar. Indeed, each commanding officer and soldier might be replaced by three people who each have a third of the knowledge and do a third of the activities as the ones they replace. But as long as the overall end states and intermediate states they accomplish are the same as before, we would not say that the goals of the unit have changed—even though the particular representations and goals of *each* of the people involved had changed. The people involved in a group representation each have their own representations, but these representations need not be identified as the representations that the overall unit has.

Groups, then, could have belief-like states different from those of the individuals in them. What's more, if the above argument is correct, there is no reason that *groups of groups* cannot have goals and representations as well. If the army example shows how clusters of people can meet the criteria for instantiating goals and representations, then it's easy to see how clusters of armies could do the same thing. A cluster of different armies could join forces to defeat a common powerful enemy. A subgroup of this supergroup—a unit made up of four different armies, could be responsible (via various means) for the subgoal of knocking out the enemy's artillery. A coalition of five armies could coordinate activities to capture the enemy king and structure their conditional activities in a way that constitutes a representation of the king's possible escape routes. In theory, whatever a group can do, a group of groups can do. With the above definition of an intentional system, as in functional role theories generally, it doesn't matter how the requisite activities are performed—with metal parts, organic parts, individuals, or groups of individuals—it just matters that they get performed. Again, I see no in-principle obstacle to a group or a group of groups fulfilling all the criteria for being an intentional system.

5   The Formation of Sustained Intentional Groups

How can a group that could be thought of as an intentional system (henceforth an i-group) come to exist? Organisms with intentionality could come to exist and continue to exist when systems appear that have a robust disposition (through various means) to produce end states that happen to help that system continue to exist or reproduce itself. I-groups, then, could come to exist and continue to exist when there are groups of individuals with a robust disposition (through various means) to produce end states that happen to help that arrangement of people continue to exist or reproduce itself. There seems to be three general (overlapping) ways that individuals initially come to cluster together in i-groups. Individuals doing various activities could come to cluster together in an i-group through *random* trial and error. They could also move into a group and begin performing the activities leading to a robustly disposed i-group because they think that *putting themselves* in such positions will help them achieve their goals. They could also move into certain places and begin performing certain i-group-constituting activities because *other people* reward them for doing so and punish them for not doing so. In general, entity A has power over entity B, when A can make it costly (in terms of goal-achievement) for B not to do what A wants it to. An A-entity can make activities costly to a B-entity by its ability to inflict punishment, or its ability to deny rewards that it is in a position to give (see also Emerson 1962). Individuals often engage in activities because of the rewards and punishment that other people will give them, rather than rewards that they see beforehand that nature will give them, or rewards they happen to get from nature for activities they randomly stumble into. Hierarchies develop when an individual has power over a set of individuals, but there are other individuals in turn, with power over him or her.

Through random forces, self-control, and controller-control, then, individuals could come to engage in certain activities in certain places and time that produce i-groups. The next question is what could cause or enable such activities to stably *continue*. Again, the answer is similar to what we find in organism evolution. Creatures with goal-seeking dispositions continue to exist because certain clusters of dispositional mechanisms happen to interact in a way that produces results that *help that cluster* of dispositional mechanisms (or its replicas) continue to exist. Clusters of organisms, too, can continue to exist because of the way that clustering enhances the survival of that cluster (see Wilson and Sober 1994 for a review article in which they mention over 200 articles that discuss group selection). Writes biologist Tom Seeley:

By virtue of its greater size and mobility and other traits, a multicellular organism is sometimes a better gene-survival machine than a single eukarytic cell. . . . Likewise the genes inside organisms sometimes fare better when they reside in an integrated society of organisms, rather than in a single organism because of superior defensive, feeding and hemostatic abilities of functionally organized groups. (Seeley 1989, 546)

Biologist Richard Dawkins (1976) calls any stable interacting assembly of traits a *vehicle* that natural selection can operate on. The example he uses to explain this concept is instructive for our purposes. A vehicle, he writes, is like a rowing team in which the success of any individual member is dependent on coordinating activities in such a way that the team as a whole wins the race. An i-group could continue to exist because of the way that clustering of individuals, as a vehicle, enhances the continued survival of that cluster.

Examples of possible i-groups in which people coordinate activities in ways that enable the group to continue engaging in just those activities include people who cooperate to *extract* consumable resources from the Earth. Hunting, gathering, farming, mining, and herding groups do this. A different type of group, one that can thrive only in the environment of the right sorts of other groups, is a *trade* group. Trade groups are composed of individuals that benefit by cooperating in taking materials and transforming them into various consumer goods and services, not for themselves, but to trade and sell to other groups and individuals in exchange for other goods and services. There is a myriad of organized groups engaged in this type of organization, from toolmakers to software companies. The trade groups that come together can continue to exist for a long time because their activities give benefits to group members, which, in turn, encourage them to continue to engage in those activities.

In environments where people's basic metabolic needs are already taken care of by certain activities, other types of groups could form whose activities are sustained because of their ability to *assuage the pain* and stress of the members that compose them, or *enhance the pleasure* of these members. I call such groups noneconomic support (NES) groups. In NES groups, members benefit by joining together not to produce goods and services for themselves and others, but to give each other emotional support or enjoyment. A person can benefit by knowing that there are other people around who can help him through a range of potential problems or who can enhance his enjoyment of various things by using their knowledge to help focus his attention in useful directions. Groups with the emotional support function include Alcoholics Anonymous, Gay Men's Health Crisis, and the National League of Families of Prisoners. Groups with the "share enjoyment" function include the Girl Scouts, softball teams, Masons, Knights of Columbus, and book discussion groups. The American Association of Retired People, like many other groups, seems to be set up to serve both functions.

Note that the general forces sustaining these groups could be the same ones that put the dispositional mechanism together in the first place. Rewards for staying together could be bestowed on lucky individuals whose coming together happens to be beneficial for each of them. Individuals could also steer themselves toward continuing to engage in certain coordinated activities because they see that acting that way will give them certain benefits. Or powerful individuals can punish people for not continuing to engage in certain activities (or reward them for doing so). All three can certainly occur at the same time.

If resource-extracting groups, trade groups, and NES groups could bear similarities to individual organisms in that they are self-sustaining units that survive because they benefit from that arrangement of component parts, other types of groups can be more analogous to the *organs* of organisms. Recall, that, over time, goal-seeking creatures develop specialty organs (and organ parts) with subgoals of their own. These parts produce portions of the end state, produce states intermediate to the end state, or just enhance some of the activities that help produce either of these. These parts continue to exist (and to evolve) because of the benefits they provide to the overarching group that contains them. Over time, groups of people could develop specialized subgroups that do analogous things. In organisms, some of the most important organs with subgoals are ones that function to protect the organism. Similarly, among the most important specialized subgroups are those devoted to the activity of *protecting* the larger group from forces that would jeopardize its existence. Groups like armies protect a given group from outside forces like invading parties. Shelter-building subgroups protect group members from the hostile forces of heat and cold. Other groups, like the police, protect members from threats that result from the activities of other group members. (Note that members of these subgroups might well be members of other subgroups, too.)

Related to protection groups are groups dedicated to ensuring the harmonious *coordination* of other group members. In organisms, the subpart called the brain is an organ that helps make sure the body's other activities are successfully coordinating with each other. In human groups, even small organizations usually develop governing subparts whose task it is to coordinate and regulate the activities of a larger group containing them. Trade groups, for example, develop management teams to make sure the people involved are efficiently doing their part to achieve the group's goals. The larger the group, the more likely it is to further divide governing subgroups into specialized sub-subgroups. Large communities, for example, often have councils or parliaments that specialize in making pronouncements about which actions should be forbidden and which are obligatory. These communities also often have various subgroups such as regulatory agencies that function to punish the people and groups who engage in forbidden activities.

Protection groups and governing groups often directly benefit a larger group containing many different subgroups. Other subgroups most directly benefit the subgroup that contains them. Some soldiers are part of a ground repair team subgroup of an air strike unit subgroup of the Marines (itself a subgroup of the armed forces). Some auto factory workers specialize in producing parts for subgroups that produce motors. Some girl scouts are on subcommittees of recruitment committees dedicated to minority outreach. As in organismic evolution, where goal-seeking entities can develop numerous subgoal-seeking entities, the existence of certain i-groups could lead to the development of increasingly specialized subgroups, which themselves might meet the definition of an i-group. Over time, within a community, one could expect to find numerous i-groups forming and numerous sustainable i-groups continuing to exist. As the biological world is populated with various sorts of goal-seeking creatures (and organs), we should expect the social world to be populated with various sorts of intentional system groups.

In biological systems, meanwhile, we also find that certain organisms can eventually evolve that have goals and subgoals beyond survival, maintenance, and reproduction. A farmer can trade a shepherd for mutton, planning to consume it. But he can also plan to only purchase mutton that has been killed and cleaned in a certain way, he can plan on forming a long-term trade pact with the shepherd, and he can plan on refraining from trading with the shepherd's enemy. Similarly, we can expect that certain i-groups like corporations might also develop elaborate goals, plans, and representations directed at achieving far more complex ends than their own survival and profitability. When organisms are complex enough, their goals and plans become the subject of moral evaluation. In the following final section, I will briefly discuss extending the same kind of moral scrutiny to groups with complex plans and goals.

6 Intentional and Moral Agency

Throughout everyday conversation, journalistic reports, and the social sciences, we talk of groups having beliefs and desires. In this discussion, I have shown that this need not be just loose, idle talk. It is quite possible for collections of people to have goals and representations if they are organized similarly to intentional creatures. Intentional biological organisms are cooperating clusters of cells that, over time, develop capacities to survive and flourish by becoming increasingly good at achieving their goals in their particular environments. There is no reason to believe that cooperating clusters of people can't come to be organized in a similar manner. It is metaphysically possible for groups to be full-blown intentional agents.

If groups could *not* be intentional agents, there would be no way for them to be moral agents. What I wanted to do in this essay was to show how they could be intentional agents. Seeing this, we are now in a better position to consider whether and how they could also be moral agents. Examining this further question in detail is well beyond the scope of this essay. Still, some remarks are in order.

One way we can examine whether groups can be moral agents is to look at what our best moral theories say about what additional features intentional agents need in order to be full-blown moral agents. We could then look at whether there are any i-groups that possess these additional features. We might, for example, adopt Frankfurt's (1971) view that moral agency requires our second-order desires to be in harmony with our first-order desires. We would then ask whether and how it is possible for certain groups to have second order-desires.

Given our current lack of consensus about what are the requirements for being a morally responsible agent, I would favor a different type of approach. At our current stage of knowledge, I think it would be useful to simultaneously look at what various theories of moral agency say about problematic borderline cases (including groups) while, at the same time, using these borderline cases to try to help us clarify what counts as moral agency, in a process of reflective equilibrium. One area it would be useful to look at, for example, is animal morality. How complex does animal thinking have to be before we say that animals are truly moral agents? Looking at what we learn from these cases could help us develop a theory of moral agency rich enough to tell us what we should believe about intentional groups. Scholars like Bruce Waller (1997) and Franz de Waal (1997) have useful and interesting things to say about animal morality. Another area that could be useful here is looking at the morality of cases in which subagents are involved. If someone with a multiple personality disorder commits a crime, is the whole person guilty? Cases like these could help us develop a theory of moral agency that could tell us something about the moral agency of groups, which are always going to be made up of subagents—subagents that may have different goals from the agent as a whole. Finally, there's a large literature about the *morality* (if not the moral agency) of corporate actions by scholars like Peter French. Looking at our judgments about the morality of corporate *actions* is likely to help us develop a theory about the relationship between moral actions and moral agency that's almost certainly going to be relevant to questions about whether groups have moral agency.

Groups, it seems, can be intentional agents. Whether, in addition, they can be moral agents is unclear. But knowing how they can be intentional agents helps give us some promising ways to find that out.

References

Bennett, J. 1990. Folk Psychological Explanations. In *The Future of Folk Psychology*, ed. J. Greenwood. Cambridge: Cambridge University Press.

Churchland, P. M. 1980. Plasticity: Conceptual and Neuronal. *Behavioral and Brain Sciences* 3:133–134.

Dawkins, R. 1976. *The Selfish Gene*. Oxford: Oxford University Press.

de Waal, F. 1997. *Good Natured: The Origin of Right and Wrong in Humans and Other Animals*. Cambridge, MA: Harvard University Press.

Emerson, R. 1962. Power-dependence Relations. *American Sociological Review* 27:31–40.

Frankfurt, H. 1971. Freedom of the Will and the Concept of a Person. *Journal of Philosophy* 68:5–20.

French, P. 1995. *Individual and Collective Responsibility*. New York: Schenkman Books.

Haugeland, J. 1990. The Intentionality All Stars. In *Philosophical Perspectives, IV: Philosophy of Mind and Action Theory*, ed. J. Tomberlin. Atsacadero, CA: Ridgeview.

Kutz, C. 2000. *Complicity*. Cambridge: Cambridge University Press.

Lyons, W. 1995. *Approaches to Intentionality*. Oxford: Oxford University Press.

May, L., and S. Hoffman. 1991. *Collective Responsibility*. New York: Rowman & Littlefield.

Seeley, T. 1989. The Honey Bee Colony as Superorganism. *American Scientist* 77:546–553.

Stich, S. 1983. *From Folk Psychology to Cognitive Science: The Case against Belief*. Cambridge, MA: MIT Press.

Waller, B. 1997. What Rationality Adds to Animal Morality. *Biology and Philosophy* 12:341–356.

Wilson, D., and E. Sober. 1994. Reintroducing Group Selection to the Human Behavioral Sciences. *Behavioral and Brain Sciences* 17:585–654.

13　Moral Judgment and Volitional Incapacity

Antti Kauppinen

Charles Doyle had let down the Mam and condemned his children to genteel poverty. He had been weak and unmanly, incapable of winning his fight against liquor. Fight? He had barely raised his gloves at the demon.

—Julian Barnes, *Arthur & George*

The central question of the branch of metaethics we may call philosophical moral psychology concerns the nature or essence of moral judgment: what is it to think that something is right or wrong, good or bad, obligatory or forbidden? One datum in this inquiry is that sincerely held moral views appear to influence conduct: on the whole, people do not engage in behaviors they genuinely consider base or evil, sometimes even when they would stand to benefit from it personally. Moral judgments thus appear to be motivationally effective, at least to an extent. This motivational success would be readily explained if they simply *were* motivationally effective psychological states, such as desires. This is what Hobbes seems to do when he claims that "whatsoever is the object of any man's appetite or desire, that is it which he for his part calleth good; and the object of his hate and aversion, evil" (Hobbes 1651/1994, VI, 28). But this is far too quick. We know that moral judgments can also fail to lead to corresponding action. For example, since it is conceptually possible—not to mention all too common in the actual world—to think that something is wrong and yet want to do it, thinking that something is wrong cannot simply consist in aversion toward it, contrary to what Hobbes seems to have thought. In this way, reflection on the various conceivable *failures* of moral motivation rules out possible candidates for explaining *successful* moral motivation. This is not an empirical psychological inquiry. We want to find out what kind of psychological state moral judgment *must* be (and what it *cannot* be) in order to have just the right kind of motivational role. What I will suggest in this essay is that a close examination of the various possible

kinds of motivational failure has important and underappreciated implications for metaethics.

In metaethics, there are two major strategies for explaining the existence
and ubiquity of the motivational success of moral judgment. According
to moral judgment *internalism*, moral judgments involve some degree of
motivation by their very nature.[1] Roughly, internalists believe there is a
conceptual connection between thinking that one morally ought to φ and
being to some degree motivated to φ (or being motivated to take what
one believes to be the means to φ-ing). Consequently, an agent who is not
at all motivated to φ does not genuinely think that she morally ought to
φ.[2] The denial of internalism is known as moral judgment *externalism*. On
externalist views, it is not the nature of moral judgment but rather human
nature that explains why judgments tend to motivate: as a contingent
matter of fact, human beings are often disposed to do what they believe
to be morally right. Thinking that something is one's duty does not as
such involve motivation, but does lead to action when combined with a
desire to do whatever is right. Internalism and externalism face opposite
challenges: internalists have an easy time with motivational success, but
difficulty with motivational failures, whereas externalists make failure
easily intelligible at the cost of struggling to explain success.

It seems to me that internalists have the upper hand in this debate. As
Michael Smith has recently argued, any externalist strategy makes morality
look like a kind of fetish.[3] After all, on the externalist picture, what we care
directly about is being moral, so that our concern with the particular things
we judge to be right is only derivative. If Smith is correct, only internalists
can leave room for nonderivative caring about what we think is good or
fair as a result of moral judgment, where "what we think is good" is read
de re—caring about reducing poverty as such, for example, as opposed to
caring about it as a way of doing whatever is good. The externalist explanation for motivational success is thus suspect. In addition, externalists
seem to allow for too radical motivational failures. On their picture,
someone who was never once in her whole life motivated to act morally
could nonetheless make genuine moral judgments. Equally, there could be
a community within which a recognizably moral language game was played
without the judgments making the slightest difference to people's actions.[4]
But neither individual nor communal comprehensive indifference to moral
judgments seems conceptually possible. At best, we could describe these
people as trying to make moral judgments, but failing to do so.

It is thus some form of internalism that holds the most promise. Traditionally, internalism has been perhaps the strongest reason for adopting

noncognitivist views about the nature of moral judgment. According to them, a moral judgment is a *conative* or *affective* state, and only such states are intrinsically motivating. If this is the case, it is easy to see why internalism is true: moral judgments have an internal connection to motivation, since they consist in some sort of motivational states. Internalist *cognitivists* face a challenge of explaining why an internal connection would obtain between merely *believing* that one ought to do something and being motivated to do it, given that on the standard story in the philosophy of action, belief alone cannot constitute motivation.[5] They have responded to this challenge in two main ways: either denying that all beliefs are motivationally inert, or by arguing for a weaker internalist thesis that beliefs with a suitable content necessarily hook up to motivation in rational agents, though not all moral agents. Here the earlier dialectic reappears: noncognitivist internalists are prima facie better placed to explain motivational success, whereas cognitivist internalists have an easier time with motivational failure.

Sophisticated contemporary forms of noncognitivism, such as Allan Gibbard's norm-expressivism, are capable of explaining certain kinds of motivational failure, like weakness of the will. However, I will argue here that the existence of the sort of radical motivational failure that Gary Watson has labeled *volitional incapacity* cannot be accounted for by *any* expressivist theory that identifies a moral judgment with a conative state. Volitional incapacity, crudely put, is the kind of disorder that Charles Doyle in my epigraph might have suffered from, supposing he genuinely judged that he should stop drinking: it is not that his desire to drink was causally stronger than his will to stop, but that he never really willed to stop in the first place—he "barely raised his gloves" at it. It is not just that he was not able to resist the temptation; he was not even able to *fight* it. This contrasts with another kind of addict, the weak-willed agent who yields to temptation in spite of meaning to stay clean. As Watson points out, this kind of incapacity is a neither a failure of judgment nor one of self-control: Charles Doyle knew what he had to do and, we may suppose, would have been able to do it had he put up a fight. Rather, volitional incapacity forces us to distinguish between *judgment* and *the will*: one is volitionally incapacitated when one's self-directed ought-judgment does not result in a corresponding intention. Just as weakness of the will shows that valuing and desire are (at least) modally separable, volitional incapacity shows that valuing and conative states like planning are modally separable and thus cannot be identical, as expressivists claim. Instead, the internal connection between moral judgment and motivation must be explained in terms rationally binding belief, as internalist cognitivists have argued. I finish with a sketch of a new kind of cognitivist and rationalist account that draws on recent developments in conceptual role semantics.

1   Expressivism and Failures of Motivation

According to any kind of noncognitivism, moral judgments consist in psychological states[6] with a world-to-mind direction of fit. These states include desires, second-order desires, intentions, plans, and the like—any psychological state whose function it is to make the world fit its content rather than the other way around.[7] The identification of moral judgment with desiderative or conative states is motivated primarily by internalism: if thinking that something is right is adopting some positive attitude toward it, it is easy to see why moral judgments essentially have a relation to motivation. As already noted, the crudest form of noncognitivism, identifying valuing with desiring, is untenable in light of the possibility of motivational failure, since it seems plain we can fail to desire what we think is right.[8] More sophisticated noncognitivists, such as contemporary expressivists, make room for motivational failure by making a distinction between noncognitive attitudes: only *some* of them constitute valuing, and having these more complex attitudes is compatible with lacking occurrent motivation.

I will focus here on Allan Gibbard's recent work, since it provides perhaps the most detailed expressivist account of ought-judgments currently available. In his *Thinking How to Live*, he begins with the observation that moral judgments, and normative judgments in general, are essentially judgments about what to do. Correspondingly, ought-questions and reason-questions are questions about what to do. To judge that something is the thing do, in turn, is on his view to *settle* on doing it or to *decide* to do it—more precisely, to rule out doing anything else (Gibbard 2003, 137). As he puts it, "When I deliberate, I ask myself what to do and I respond with a decision. Thinking what I ought to do amounts to deciding what to do" (ibid., 17). Gibbard's main goal is to argue that seeing normative utterances as expressing "contingency plans" or "hyperstates"[9] explains why they behave in many ways as would Moorean assertions about non-natural properties, but without the need to commit to queer metaphysical or epistemological theses. He claims that this is the key to solving the Frege–Geach problem about the behavior of normative predicates in unasserted contexts. I do not here take a stand on whether planning states can play this sort of role; my question is rather whether planning states play the right sort of motivational role to qualify as candidates for moral judgment in the first place.

Suppose, then, that thinking that I ought to take the dog for a walk is a planning state, a matter of adopting a plan to take the dog for a walk. Clearly this makes motivational success intelligible: if I plan to do something, then, at least ceteris paribus, I will have some motivation to do it. But how does Gibbard's view accommodate motivational failures? His first response is to deny that one wholeheartedly judges that one ought to do something if one fails to (try to) do it:

> For a crucial sense of 'ought', I say, the following holds: if you do accept, in every relevant aspect of your mind, that you ought right now to defy the bully, then, you will do it if you can. For if you can do it and don't, then some aspect of your mind accounts for your not doing it—and so you don't now plan with every aspect of your mind to do it right now. . . . And so, it seems to me, there's a part of you that doesn't really think you ought to. (Ibid., 153)

These sort of cases result from "conflicts among motivational systems" (ibid.; see also Gibbard 1990, 56–58)—here between the planning system and the more primitive one that results in fear of the bully. At other times, our plans are defeated by the grip that social norms like those of politeness and cooperation have on us even when we acknowledge other things are more important in the situation, morally speaking—Gibbard points here to Milgram's classic experiments, in which subjects continued to give electric shocks to others in spite of recognizing that it was wrong in virtue of the great pain the shocks were causing (as they were led to believe) (Gibbard 1990, 59). It seems that we can make sense of failures like weakness of the will in these terms, whether we describe it as a case of being of two minds about what one ought to do or being overcome by a desire that is stronger than the motivation provided by the planning system. If we identify the self of an agent with the totality of her higher-order planning states, as Gibbard sometimes is tempted to do,[10] the latter description is more fitting, since the competing motivation will be external to the self: *I* am not of two minds, though there is a force in me that may be causally stronger than my decision when it comes to acting.[11] To accommodate cases of listlessness or accidie, in which the problem is not the strength of a competing desire but lack of *any* desire in spite of willing (see below), Gibbard allows that a state may be a planning state even if it only *normally* issues in action (Gibbard 2003, 154).[12] (Of course, it does not make sense to say of a token state that it "normally" does anything; Gibbard must be thinking of an instance of a certain *type* of state.) Thus, there is room for certain kinds of motivational failure even if moral judgments are identified with planning states. Sophisticated expressivism can make sense of failures like weakness of will and accidie while at the same time making intelligible the internal connection between judgment and action.

Having provided an expressivist explanation of motivational success and failure, Gibbard goes on the offensive. He argues that the expressivist explanation of motivational success is superior to the internalist cognitivist one, so, given that it can handle failure equally well, we should prefer expressivist moral psychology. In effect, the argument is that once we admit that there is an internal connection between judgment and motivation, there is no point in thinking that the psychological states in question are distinct existences: "[W]hy then think that deciding and thinking what one ought to do are separate activities?" (ibid., 13). Making a distinction here merely incurs an extra explanatory debt (why would there be an internal connection between two separate states with opposed directions of fit?), so expressivism has an advantage here, if Gibbard is right.

2 The Difference between Judgment and the Will

I granted above that expressivists can accommodate certain kinds of failure of motivation. In this section I will draw on recent arguments in the philosophy of action to show that we must distinguish between two basic types of motivational failure and corresponding internal conflict, the latter of which would have no conceptual room if moral judgment were a conative state.

The Gap between the Will and Action

The most obvious failures of motivation occur between what an agent sets out to do and what she in fact does or tries to do. There are at least three possible forms here. First, it may be that the agent sets out to do one thing, but a desire to do something else is causally stronger, leading her to form at different proximal intention (the psychological state that causes and sustains the bodily movements that constitute intentional action) and thus doing something else intentionally, unless prevented by an external obstacle.[13] This is *weakness of the will*, as I understand it. Weakness of will may also consist in giving up one's original prior intention and forming a new one—that is, giving up one plan and adopting another—without changing one's mind about reasons for action. The essential thing is that it makes sense to speak of weakness of the will only when there already is a will that can be either strong or weak. To be sure, weakness of the will is often understood or even defined in slightly different terms, as acting against one's judgment about what is best. It is readily intelligible why it is commonly thought so, since as a rule what we will is what we judge best. In such cases, the weak-willed person acts *both* against her judgment *and* her will. But as I will argue, we must be careful to distinguish between the two. Consequently, we are better off restricting the term 'weakness of (the) will' to cases where the agent has already *formed* a will, that is, set out to do something, without simply assuming that this is what judgment about what is best consists in.[14]

The second form of failure of willing is accidie or listlessness, where the agent sets out to do something but is not capable of mustering any effort to achieve her goal. This seems to be the condition from which some depressives suffer, as Michael Stocker (1979) notes. Third, it may happen that the agent does what she has set out to do, but this action is in fact caused by some other source of motivation than her setting out to do so.[15] This kind of *deviant causation* is a failure of self-control that can be relevant to assessing the agent, since it raises the question about what she would have done in counterfactual situations where the causally efficacious desire would not have been present.

In each of these cases, we can say that in settling on a course of action, the agent has formed a ("prior" or "distal") *intention* to act in a certain way, a commitment that implies forming a certain causally effective proximal intention at the time of action. This commitment has a world-to-mind direction of fit and a characteristic causal-functional role of leading to proximal intention. On pain of (subjective) irrationality, it excludes commitments to contrary courses of action and can thus play an important role in coordinating and planning activities. In Alfred Mele's terms, having an intention is *having an executive attitude toward a plan* (Mele 2003, 28, 210; cf. Bratman 1987). It is natural to talk about the agent's *will* in this context. An agent who has a strong or resolute will is one who follows through on her intentions. I will use the terms 'will', 'planning state', and '(prior) intention' interchangeably in what follows.

The Gap between Judgment and the Will

It seems possible that sometimes we not only fail to do what we have set out to do, but also fail to set out to do what we think we ought to do. This amounts to a different kind of failure and inner conflict, as many in recent philosophy of action have argued. I will first try to make this difference intuitive by contrasting four different cases.

Brave Michelle

It is wartime, and Michelle is in the Resistance. There's a wireless in her room, and one day she gets an urgent message to be delivered to René, an explosives expert: "The hawk will be in the henhouse at 1900 hours tonight." There is a curfew and the town is swarming with Germans, but Brave Michelle believes it is her duty to go out and deliver the message. Consequently, she settles on leaving. Just as she's about to go, she hears a German armored car rumbling nearby, but maintains her resolve and sneaks out anyway.

Weak Michelle

Weak Michelle's situation is otherwise the same as Brave Michelle's, but when she hears the armored car rumbling nearby, she feels too scared to open the door. Her heart beats loudly as she walks around in small circles, her nerves racked. She envisions what will happen if she doesn't go and tells herself she will do it now and then it will be over, but as she puts her hand again on the handle, there's another violent sound and she can't bring herself to do it.

Listless Michelle

Listless Michelle's situation is otherwise the same as Brave Michelle's, but owing to fatal failures and loss of comrades in previous resistance activity, she has become seriously depressed. She finds it her duty to deliver the message and swears to herself she will do so, but when the time comes, she lies inert in her bed. Try as she might, she can't get her legs to move in the right direction.

Incapacitated Michelle

Incapacitated Michelle's situation is otherwise the same as before, but she has, understandably enough in the exceptional conditions, developed a severe case of agoraphobia, fear of open spaces and the outdoors. The wireless crackles out the message, and Michelle thinks it her duty to deliver it. After all, lives are at stake, and it is all up to her. But delivering the message would require leaving the house, and she can't see herself doing it. The mere thought makes her shudder. She knows she should at least make an effort, but finds herself paralyzed by the idea. Consequently, she can't bring herself to make the decision to go out, though, as we might say, she has already decided that it is what she should do.

As I would describe these cases, Brave Michelle exercises her volitional capacity by willing in accordance with her judgment and strength of will by following through with her plan in spite of the scary situation. Weak and Listless Michelle also will in accordance with their judgment, but lack strength of will, thus suffering from the type of motivational failure I discussed in the previous section. The interesting case is Incapacitated Michelle, who does not even form a will or intention to do what she judges she ought. This is the same sort of radical failure I suggested the fictional Charles Doyle might have suffered from. In neither case is there an internal struggle between two competing motivational systems. Incapacitated Michelle is, as Watson puts it in a similar case, too terrified even to try (Watson 2004a, 94). Her condition consists precisely in her inability to settle on a course of action that would involve going out.[16] As Watson notes of a similar case, "Quite apart from being unable to see clearly what is to be done, or to do what [she] wills, [she] is sometimes unable to commit herself to implementing [her] judgments."[17] In Mele's terms, we can say that in spite of her judgment, Incapacitated Michelle has a plan to go out as a sort of recipe of how to carry out her duty, but she fails to adopt an *executive attitude* toward it. (In the final section, I will return to what adopting such an attitude might amount to.) In this, she differs from Listless and Weak Michelle, who fail to follow through on a plan they have settled on executing, either through general inertia or the presence of a competing desire. Their conditions, consequently, support different counterfactuals. Were Incapacitated Michelle to form an intention, she would be able to act on it (unless she also suffers from some other motivational disorder). By contrast, Listless Michelle would be unable to act on any or most other intentions as well, and Weak Michelle would act on the intention if she only got rid of the competing desire or fear. To be sure, the difference here is subtle, and we may well be unable to tell whether Michelle is weak willed, listless, or incapacitated on the basis of a single case of inaction. But the difference can come out on the basis of a pattern in her action, or inaction, as it may be. Listless Michelle will not answer the phone either, whereas Incapacitated Michelle may have no problem with it.

The situation of Incapacitated Michelle seems to be a coherent possibility, assuming that conceivability is here a reliable guide to possibility. The lesson is that there is a potential difference between judgment and the will that is distinct from the failure to act on one's plans or intentions (the failure of Weak Michelle), but a failure to adopt an executive attitude to what one takes to be the best supported plan in the first place. This distinct failure is *volitional incapacity*, the inability to will as one judges best.

Distinguishing between ought-judgment and the will is not an ad hoc move to make sense of volitional incapacity. It does other work as well.

Watson argues that it leaves room for the "work of the will" in cases where it is necessary to form an intention even though the balance of reasons is even or unclear, leaving the normative issue open. Perhaps I cannot decide whether it is better to stay or to go, but I must do either, and so I will.[18] Second, Jay Wallace argues that a realistic account of normative motivation must leave room for counternormative intentions. This is manifest in the fact that there doesn't seem to be a Moorean paradox involved in saying "I really ought to do x, but I'm going to do y instead" or "I've chosen to do y, though it's not in fact the best alternative open to me," as one would expect if there were no possible gap between ought-judgment and intention.[19] (There is still something odd about such statements; I will return to this below.) Finally, Al Mele points out that there may be a temporal gap between judgment and decision (understood as settling on an action). For example, we can imagine that Joe deliberates on New Year's Eve about whether or not to continue smoking, and judges it best to stop smoking at midnight; that will be his New Year's resolution (Mele 2003, 199). But he may not *yet* have resolved to stop, Mele argues.

All these cases support distinguishing normative judgment and planning states, though in most situations the two are closely aligned. Both ought-judgment and settling on a plan involve a verdictive, all-things-considered stance on action. That is why it is natural to talk of "decision" in each case. But they are different kinds of decision. The decision involved in reaching a first-personal ought-judgment could be called a *cognitive decision*, a verdict that all things considered, the balance of reasons in the case favors a particular course of action.[20] Forming the will or adopting a plan, by contrast, amounts to a *practical decision*, actually settling on a course of action. Thinking about a court case should make this distinction clear.[21] The jury deliberates whether the defendant is guilty or not, weighing the evidence pro and con. Let us assume that in the end, it *decides that* the defendant is guilty. As a result, the judge *decides to* send the defendant to prison for, say, eight years. Here, the jury's decision is a *belief* that, in the context of legal practice, has practical consequences, calling for action on the part of the judge—that is the whole point of forming the belief. Nonetheless, it can be true or false, depending on whether the defendant actually is guilty or not. The judge's decision, by contrast, is an announcement of an (institutional) *intention* or plan to punish the defendant in a certain way. It cannot be true or false, though we can agree or disagree with it. This process can malfunction in two ways, analogous to the motivational disorders: the judge may fail to issue a verdict corresponding to the one given by the jury (perhaps she is bribed) or the wheels of the institution may grind to a halt (prison guards don't do their job properly and the prisoner walks free).

3 From Noncognitivist to Cognitivist Internalism

I argued in the previous section that we must separate ought-judgment and volitional states from each other to make volitional incapacity and related phenomena intelligible. This is very bad news for noncognitivist forms of internalism, Gibbard's expressivism included. The argument is quickly stated. Gibbard claims that we should think of ought-judgments as consisting of contingency plans, decisions to act in a certain way in a certain situation. But this cannot be the case: were normative judgments planning states, the sorts of failure I discussed in the previous section would be inconceivable. To borrow a term from Michael Smith, who uses a similarly structured argument to argue against the identification of moral judgments with desires, the existence of volitional incapacity and the like shows that normative judgments and planning states are *modally separable*, so that their relationship cannot be either identity or logical connection. Moral judgment must be different from practical decision or adopting a plan.

The internal connection between ought-judgment and motivation cannot, then, be explained by identifying the judgment with a conative state. It must instead be a cognitive state that is in some way special in terms of giving rise to plans and actions. It cannot be an ordinary belief like a belief that there is milk in the fridge, since the ordinary belief has motivational effects only contingently, given one has an appropriate desire, such as the desire to drink milk. The whole point of the practice of making moral judgments and persuading each other of them seems to be making a difference to action and attitude. (In this respect, a moral judgment is like the jury's verdict of guilt, discussed above.) It is just this difference between moral judgments and ordinary beliefs that externalism misses. What we need, then, is a cognitive state that has a noncontingent but defeasible tie to the will and corresponding action. The story should go something like this. Suppose that I am being threatened by a schoolyard bully who wants me to do his homework. I weigh the practical reasons bearing on the situation and reach the conclusion that all things considered, I ought to just walk away. Insofar as I successfully exercise my volitional capacities—insofar as my will listens to my reason, to put it in Aristotelian terms—I form the intention to walk away.[22] The intention to walk away, in turn, leads me to intentionally walk away (as a causal result of forming the relevant proximal intention) insofar as I successfully exercise my strength of will. The various motivational disorders and inner conflicts show that the required capacities can fail to function at both junctions. When judgment fails to lead to willing, I suffer from volitional incapacity. My will stands opposed to my reason. On the other hand, if, for example, a causally stronger desire to avoid risk intervenes between my will and action, I either form a different proximal intention than I had intended or go a step back and form a different intention altogether, with the result that I (intentionally) do the bully's work rather than walk away. If my will misfires entirely and I remain passive in spite of my intention, I suffer from accidie. In these cases, some of my desires stand opposed to my will. Acting on a *moral* ought-judgment is simply a special case of normative control, as are failures to do so.[23]

The picture I have presented is supposed to be a weakly internalist one. But how can that be the case, if ought-judgment is at least two steps removed from action? As Michael Smith observes, talk of internalism in the absence of necessary connections makes sense if (and perhaps only if) volitional capacity and strength of will are distinctively *rational* capacities, so that judgment, will, and action go necessarily together *for rational agents* (cf. Smith 1994, 177–180). A verdictive, all-things-considered ought-judgment, after all, is a judgment that I have most reason to do this. This would also explain the pragmatic oddity of claims like "I really ought to do x, but I'm going to do y instead"—they amount to avowals of practical irrationality on one's own part, admitting that one cannot justify one's behavior to others. This seems to be the most promising *form* of an internalist cognitivist account.

Are volitional capacity and strength of will rational capacities, then? For Smith, the paradigm rational capacity is the logical capacity of improving the *coherence* of our beliefs (Smith 1997, secs. 5–6). Consequently, he argues that what corresponds to volitional capacity (or strength of will—Smith's model does not distinguish between the two) in his Humean model is a rational capacity only if the content of the belief that one ought to φ (that is, one has most reason to φ) is such that when the belief is present, one's psychology is more coherent if it includes the desire to φ than if it lacks it. He claims that this is the case only if the belief itself is a belief about desires—more precisely, the belief that one's ideally informed and perfectly coherent self would desire one to desire to φ. On this analysis, to believe one ought to φ is to believe that one's ideal counterpart would desire one to φ, and forming this belief leads an agent with a disposition toward coherence to desire to φ.

Smith's proposal involves strong assumptions about the content of our moral beliefs (do we really form causally effective beliefs about an ideal counterpart?) and the role of coherence in rationalizing attitudes (could not acting against an ought-judgment cohere better with the rest of one's psychology in some cases?), among other things.[24] These and other problems are now well known, so instead of discussing the virtues and vices of Smith's account, I want to finish with a sketch of a promising alternative model that treats *inference* rather than coherence as the basic rational capacity. According to inferentialism, or more broadly, conceptual role semantics, the content of a belief is to be understood in terms of how it fits into the context of other mental states, perceptual inputs, and behavioral outputs; that is, what it properly follows from and what properly follows from it. The version that seems to me the most promising is developed in detail by Robert Brandom in *Making It Explicit* (1994) and other works.

The key ideas of inferentialism, in short, are the following. First, sounds, inscriptions, and tokenings of mental states acquire content by being caught up in the right way in a social practice of giving and asking for reasons. Second, the distinctive feature of the game of giving and asking for reasons is the deontic score that all participants attribute to each other, a record of which linguistic and nonlinguistic performances each of us is committed and entitled to. On Brandom's social pragmatist picture, these deontic statuses of commitment and entitlement result from deontic attitudes—treating someone as committed or entitled. In simplest terms, to treat someone as *entitled* to φ (that is, to attribute an entitlement to φ -ing) is to *positively* sanction φ -ing—for example, treating a ticket-holder as entitled to enter a concert may consist simply in allowing only ticket-holders in. Treating someone as *committed* to φ, in turn, is a matter of *negatively* sanctioning *not* φ-ing—for example, treating a library user as committed to returning a book in time may consist simply in revoking library privileges in case of failure to return the book in time.[25] Importantly, undertaking a commitment can be understood in these terms as entitling others to negatively sanction failure to perform; I will develop this idea below.

Third, the *pragmatic significance* of speech acts consists in the difference they make to deontic scores—what commitments and entitlements they give rise to, what commitments preclude entitlement to them, and so on. Fourth, the *semantic content* of expressions, their inferential role, is understood in terms of their pragmatic significance. Crudely, to know what something means is to know (in the sense of being able to discriminate in practice) what entitles one to it, what it commits one to, and what is incompatible with it in terms of precluding entitlement. This is to know the material inferential role that the expression has. Finally, *logical vocabulary is expressive*: its function is to make explicit the material inferences that give content to nonlogical vocabulary. Asserting (or thinking) that Matilda is a cow commits one to thinking that Matilda is an animal, since licensing that (material) inference is part of what gives the concept the content it has. Using the conditional to say "If Matilda is a cow, Matilda is an animal" or the negation to say "Cows are not horses" *makes explicit* part of the concept's content, rather than underwriting the correctness of the inference.[26]

Though inferentialist accounts are inspired by Gentzen-style definitions of logical connectives in terms of introduction and elimination rules,[27] the circumstances and consequences of proper application that define the inferential role of a commitment need not be limited to other commitments. For example, one can acquire entitlement to "That car is red" by being in the right kind of causal commerce with the world and having the right kind of discriminatory abilities. Indeed, this is how concepts come to have empirical content, even broad content—the broad inferential role of "water" is not the same in the actual world and on Twin Earth, since the proper circumstances of application on Twin Earth involve different stuff. Importantly, the same goes for nonlinguistic output. It can be a part of the inferential role of an expression that it commits one to *act* in a certain way. Rational agency, on Brandom's view, is a matter of responding to the acknowledgment of such a commitment with the suitable behavior. For example, "I shall open the door at ten o'clock" expresses a practical commitment of this kind; an agent who undertakes such a commitment will open the door at ten o'clock, insofar as she is practically rational (disposed to respond to acknowledging a commitment with appropriate behavior) and the performance is in her power. To be more precise, there are two kinds of practical commitments, future-directed and present-directed ("I shall open the door *now*"), which correspond to prior and proximal intentions, respectively. The difference is that they are defined in normative rather than causal-functional terms.

What, then, is the distinct inferential role of moral ought-beliefs—what is it to think ought-thoughts? Let us begin with the language that makes these thoughts explicit. Brandom's original and at first sight unlikely idea is that normative vocabulary is akin to logical vocabulary in its function, indeed a species of it: it, too, makes explicit proprieties of inference. What is specific about it is that it makes explicit inferences from doxastic commitments (beliefs) to practical commitments—that is, in Brandom's terms, proprieties of a kind of *practical reasoning*. To illustrate this with a nonmoral case, let us imagine that Al and Sean volunteer as firemen in their small village. Suppose that Abe treats firemen as committed to rush to the fire station when the fire bell rings—that is, he negatively sanctions them for failing to do so, say, in the form of disapproval and not inviting them to a party, and takes everyone else as being entitled to do the same. This is a matter of Abe taking anyone, himself included, to be entitled to a pattern of inferences like the following: (Al fails to rush to the fire station when the bell rings → I shall not invite Al to the party), (Sean fails to rush to the fire station when the bell rings → I shall not vote for Sean in the election), and so on for any number of (social) sanctions and for anyone who might volunteer to be a fireman. In the pattern, the antecedent is a belief about nonperformance of an action in a situation, and the consequent a practical commitment to a form of sanctioning. At the same time, Abe takes responding to a belief that the fire bell rings with a practical commitment to rushing to the fire station to be an instance of good practical reasoning on Al and Sean's part—that is, he takes them to be entitled, not simply committed, to making this move.[28] One can presumably be disposed to draw such inferences without possessing explicit normative vocabulary. But when one does possess normative vocabulary, one is able to express one's commitment to endorse all these inferences by simply saying "Firemen *ought* to rush to the fire station when the bell rings."

Provided that Sean, for example, possesses the relevant vocabulary, he, too, can say or think "I *ought* to rush to the fire station when the bell rings." On the inferentialist view, to say or think "I ought to φ" amounts to explicitly acknowledging the appropriateness of the kind of pattern of inferences by oneself and others I sketched above. It is *not* itself to undertake the practical commitment—in traditional terms, form the intention—to φ. That would be expressed by "I will φ" (in the committive rather than predictive sense) or "I shall φ." Ought-talk makes explicit *inferential commitments*, not practical ones. These commitments fall into two classes that together make it intelligible why first-personal ought-judgments are *rationally binding* for the will. First, the *rationality* of the binding must be understood in the inferentialist picture in terms of entitlement-preserving inferences. Crudely, to think that the balance of reasons favors φ-ing is to think that anyone in *this* situation is entitled to φ. That is, anyone who is entitled to my doxastic commitments, whatever they are, is also entitled to form the practical commitment to φ—to reason practically to the conclusion expressed by "I shall φ."[29] But this does not yet capture an ought, since one could be entitled to do many incompatible things. So, second, the *bindingness* of the ought-judgment is manifest in the fact that it excludes entitlement to do anything else (to undertake other practical commitments). To take myself to be committed to φ-ing is to take anyone, myself included, to be entitled (and perhaps committed, too) to negatively sanction my failing to φ.

In my view, this is all we can say about generic ought-judgment as such. What are sometimes called moral or prudential or institutional oughts are just ought-judgments grounded in different reasons or norms, and consequently entitle different kinds of sanctions.[30] The specific motivational role of first-personal *moral* ought-judgments must be understood in terms of the specific nature of moral reasons and moral sanctions. Let us return to the case of Michelle to get a grasp of them. When she forms the belief that she ought to go out and deliver the message to René, she commits herself to a pattern of practical reasoning, both in the first person and in the third person. She takes it that anyone in her situation would be entitled to (make the practical commitment to) deliver the message. This she takes to be licensed by the moral wrongness of not delivering it. The inferentialist account as such leaves open how to think of moral wrongness. Perhaps to think something is morally wrong simply is to think that its nonmoral properties license the inference to a practical commitment of a moral kind—to think that staying in the house is wrong is just to think that one ought not stay in the house, on pain of moral sanctions.[31] This approach would rest all the specificity of moral judgment on the sort of practical commitments licensed. Or maybe thinking that something is wrong is ascribing to it a nonnatural property that grounds an obligation, or a particular sort of natural property, like causing more pain to a creature capable of suffering than other open alternatives. Each of these theories of the proper circumstances of application of a moral ought is compatible with inferentialism.

In making the ought-judgment, Michelle also takes herself to be committed to delivering the message, that is, not entitled to do anything else. As we have seen, that means that she positively sanctions anyone negatively sanctioning her not delivering the message. And in the moral case, this means that anyone is entitled to adopt a particular emotional posture toward her, namely, that of *blaming*. She herself is entitled, and perhaps also committed, to blame herself—in other words, to feel guilt.[32] Moreover, insofar as the commitment is grounded in moral wrongness, she takes herself to have it independently of anything that she herself has done.

Let us, then, suppose that to judge that one (morally) ought to do something is to make such an inferential commitment. How does this view fare with the task of explaining motivational success and motivational failure? To begin with the success, on the inferentialist picture to think that one ought to φ is to think both that one is entitled to form a practical commitment to φ and that one is not entitled not to form a practical commitment to φ. Clearly, commitment to the correctness of this inference gives rise to the practical commitment in question insofar as the agent is a rational one, since an essential part of being rational is just being disposed to match one's psychology to one's entitlements. And once the practical commitment is adopted by the agent, the agent will act accordingly, again insofar as she is rational. Thus, motivational success in rational agents is easily explained and predicted by the inferentialist model.

What, then, of the various kinds of failure? To understand weakness of will, we must bear in mind the distinction between the two different kinds of practical commitments, future- and present-directed ones. It seems natural to understand weakness of will as the failure of present-directed practical commitments to match the future-directed ones, or failure to maintain a future-directed commitment in the face of a contrary desire. In either case, the result is that one fails to do what one has set out to do. In paradigmatic cases, the explanation for the failure is that a causally stronger desire disrupts the rational causal mechanism that standardly translates practical commitments to actions. Volitional incapacity and the like, in turn, are on this model failures to respond to inferential commitments by adopting the corresponding (future-directed) practical commitment while acknowledging the doxastic commitments that serve as the antecedent.[33] Rationally speaking, this is the same sort of failure as believing that p, endorsing the inferential commitment expressed by "p implies q," and not believing that q. It can have various kinds of explanations—in Michelle's case a deep psychological disorder, in Charles Doyle's case his "weak and unmanly" character.[34]

The inferentialist story that I have sketched has some obvious affinities with both Smith's and Gibbard's views. I hope its advantages in naturally accommodating various motivational failures while making intelligible the rationality of the transitions are clear at this point. Still, a few words may be in order to distinguish it from the expressivist model. On the inferentialist picture, to make an ought-judgment is in effect to locate oneself in the space of reasons, understood as a space of inferentially articulated commitments and entitlements. These commitments and entitlements, in turn, are understood in terms of deontic attitudes. Does this undermine the claim that the account is a *cognitivist* one? Not so, for the deontic metalanguage applies across the board. Surely we can *believe* that cows are not horses, even if the content of that belief is understood in terms of commitments and entitlements,[35] and those in terms of deontic attitudes. Cognitivism is thus compatible with construing ought-judgments as inferential commitments. What is essential is that they are not understood as practical commitments, as expressivists would have it. Moreover, there is nothing to prevent inferential commitments from being *true*—just as it can be true that if p, then q—nor having the sort of phenomenology that is commonly associated with moral convictions. No doubt further argument is needed, but we have at least a prima facie case for the inferentialist account being a form of cognitivism.

In short, it seems that an inferentialist account of the content of moral beliefs provides a basis for a rationalist, weak internalist cognitivism that leaves room for the different kinds of motivational failure while also making it intelligible why motivational success can be expected from rational agents, since it shows how ought-judgments can be rationally binding. Given that the modal separability of moral judgment and planning states is a fatal problem for expressivism, this version of internalism deserves serious consideration.

Acknowledgments

I have greatly benefited from comments by Sven Nyholm, Lilian O'Brien, Geoffrey Sayre-McCord, James Skidmore, and Jussi Suikkanen.

Notes

1. The term 'internalism' is used for a wide variety of views in metaethics, more than can be covered in a note; I will use it only for moral judgment internalism, as defined in the text.

2. I omit an important intermediate step here, namely, the move from thinking that something is morally obligatory in my situation to thinking that I ought to do it, or conversely from thinking that something is morally wrong to thinking that I ought not do it. I return to this briefly in the final section.

3. Smith 1994, 1997. For a defense of Smith against critics, see Toppinen 2004.

4. For this kind of argument, see Blackburn 1998 and Lenman 1999.

5. This challenge, in effect, is what Michael Smith calls "the moral problem" (Smith 1994).

6. It should be noted that we talk about "judgment" in two different though related senses: judgment as a linguistic expression (an utterance like "Cheating on one's girlfriend is morally wrong") and judgment as a psychological state (the thought that cheating on one's girlfriend is morally wrong). On the standard picture, sincere moral judgments in the former sense conventionally express moral judgments in the latter, constitutive sense. It this constitutive sense of judgment that we are concerned with; it would be a category mistake to say that an utterance is inherently motivating.

7. For a well-known attempt to cash out the notion of direction of fit, see Smith 1987. For persuasive criticism, see Tenenbaum 2006. I will not press the point here.

8. Another cautionary note: though I follow here the convention of speaking loosely about valuing and ought-judgments in the same breath, they are prima facie distinct precisely in terms of their motivational consequences. Moral judgments fall into two basic kinds, evaluative ("Helping the poor is good") and deontic ("I ought to help the poor" or "Not helping the poor is wrong"). Though the relationship between the two is a matter of dispute—it is one of the things at issue in the buck-passing debate, for example—we can say that prima facie, (first-personal) deontic judgments have a more direct relation to motivation and action. They are *verdictive* in nature, amounting to an all-things-considered take on the (moral) reasons present in the situation, whereas value judgments are of a *contributory* nature—they are judgments about which features of the situation weigh in which direction. Although it is debatable whether merely thinking that something would be good necessarily involves motivation (can I not see *some* good in quitting philosophy without having the slightest desire to do so?), it seems that moral verdicts do push toward an action—at least in the sense that if they do not result in corresponding behavior, it makes sense to speak of a motivational *failure*.

9. Hyperstates are idealized states in which one has decided what to do with regard to every possible factual circumstance (Gibbard 2003, 53–59).

10. See Gibbard 1990. In a similar spirit, Michael Bratman argues for understanding the self in terms of a special kind of plans, "self-governing policies," in various papers in Bratman 2007.

11. Indeed, Gibbard's explanation of the bully case is somewhat bizarre from this perspective: if my fear or desire to please leads me to submit against my decision to stand up for myself, it is surely not true that there is a part of me that thinks I *ought* to submit. To be sure, Gibbard does not exactly say this, but only that "there's a part of you that doesn't really think you ought to" (Gibbard 2003, 153). Still, why bring up oughts and plans when the part of me that leads me to submit is neither involved with nor responsive to ought-thoughts and plans?

12. Defining functional roles in terms of statistical normality seems too weak; in the case of the depressive, it may be that it is *normal* for her planning states to fail

to lead to action. In the spirit of Gibbard's earlier work (Gibbard 1990), one might appeal to the reason why the capacity to form planning states was selected for in the course of evolution, which is plausibly intelligent action in pursuit of long-term goals. In this sense, it is "normal" that plans lead to action. But this alone does not suffice for explaining why failures of motivation are *normatively* criticizable—why it is a kind of failure on the *agent's* part not to follow through on plans, something for which *she* is responsible.

13. For the notion of proximal intention, see Mele 1992.

14. For another view according to which weakness of the will is a matter of giving up one's intentions rather than acting against one's best judgment, see Richard Holton 1999.

15. Perhaps I have decided to treat myself to a doughnut, but the very sight of a Dunkin' Donuts sign arouses in me a desire that takes over control of my steps, rendering my original plan irrelevant.

16. If Gilbert Harman (1975) is correct in claiming that intention involves the belief that one will act as one intends (or at least the absence of the belief that one won't), the reason why Incapacitated Michelle fails to intend to leave may be that she believes she won't anyway.

17. Watson 2004a, 95. Watson talks, in fact, about "judgments or prior intentions," but this is misleading in my context.

18. See Watson 2004b, 134–135. Here "deciding what is better" is a *cognitive* decision, as explained below.

19. Wallace 2000, 10–12. I don't agree with the conclusions that Wallace draws from this phenomenon.

20. For this terminology, see Mele 2003, ch. 9.

21. I may owe this analogy to Lilian O'Brien's unpublished work on intention.

22. On this simplified picture, means–end deliberation is part of the process of forming the ought-belief. Some actions may be best represented as resulting from a process where the belief that one ought to φ combines with the means–end belief that x-ing is the best (or sufficient) means to φ-ing to lead to an intention to x. Smith (2005) takes this to be the standard case (and misleadingly talks about desire for an end rather than intention; see the next note).

23. There's a conspicuous absence from this story: desire as an independent psychological state is nowhere mentioned in the success story. This is no accident. Once we have intentions in the picture, we have no need for desires; indeed, it is hard to see where they would fit in. However we understand desire, it is what we might call a *partial* pro-attitude or stance toward its object, in contrast to intention, which is an all-things-considered attitude that is able to play a central role in

the coordination of action. They are conduct-*controlling*, not merely conduct-influencing attitudes, as desires are (Bratman 1987, 15–16). Intentions do all the work that desires were supposed to do on the Humean picture, and they do it better, since they make irrationality intelligible in virtue of the commitments they embody. To be sure, there is still room for consequential attribution of desire: whenever A φs intentionally, we can attribute to A a desire to φ, as Nagel famously argued (Nagel 1970, 29). But this is to say nothing of the etiology of the action.

24. For critical discussion of Smith, see Sayre-McCord 1997; Arpaly 2003, ch. 2; and Dancy 2004, ch. 6.

25. As the latter case shows, the sanctions involved need not be external to the practice in question. This point is of fundamental importance for Brandom, since it makes possible understanding conceptual practice as "normative all the way down."

26. So, for Brandom, the inference (Matilda is a cow → Matilda is an animal) is not enthymematic; it does not need the conditional as a premise in order to be valid. See Brandom 2000, ch. 1.

27. See not only Brandom 1994, but also Peacocke 1992 and Wedgwood 2001.

28. By emphasizing the commitment and negative sanctions involved, I depart from Brandom, who defines what he calls an "institutional ought" solely in terms of entitlement: "Taking it that there is such a norm or requirement [in Brandom's example, the bank employees wear neckties] just is endorsing a patter of practical reasoning—namely taking [the inference from going to work in a bank to putting on a necktie] to be an entitlement-preserving inference for anyone who is a bank employee" (Brandom 1994, 250–251). But bank employees are not just *allowed* to wear neckties, but precisely *required* to do so, and talk of entitlement does not capture that essential aspect. More on this below.

29. The relevant doxastic commitments must be picked out demonstratively, as it were, since the thought I ought to rush to the fire station does not as such involve any particular grounds for rushing there. If my house is on fire, the reason why I ought to rush to the fire station may be that I need help putting out the fire. The relevant doxastic commitment, the entitlement to which I take to entitle anyone to rush to the fire station, turns out in this case to be the belief that one's house is on fire.

30. For this sort of view, see also Broome 2004; Wedgwood 2006.

31. This resembles so-called buck-passing theories of value, such as Thomas Scanlon's (1998) view. According to buck-passers, for something to be good is just for it to have nonevaluative properties that give reasons to adopt positive or negative attitudes toward it. For criticism and defense, see, e.g., Väyrynen 2006; Suikkanen 2005.

32. This is obviously a *very* simplistic story about moral emotions, but I lack the space for a proper discussion here. One thing to note is that the inferential commitment to accept blame does not entail that one *will*, in fact, accept it—as it is with commitments in general, it is always possible to fail to act accordingly. Thus you may very well get upset when someone criticizes you for something you yourself acknowledge you should have done.

33. Here my story departs significantly from Brandom, who describes weakness of the will in much the same terms as I discuss volitional incapacity (Brandom 1994, 267–271). This is at least in part because he takes conative, not just normative, vocabulary to express inferential commitments; I disagree, but cannot pursue this here.

34. The nature of the explanation has major implications for whether volitional incapacity excuses from responsibility. We would be far more likely to blame Charles Doyle than Michelle, and perhaps blame him more than the "manly" alcoholic who would at least put up a fight and only then succumb to temptation.

35. Namely, that commitment to something's being a cow precludes entitlement to the commitment that it is a horse.

References

Arpaly, N. 2003. *Unprincipled Virtue*. Oxford: Oxford University Press.

Barnes, J. 2006. *Arthur & George*. London: Jonathan Cape.

Blackburn, S. 1998. *Ruling Passions: A Theory of Practical Reasoning*. Oxford: Clarendon Press.

Brandom, R. 1994. *Making It Explicit*. Cambridge, MA: Harvard University Press.

Brandom, R. 2000. *Articulating Reasons*. Cambridge, MA: Harvard University Press.

Bratman, M. 1987. *Intentions, Plans, and Practical Reason*. Cambridge, MA: Harvard University Press.

Bratman, M. 2007. *Structures of Agency*. Oxford: Oxford University Press.

Broome, J. 2004. Reasons. In *Reason and Value*, ed. J. Wallace, M. Smith, S. Scheffler, and P. Pettit. Oxford: Oxford University Press.

Dancy, J. 2004. *Ethics without Principles*. Oxford: Oxford University Press.

Gibbard, A. 1990. *Wise Choices, Apt Feelings*. Cambridge, MA: Harvard University Press.

Gibbard, A. 2003. *Thinking How to Live*. Cambridge, MA: Harvard University Press.

Harman, G. 1975. Practical Reasoning. In *The Philosophy of Action*, ed. A. Mele. Oxford: Oxford University Press.

Hobbes, T. 1651/1994. *Leviathan*. Ed. E. Curley. Indianapolis: Hackett.

Holton, R. 1999. Intention and Weakness of Will. *Journal of Philosophy* 96: 241–262.

Lenman, J. 1999. The Externalist and the Amoralist. *Philosophia* 27:441–457.

Mele, A. 1992. *Springs of Action*. Oxford: Oxford University Press.

Mele, A. 2003. *Motivation and Agency*. Oxford: Oxford University Press.

Nagel, T. 1970. *The Possibility of Altruism*. Oxford: Oxford University Press.

Peacocke, C. 1992. *A Theory of Concepts*. Cambridge, MA: MIT Press.

Sayre-McCord, G. 1997. Michael Smith's *The Moral Problem*. *Ethics* 108:77–82.

Scanlon, T. 1998. *What We Owe to Each Other*. Cambridge, MA: Harvard University Press.

Smith, M. 1987. The Humean Theory of Motivation. *Mind* 96:36–61.

Smith, M. 1994. *The Moral Problem*. Oxford: Blackwell.

Smith, M. 1997. In Defense of *The Moral Problem*. *Ethics* 108:84–119.

Smith, M. 2005. The Structure of Orthonomy. In *Agency and Action*, ed. J. Hyman and H. Steward. Cambridge: Cambridge University Press.

Suikkanen, J. 2005. Reasons and Value—In Defence of the Buck-Passing Account. *Ethical Theory and Moral Practice* 7:513–535.

Stocker, M. 1979. Desiring the Bad. *Journal of Philosophy* 76:738–753.

Tenenbaum, S. 2006. Direction of Fit and Motivational Cognitivism. *Oxford Studies in Metaethics* 1:235–264.

Toppinen, T. 2004. Moral Fetishism Revisited. *Proceedings of the Aristotelian Society* 104:305–313.

Väyrynen, P. 2006. Resisting the Buck-Passing Account of Value. *Oxford Studies in Metaethics* 1:295–324.

Wallace, R. J. 2000. Normativity, Commitment, and Instrumental Reason. *Philosophers' Imprint* 1. http://www.philosophersimprint.org/.

Watson, G. 2004a. Volitional Necessities. In *Agency and Answerability*. Oxford: Oxford University Press.

Watson, G. 2004b. The Work of the Will. In *Agency and Answerability*. Oxford: Oxford University Press.

Wedgwood, R. 2001. Conceptual Role Semantics for Moral Terms. *Philosophical Review* 110:1–30.

Wedgwood, R. 2006. The Meaning of 'Ought'. *Oxford Studies in Metaethics* 1:127–160.

14 "So Sick He Deserves It": Desert, Dangerousness, and Character in the Context of Capital Sentencing

Robert F. Schopp

1 Introduction

Discussions of criminal responsibility sometimes frame the inquiry as one regarding the most defensible standard for categorizing an offender as either bad or mad (Morse 2003, 165; Resnek 1997, 1–2; Schopp 2003, 324). Although the insanity defense calls for a dichotomous categorization of offenders as either bad (criminally responsible) or mad (not guilty due to insanity), some capital sentencing statutes include as a mitigating factor psychological disorder that is not sufficient to preclude criminal responsibility but renders the offender less culpable than unimpaired offenders who commit similar crimes (Model Penal Code §210.6[4][g] [1962]; 18 United States Code §3592 [a][1] [2000]; Wyoming Statutes Annotated §6-2-102 [j][ii], [vi] [2003]). These provisions recognize that psychopathology can vary in type and degree, and thus, that serious but relatively less severe disorder can reduce the culpability of some offenders without precluding criminal responsibility.

An offender was recently executed for the vicious murders of two children in circumstances that suggested extremely depraved and perhaps paraphilic motivation (*State v. Joubert* 1986, 241–243, 251–252).[1] One common attitude in the public discussion approaching the execution was captured by the characterization of the offender as "so sick he deserves it." Taken on its face, this statement apparently represented the view that the offender manifested psychopathology but that this disorder was of a type that exacerbated rather than mitigated culpability.

Can we articulate any clear interpretation of the claim that an offender is "so sick he deserves it"? That is, can we identify any circumstances in which psychopathology can legitimately serve as an aggravating factor that increases the level of punishment deserved? If we can articulate such an interpretation, can we reconcile that interpretation with the Supreme

Court opinions that apparently require sentencing in proportion to culpability and with the opinions that accept dangerousness as an independent sentencing consideration supporting increased severity of punishment? That is, can sentences predicated partially upon judgments of dangerousness, and particularly upon dangerousness associated with psychopathology, conform to a requirement that sentences are proportionate to culpability or desert? If we can articulate and reconcile such an interpretation, does that interpretation reflect any defensible justification of criminal punishment?

This essay represents an initial attempt to address these questions. Section 2 provides a brief explication of some relevant Supreme Court opinions and of an apparent tension raised by those opinions. Section 3 examines the relevant conception of "sick," and interprets the claim that offenders can deserve punishment or more severe punishment because they are sick in this sense. Section 4 interprets the Supreme Court opinions discussed in section 2 and the interpretations discussed in section 3 as consistent with a form of character retributivism. Section 5 defends character retributivism against one form of criticism to support the contention that character retributivism is at least plausibly defensible, and section 6 concludes the analysis.

2 Central Court Opinions

Supreme Court opinions addressing capital punishment interpret the Eighth Amendment as prohibiting the gratuitous infliction of pain, and thus, as requiring that punishment serve some legitimate penal purpose (*Roper v. Simmons* 2005, 1196; *Atkins v. Virginia* 2002, 318–320; *Gregg v. Georgia* 1976, 183–186). Early opinions identify retribution, deterrence, and incapacitation as legitimate purposes, although some later opinions emphasize retribution and deterrence, raising some questions regarding the sufficiency of incapacitation as a justification for capital punishment (*Atkins v. Virginia* 2002, 350 [Scalia, J., dissenting]; *Ring v. Arizona* 2002, 613–619 [Breyer, J., concurring]; *Gregg v. Georgia* 1976, 83n29). These opinions apparently preclude only punishment that serves no legitimate purpose and accept punishment that serves any legitimate purpose. Other opinions apparently require punishment in proportion to culpability or moral blameworthiness, however, although it is not clear whether these opinions are most accurately understood as requiring punishment in proportion to culpability (positive retribution) or as limiting punishment to the severity defined by culpability but allowing less severe punishment (negative retribution) (*Penry v. Lynaugh* 1989, 319; *California v. Brown* 1987, 545 [O'Connor, J., concurring]; Audi 1999, 759 [positive and negative retributivism]).

Insofar as these cases require sentence severity as defined by positive or negative retributivism, they appear to conflict with the sentencing provisions that accept dangerousness as a sentencing criterion or factor that can render an offender eligible for a more severe punishment than that for which he would be eligible if he were not dangerous (Idaho Code §19-2515[3][b], [9][h] [2004]; Oklahoma Statutes Annotated tit. 21 §§701.11, 701.12[7] [2002]; Oregon Revised Statutes §163.150[1][b][B], [2][a] [2003]; Texas Criminal Procedure Code Annotated Art. 37-071 §2[g[[2004–05]; Wyoming Statutes Annotated §6-2-102[e], [h] [xi] [2003]). By limiting severity of punishment to that which is proportionate to culpability or desert, these opinions apparently allow determinations of dangerousness to increase the severity of punishment only if the considerations that support the determinations of dangerousness also support judgments of increased culpability. Upon initial reflection, dangerousness due to characteristics ordinarily classified as forms of psychopathology does not seem to support a judgment of increased culpability. Thus, it is difficult to reconcile these two sets of opinions with each other or with the judgment captured by the contention that an offender was "so sick he deserves it."

3 "So Sick He Deserves It"

3.1 Disorder and Desert

Although one might ordinarily think of psychological impairment as a condition that precludes or reduces culpability, the contention that the offender was "so sick he deserves it" suggests that the speaker believed that the offender's psychopathology exacerbated his culpability. This assertion occurred in the context of informal discussion among ordinary people commenting on an event regarding which they had no specific role or expertise. Thus, one should be cautious about interpreting it as if it purported to represent a technical judgment of legal culpability or of psychological functioning. The purpose of the current analysis is not to speculate about what individuals involved in such discussions had in mind. Rather, this analysis reflects on the phrase in order to consider whether it might provide some insight into relevant judgments that some ordinary people might make.

They could have used more familiar terms of condemnation such as "wicked" or "evil," however, or less formal terms such as "rotten" or "worthless." Assume for the purpose of this analysis that the selection of the term "sick" reflects some intuitive judgment that this term approximates. Ordinarily, persons are considered sick when they are "affected by illness; unwell, ailing . . . of a part of the body: not in a healthy state" (*The New Shorter Oxford English Dictionary* 1993, vol. II, 2851; hereafter *NSOED* II 1993). As applied to psychological functioning, the term suggests mental illness or disorder (*NSOED* II 1993, 2851). The core meaning of the term involves physical or psychological dysfunction. The case that elicited these statements provided no suggestion of physical illness and no indication that such illness if present would be relevant to the criminal sentence.

As previously discussed, mental illness in the context of criminal responsibility is ordinarily interpreted as exculpatory or mitigating in that it can preclude or reduce the offender's culpability for the offense. Thus, it is not obvious in what sense the perception of an offender as sick would support a judgment of increased desert. Alternately, perhaps the term was intended to refer not to physical or mental illness but to sickness of the soul as "[s] piritually or morally unsound; corrupt" (*NSOED* II 1993, 2851). Perhaps the speakers were suggesting that the offender was corrupt as "[d]praved; inflicted with evil" (*NSOED* I 1993, 518).

Are the interpretations of "sick" as disordered and as depraved mutually exclusive? Suppose, for example, that Smith commits a major property crime for the purpose of eliciting a large profit. He breaks into a house in order to steal a very valuable piece of art for which there is a highly profitable illicit market. He planned to break into the house when the occupants were away, steal the artwork, and set a fire that would conceal his crime by giving the appearance of an accidental fire that destroyed the house, including the stolen piece of art. Perhaps most people would say that Smith is greedy, evil, or wicked, rather than sick. Suppose that while setting the fire, Smith realized that the house was not empty. Two children were asleep in one of the bedrooms. Having already secured the work of art, he decided that he could not risk changing the plan at this point, so he set the fire. He realized that the children would probably be killed, and that he might even regret it, but he was more concerned with protecting his profit and freedom than with avoiding harm to the children.

Perhaps most citizens would describe Smith as selfish, callous, wicked, evil, or some other description reflecting condemnation as extremely culpable due to his willingness to inflict severe harm on children in order to protect his interests. There appears to be an important difference between Smith and the previously discussed child murderer, however, in that Smith's crime was not motivated by a desire to inflict pain or to kill or harm the children. In contrast to the child murderer, Smith was motivated by an ordinary desire for profit. His crime was very serious, but it was not the product of desire or paraphilic sexual arousal that would ordinarily be considered disordered. His culpability reflects his willingness to inflict harm in order to satisfy his ordinary desires, but it does not reveal distorted or pathological desires or arousal.

Arguably, Smith was very culpable rather than sick because in contrast to the child murderer, his crime did not reveal distortion of desire or arousal. Compare Jones, who commits no crime but engages in prolonged fantasies involving sadistic sexual activity with children. This activity was discovered only because an accidental fire occurred in his apartment complex, and firefighters inadvertently discovered his diaries that detail these fantasies. In contrast to Smith, who many might characterize as culpable rather than as sick, Jones might be characterized as sick, although he is culpable of no crime. The child murderer was characterized as sick as well as extremely culpable because the severely harmful crime for which he was fully culpable was motivated by distorted forms of desire and arousal.

According to this interpretation, an offender is sick in this sense insofar as his crimes reveal pathological desires or patterns of arousal that motivate those crimes. These desires or patterns of arousal represent psychological defects in the person that motivate certain types of crimes. These distortions of character are more general than this specific crime. In contrast to Smith, the offender who is sick in this sense is not merely willing to inflict suffering in order to complete his crime. Rather, he is motivated to commit the crime at least partially by pathological desires or arousal. His crime reveals culpable willingness to harm others in order to satisfy his wants, and it reveals pathological wants.

3.2 "So Sick He Deserves It"

The suggestion that an offender deserves more severe punishment because he is sick in this sense reflects the premise that appropriate severity of punishment can depend at least partially on the general characteristics or dispositions of the person, rather than entirely on his culpability for this particular crime as defined by legally recognized culpability elements such as purpose, knowledge, recklessness, or other mental states specified as offense elements (Model Penal Code §2.02 [1962]; *Black's Law Dictionary* 2004, 1219). Statutes that identify dangerousness as a sentencing criterion or factor apparently adopt a similar premise in that they recognize a general property of the person as a legitimate basis for increasing the severity of the punishment. Culpability and dangerousness might converge in any particular case in that the considerations that render an individual highly culpable for the instant offense might also be interpreted as evidence that he presents a high risk of committing further offenses. At least some of these provisions do not require this convergence, however, because they identify dangerousness as a criterion or factor for severe sentencing in terms that do not require a corresponding elevation in culpability.

Can any interpretation of the Court's opinions discussed in section 2 render those that require punishment in proportion to culpability, or that limit punishment to a degree no greater than proportionate to culpability, consistent with the sentencing provisions and Court opinions that accept dangerousness as a criterion or as a factor that supports more severe sentences? If one can provide such an interpretation, can that interpretation accommodate the judgment that an offender is sick in the sense discussed previously as a legitimate basis for increasing the severity of sentences?

3.3   Sick or Dangerous as Defects of Character

If one understands a person's moral character as that person's comprehensive set of dispositions to manifest attitudes, emotions, and behavior that are relevant to the assessment of the person as a moral agent, then the distortions of desire or arousal previously identified as those likely to be informally characterized as "sick" constitute defects of character (Audi 1997, 159–160; Audi 1999, 130; *NSOED* I 1993, 373). Although some traits or dispositions that render one dangerous constitute elements of moral character, others fall outside this category. One who is dangerous because he is prone to violence due to vicious, selfish, or callous dispositions, for example, would reasonably be considered dangerous due to defect of moral character. Such traits qualify as defects of moral character in that they are dispositions to engage in wrongful conduct for which the actor remains fully responsible because these dispositions do not involve impairment of the capacities of responsible agency.

Other individuals qualify as dangerous due to characteristics that do not constitute defects of moral character. Those who present elevated risk of harm to others due to mental retardation, persecutory delusions, or vulnerability to unanticipated seizures, for example, might qualify as dangerous in ordinary discourse or for specified legal purposes in that they represent an elevated risk of injury to others. The traits that generate this elevated risk would not ordinarily be considered defects of moral character, however, because they are not susceptible to direction or modification through the exercise of the capacities of responsible agency (Schopp 2001, 144–148). The criminal law accommodates such impairment through exculpatory defenses such as insanity or failure of proof defenses regarding culpability elements or voluntary act requirements (Robinson 1984, §§22, 173).

Some individuals might remain responsible for generating risk to others, although they would not be immediately responsible for the behavior that directly causes harm. One who operates a motor vehicle despite awareness of vulnerability to seizures and injures or kills others when a seizure causes him to lose control of the vehicle would not possess the capacities of legal or moral responsibility at the time he harmed others as a result of the seizure. He would have been responsible for creating the risk to others, however, because he began operating the vehicle despite awareness of his vulnerability. His vulnerability to seizures would not constitute a defect of character, but his willingness to subject others to the risk of harm generated by that vulnerability would constitute a defect of character in ordinary circumstances. He would remain criminally responsible for harm caused by his conscious disregard of that risk (*People v. Decina* 1956).

Some dispositions might preclude or reduce the individual's capacity to responsibly direct his conduct through the exercise of responsible agency without precluding or reducing attributions of responsibility for the resulting harm because the individual remains responsible for having developed those dispositions. Some evidence indicates that capital sentencing jurors do not attribute mitigating force to impairment caused by substance abuse (Garvey 1998, 1555–1565). Common legal standards allocate only limited exculpatory or mitigating significance to intoxication, but this limited effect is somewhat more available for involuntary intoxication and almost entirely unavailable for voluntary intoxication (Dressler 2001, §§24.02–24.06; LaFave 2003, §9.5). This evidence and these standards are consistent with the interpretation that an individual is ordinarily held accountable for risk or harm caused by impaired capacities to the extent that he is responsible for generating that impairment with notice that the impairment exacerbates risk.

Suppose, for example, that one individual has a history of impulsive hyperactivity since childhood. He is prone to disproportionate anger and impulsive aggression in response to insult or frustration, and there is evidence that this lifelong pattern may be associated with neurological dysfunction that limits his ability for reasoned reflection but does not render him unable to meet the requirements of criminal responsibility (American Psychiatric Association 2003, 85–93, 663–667). A second individual is prone to similar patterns of responsiveness due to ongoing abuse of methamphetamine. Both engage in armed robberies during which they kill their victims, and neither experiences impairment that precludes criminal responsibility. Reasonable sentencers might conclude that both are guilty of homicide and that their tendencies toward anger and aggression render them likely to reoffend. Those reasonable sentencers might also conclude, however, that the second offender presents risk due to defects of character that he is fully responsible for generating whereas the first offender presents similar risk due to dispositions that he is less responsible for generating. Those sentencers might reasonably conclude that the risk presented by the second offender justifies a more severe sentence enhancement than the comparable risk generated by the first offender.

This analysis suggests that for the purposes of criminal sentencing: (1) individuals are accountable for risk to others that they generate through defects of character when they manifest those dispositions through culpable criminal conduct; and (2) that risk justifies enhanced criminal sentences to the extent that: (A) the individuals retain unimpaired capacities of criminal responsibility, or (B) they are responsible for developing those dispositions.

3.4   Responsibility for Developing One's Character

This analysis suggests that the appropriate punishment for an offender depends partially on his responsibility for the crime and partially on his responsibility for his dispositions that contributed to his committing the crime. According to one traditional account, individuals are responsible for their characters because they shape their characters by engaging in conduct that promotes habits or dispositions to engage in conduct of certain types. Individuals develop virtuous or vile characters by engaging in patterns of behavior that promote virtuous or vile habits and that promote the tendency to derive pleasure from behavior of that type. By engaging in conduct of the right type for the right reasons, individuals develop virtuous characters, including the disposition to engage in such conduct and to experience satisfaction from engaging in such conduct. Thus, an individual is responsible for his character because he develops that character by engaging in a pattern of conduct that manifests and promotes certain feelings, desires, and dispositions. That individual might not be able to immediately alter his character simply by deciding to do so, but he remains responsible for his character, the actions that contributed to that character, and further actions manifesting that character insofar as he developed that character by engaging in a series of decisions and actions(Aristotle 1985, 33–35 [1103a15–1103b25], 44–53 [1107a–1109a25], 66–68 [1113b5–1114a30]).

Some dispositions of character begin early in life, however, raising questions regarding an individual's responsibility for dispositions produced by patterns of experience and conduct that began before that individual was old enough to understand the significance and likely consequences of such conduct. Some evidence suggests, for example, that the juxtaposition of trauma or abuse with sexual arousal in childhood may promote violent fantasies, the association of violence and sexual arousal, and the propensity to engage in violence toward animals or humans (Johnson and Becker 1997, 336–341; Laws and Marshall 1990, 220–221; MacCulloch, Gray, and Watt 2000, 412–414). An extended pattern of such experiences and fantasies, in combination with masturbation, has been identified as a process through which some individuals develop paraphilic dispositions that generate a progression of "tryouts" of conduct reflecting those dispositions. These "tryouts" consist of behavior related to the fantasies that gradually approximates more closely the sexual violence of the fantasies. For some individuals, this pattern of fantasy and related behavior culminates in sexually motivated crimes of violence (Gray et al. 2003, 1025–1028); Johnson and Becker 1997, 343–344; Laws and Marshall 1990, 215–223; MacCulloch, Gray, and Watt 2000, 405–409; MacCulloch et al. 1983, 23–27; Prentky et al. 1989, 890).

If individuals develop their dispositions by engaging in reciprocal patterns of fantasy and behavior that begin at an early age before those individuals can understand the significance of those patterns and the risks they generate, can they justly be held responsible for developing these dispositions of character or for acting on them? Even if one limits the inquiry to dispositions that do not undermine the capacities required for legal or moral responsibility, and thus addresses only conduct for which the individual remains responsible, can those individuals justly be held responsible for their dispositions of character in a manner that justifies considering those dispositions as aggravating factors for the purpose of criminal sentencing?

Consider an offender who commits a sexually motivated murder as a culmination of an extended pattern of anger, fantasy, masturbation, and tryouts that began in childhood before he possessed the capacities of criminal or moral responsibility and before he could reasonably be expected to foresee the consequences of engaging in that pattern of fantasy and behavior. Assume that this pattern began in response to the experience of sexual or physical abuse in childhood (Johnson and Becker 1997, 343–344; Laws and Marshall 1990, 210–222; MacCulloch, Gray, and Watt 2000, 405–414; MacCulloch et al. 1983, 20–27). Assume further that this offender cannot reasonably be held responsible for the early experience that initiated this pattern or for the early reactions of anger and arousal in response to this experience.

Responsibility for character is both generative and retentional in that one can be responsible for engaging in conduct that initially generates such dispositions or for continuing to engage in an extended pattern of conduct that retains and exacerbates those dispositions. Individuals can be responsible for acting on and promoting dispositions, even if they were not responsible for the early experience and conduct that initially generated those dispositions (Audi 1997, 159–164).

Those who initially develop paraphilic dispositions in response to early experience of abuse might initially generate those dispositions at an age and in circumstances that do not support attributions of generative responsibility. Maintaining and exacerbating those dispositions may involve extended patterns of fantasy, masturbation, and tryouts that gradually increase in intensity and in approximation to the criminal conduct (Johnson and Becker 1997, 343–344; Laws and Marshall 1990, 215–223; MacCulloch, Gray, and Watt 2000, 405–414; MacCulloch et al. 1983, 20–27; Prentky et al. 1989, 890). As these individuals develop the capacities of responsible agency, and their patterns of conduct more closely approximate violence or exploitation, they provide themselves with increasingly explicit notice that they are developing propensities to engage in criminal conduct. As this combination of developing capacities and increasingly explicit notice progresses, they become increasingly responsible for continuing along a pattern of conduct that more closely approximates criminal violence and more clearly reveals the trend toward violence.

Some individuals might avoid reflecting on this pattern, or they might persuade themselves that they will halt the progression prior to inflicting harm on others. One important component of responsible agency involves the capacity to reflect on one's desires, conduct, and principles and to ask whether one ought to continue indulging those desires, engaging in such conduct, and pursuing such a pattern of life. Responsibility for self includes responsibility for specific decisions and acts, but it also involves responsibility to reflect on the desires that one ought or ought not attempt to fulfill and the dispositions that one ought or ought not indulge and promote. Thus, the responsible agent is accountable for embracing the desires he acts on and for developing the dispositions that he engenders through his decisions. If he does not engage in evaluative self-reflection, he remains morally accountable for refusing to do so (Audi 1997, 164–170; Taylor 1976, 281).

When an individual commits a criminal offense, he subjects himself to public evaluation and punishment in a manner justified by his culpable criminal conduct and by the public interest in avoiding crime. The paraphilic criminal who promoted his tendency to commit such crimes in the manner described is responsible for his crime and for engaging in the pattern of fantasy, masturbation, and conduct that led to the crime. He is responsible either for recognizing but failing to address the escalating risk produced by his pattern of conduct or for refusing to reflect on, evaluate, and modify this pattern. Thus, he is sick in the sense that he experiences pathological patterns of arousal, and he is responsible for promoting the development of this pattern and for acting on it. This pathological pattern exacerbates, rather than ameliorates, his culpability insofar as he continued to promote this disposition after his age and experience provided him with notice of the risk he was creating and with the capacities needed to resist the development of that pattern.

Although such dispositions incline one to engage in such conduct, they do not undermine the capacities of responsible agency required to render one criminally responsible for acting on those dispositions (Schopp 2001, 144–148). Similarly, they do not preclude responsibility for continuing to engage in the noncriminal conduct that exacerbates the dispositions and the likelihood of criminal conduct. The abilities to reflect on one's desires, conduct, and principles and to ask whether this is the kind of life one should live and the kind of person one should be provides the basis for one's responsibility to take action to cease promoting dispositions that generate risk to others and to refrain from acting on them.

The paraphilic individual might not be able to eradicate the desires or intrusive fantasies, but he remains responsible to refrain from promoting those desires and fantasies and from acting on them. He remains responsible to avoid behavior and circumstances that increase the inclination to act on them. He might avoid, for example, alcohol or drugs that reduce his inhibition, potential victims such as children for pedophiles or vulnerable individuals for sadists, or circumstances in which he has opportunities to act on his paraphilic desires.

Insofar as an individual develops the capacities of criminal and moral responsibility yet continues to indulge and promote paraphilic dispositions, he can reasonably be held accountable for the pattern of decisions and conduct that exacerbates the risk he presents to others. An individual who endangers others by conduct performed in conscious disregard of a substantial and unjustified risk commits the criminal offense of reckless endangerment (Model Penal Code §211.2 [1962]). The individual who continues to promote his paraphilic tendencies but does not engage in any overt conduct that endangers others promotes increased risk to others in an analogous manner, although he is not subject to criminal punishment in the absence of some act or omission that fulfills the requirements of a criminal offense definition. If he then acts criminally on the dispositions he has recklessly promoted, he can reasonably be held liable to criminal punishment that expresses condemnation proportionate to his culpability for the crime and for the extended pattern of conduct through which he exacerbated the risk to others by embracing and developing those dispositions (Feinberg 1970, 95–118; Schopp 2001, 144–148).

The paraphilic criminal differs in a critical manner from the paraphilic individual who refrains from criminal conduct. The latter individual may experience paraphilic desires and the distress associated with those desires, and he may have promoted those desires and the resulting distress through a pattern of fantasy and behavior. He has not, however, inflicted those dispositions on others in the form of criminal conduct. Thus, he may qualify as sick in the sense that he experiences pathological patterns of arousal and resulting distress, but he does not engage in conduct that injects his psychological state into the public domain (see the Jones example in section 3.1 above).

4   Retributive Punishment and Dangerousness

4.1   Dangerousness
A determination that an individual is dangerous for a specific legal purpose requires an assessment of risk presented by the person in the circumstances and justificatory judgments of quantitative and qualitative sufficiency. Insofar as relevant information is available, the assessment of risk can include estimates of the probability, severity, and type of harm in the relevant circumstances. This assessment can include explanation regarding the manner in which the individual generates the risk and regarding the manner in which available risk management strategies might ameliorate that risk (Schopp 2006, 78–80; 2001, 216–229). The judgment of quantitative sufficiency involves the justificatory judgment that the probability and severity of harm is sufficient in quantity to justify the legal intervention or liability at issue. The judgment of qualitative sufficiency involves the justificatory judgment that the individual generates this risk in a manner

that justifies the specific legal intervention or liability at issue (Schopp 2006, 78–80). Civil commitment, for example, requires dangerousness that is associated with mental illness in the manner required by the applicable statute (Schopp 2006, 72–75).

Criminal punishment expresses condemnation of the crime as a wrong rather than a mere harm and of the criminal as a culpable wrongdoer (Feinberg 1970, 95–118; Schopp 2001, 144–148). Justified punishment must be proportionate to the crime and to the culpability of the wrongdoer at least in the sense that it expresses condemnation that is no more severe than that which is justified by the severity of the wrong and the culpability of the wrongdoer. Similarly, some of the Supreme Court opinions discussed in section 2 require that punishment is proportionate to culpability at least in the sense that culpability places a limit on the severity of punishment. Therefore, risk that qualifies as dangerousness for the purpose of justifying increased severity of punishment must be quantitatively and qualitatively sufficient to justify the increased condemnation expressed by that punishment. For the purpose of this analysis, I focus on qualitative sufficiency.

4.2 Dangerousness and Culpability

As previously noted, some evidence indicates that many people do not attribute mitigating force to impairment at the time of the offense if that impairment was the product of intoxication. Consider, for example, four individuals who engage in criminal conduct under the influence of drugs that exacerbate the intensity of their emotional responses.

W ingests prescription medication. The medication unexpectedly induces a psychotic state involving intense fear associated with delusions that others he encounters are conspiring to kill him. When he is approached on the sidewalk by others walking in the opposite direction, he attacks them in delusional "self-defense."

X habitually abuses hallucinogenic drugs. He sometimes has "good trips" during which he hears friendly voices and experiences euphoric emotional states. On other occasions, he has "bad trips" during which he hears hostile, threatening voices and experiences persecutory delusions with extreme fear. During some of the latter episodes, he has attacked innocent parties in delusional "self-defense." X ingests the drug, has a "bad trip" and attacks an innocent person in delusional terror that this person is about to kill him.

Y routinely abuses methamphetamine and is aware that when he does so, he frequently becomes extremely angry and aggressive in response to minor frustrations. Y consumes methamphetamine along with a substantial amount of alcohol. When he runs out of money, he tells an acquaintance to loan him some money to buy more alcohol. The acquaintance refuses, and Y attacks him in extreme anger.

Z ingests a prescribed medication that he has not previously taken. The medication unexpectedly renders him subject to markedly exaggerated emotional responsiveness. The medication does not distort his capacities for comprehension and reasoning that are ordinarily associated with criminal responsibility, but it generates intense and labile emotional responses to frustration. Z becomes involved in an argument with another person over a parking space, and he attacks that person in a state of extreme anger.

As interpreted in section 3.3: (1) risk to others is qualitatively sufficient to constitute dangerousness for the purpose of criminal sentencing when it is associated with dispositions that the offender manifests through culpable criminal conduct; (2) dangerousness justifies enhanced criminal sentences to the extent that: (A) the offender retains unimpaired capacities of criminal responsibility; or (B) the offender is responsible for developing these dispositions. Reasonable people might absolve W of all responsibility for his offense because he lacked the capacities of criminal responsibility at the time of the offense (1). Had W retained minimal capacities of criminal responsibility at the time of the offense, the risk he presented would not justify increased punishment because the medication impaired those capacities to a substantial degree (2A), and W was not responsible for inducing that impairment (2B). Those reasonable people might conclude that X resembles W insofar as both lacked the capacities of criminal responsibility at the time of their attacks (1), but they might hold X at least partially responsible for inflicting harm because he knowingly induced the state of intoxication with awareness that doing so created a risk of inducing a state of severe impairment leading to aggression. Thus, by ingesting the hallucinogen that he knew promoted the risk that he would engage in violence, X injected his disposition to engage in violence into the public domain (1), and he culpably promoted this disposition that increased risk to others (2B).

Those reasonable people might hold Y fully responsible for his criminal attack because he retained unimpaired capacities of criminal responsibility at the time of the attack (1, 2A), and he is reasonably held responsible for inducing his state of vulnerability to extreme anger that elevated his inclination to engage in such behavior (2B). Finally, those reasonable people might hold Z responsible for his crime (1), but they might conclude that the unanticipated effects of the medication on his emotional state mitigated his culpability for the offense because it made it much more difficult for him to refrain from acting on his anger (2A), and he had no notice that he was inducing this state by taking the medication (2B).

In short, reasonable people might well assess responsibility for the attacks and for inducing the states that increased the risk of such attacks as two distinct bases for holding the offenders accountable. They would hold Y most culpable because he retained unimpaired capacities of criminal responsibility regarding the attack, and he was responsible for promoting the disposition to respond with extreme anger and aggression that increased the risk of attack. They would absolve W of responsibility because he lacked the capacities of criminal responsibility at the time of the attack, and he was not responsible for creating the condition that disposed him to commit such an attack. X and Z would be considered less culpable than Y but more culpable than W because each was responsible either at the time of the attack or for inducing the condition that increased the risk but not for both. The degree to which X is seen as less culpable than Y would depend partially on the degree to which his delusional reaction was foreseeable.

Although these cases involve substance-induced dispositions, the paraphilic child murderer discussed earlier arguably resembles Y insofar as he was criminally responsible for the crime, and he engaged in a pattern of fantasy, masturbation, and tryouts that promoted the dispositions that exacerbated the risk he presented to others and that provided him with notice that he was exacerbating that risk. Insofar as this pattern began at an early age or the offender suffered some impairment that limited his ability to recognize the risk he was promoting, he would resemble Z to the degree that he was less able to foresee the risk. These examples suggest that offenders are reasonably held responsible for the criminal conduct they perform with the capacities of criminal responsibility and for engaging in prior conduct that foreseeably promotes their dispositions to engage in such conduct.

5   Character Retributivism and Liberal Society

5.1   Punishment for Character
Sentencing partially upon the dispositions of a person's character raises the concern that it authorizes the state to extend beyond the range of legitimate state jurisdiction and intrude into the nonpublic domain of the individual's internal states and dispositions. Insofar as liberal principles of political morality define distinct public and nonpublic domains and limit

the state's authority to apply coercive force to the public domain as defined by the harm principle or some variation on this principle, it might seem that punishment based partially on character must intrude into the non-public domain (Murphy 1995, 79–84, 88–93). Suppose, for example, that one justifies the harm principle as protecting the individual's right to a nonpublic domain of individual sovereignty (Feinberg 1988, 3–8). Does a retributive theory of punishment that defines the severity of punishment at least partially by evaluation of the offender's moral character violate the boundary between the public and nonpublic domains?

Joel Feinberg describes the criminal justice system as a "great moral machine" that prohibits wrongs and subjects culpable wrongdoers to the condemnation inherent in criminal punishment (Feinberg 1988, 155). According to Feinberg's interpretation, liberal principles of political moral-ity do not prohibit the enforcement of morality. Rather, they limit the enforcement of morality through criminal punishment to those who culpably commit wrongs that violate the rights of others. Thus, the liberal state defines a range of grievance morality that falls within the public domain but protects a nonpublic domain of morality within which indi-viduals retain sovereignty to develop individual human lives and personal relationships. The harm principle, or some variation of that principle, defines the boundary between grievance morality and personal morality that remains beyond the public jurisdiction (ibid., 144–155). Those who defend this liberal boundary between the public and nonpublic domains might reasonably ask whether any substantial domain of individual sovereignty remains if an individual's inner character is subject to state evaluation for the purpose of criminal punishment.

5.2 Reconciling Liberal Political Morality and Character Retributivism

A liberal in the tradition of Feinberg would agree that an individual's character falls within the nonpublic domain and beyond the reach of state intrusion. When the actor engages in culpable criminal conduct, however, he forfeits a range of protected liberties, including, for example, the liberty from physical restraint by the state. By committing crimes, the offender injects those aspects of his character that generate harm or risk to others into the public domain.

The child murderer discussed previously, for example, injected his disposition toward violence into the public domain when he culpably committed the crimes that rendered these traits directly relevant to the public safety. In doing so, he rendered these dispositions subject to public evaluation and response, and he justified criminal punishment designed to protect the public from the risk created by those dispositions. The nature of the legitimate protective sanctions depends partially on the risk presented and on his culpability for generating that risk. Thus, the sentencer may legitimately consider his disposition to repeat such offenses and his responsibility for promoting that disposition with its resulting risk to others in setting the punishment at a level of severity that expresses condemnation reflecting the wrongful harm done and the risk culpably generated and imposed on others.

Contrast W who injects his mental states into the public domain by engaging in acts of violence for which he is not guilty by reason of insanity. Due to his severe psychopathology at the time of the offense, he is not eligible for the condemnation inherent in criminal punishment because he lacks culpability for the attack. Furthermore, he was not responsible for generating the conditions that led to the attack because he lacked notice that the medication might produce this effect. Thus, if the state is justified in exercising protective coercive force, it must do so through an institution that does not express condemnation. If he remains similarly impaired at the time of acquittal, he is appropriate for post-acquittal commitment, rather than criminal punishment, precisely because he lacks the psychological capacities that would render him eligible for the condemnation inherent in criminal punishment either for his harmful conduct or for the risk he imposes on others. Thus, both W and the child murderer render their psychological processes and character dispositions subject to public evaluation and response by injecting those processes and dispositions into the public domain through criminal conduct. They differ in that the child murderer's culpable offense and his conduct that promoted the disposition to commit such offenses justify public condemnation because he engaged in that conduct with the capacities of responsible agency and with notice of the harm or risk he was promoting. W's lack of culpability for his offense and for the behavior that generated the risk of such an offense justifies nonpunative protective intervention.

Recall the discussion in section 3.1 of Jones, who engaged in sadistic fantasies involving crimes similar to those committed by the child murderer and maintained diaries that document those fantasies. Those diaries were discovered by firefighters during a fire in his apartment complex. He is not subject to criminal punishment for his character defects involving sadistic fantasies because he has not injected his character into the public domain by engaging in criminal behavior.

In short, character retributivism of this type defines the severity of punishment partially by evaluating the dispositions to commit criminal offenses that the individual is responsible for developing and that the individual has injected into the public domain through criminal conduct. Character retributivism and the liberal harm principle share a common foundation in that both reflect respect for uniquely human capacities such as comprehension, reasoning, and self-reflection. The harm principle protects a domain of individual sovereignty within which the individual can exercise those capacities in order to define and pursue an individual human life. When that individual exercises those capacities in such a manner as to inject his character into the public domain through culpable criminal conduct, he renders himself subject to criminal punishment with its inherent expression of condemnation as the form of coercive behavior control appropriate to persons who possess those capacities (Feinberg 1988, 144–155; Schopp 2001, 144–148). The sentencer legitimately evaluates the offender's exercise of these capacities in performing criminal conduct and in promoting the dispositions to engage in such conduct.

Interpreted in this manner, responsibility for character is not opposed to or entirely distinct from responsibility for conduct or choice (Hurd and Moore 2004, 1129–1138; Moore 1997, 548–592).[2] Individuals are responsible for their characters insofar as they have developed their characters by making decisions and engaging in conduct that promotes dispositions of character. To the degree that they make these decisions and engage in this conduct with relevant information and the opportunity to apply the capacities of responsible agency, they are accountable for the dispositions of character they promote through these decisions and actions. When they manifest these dispositions by engaging in culpable criminal conduct, they inject their characters into the public jurisdiction. Thus, responsibility for character in the context of criminal sentencing is compatible with responsibility for decision and action insofar as the individual manifests that character in culpable criminal conduct and has developed that character by engaging in a series of decisions and actions for which he is accountable (Hurd and Moore 2004, 1130–1137).[3]

Offenders such as X and Y who knowingly abuse substances that incline them toward violence provide relatively clear cases of responsibility for engendering dispositions that endanger others. Those who engage in the pattern of fantasy, masturbation, and tryouts discussed in section 3.4 become responsible for promoting dispositions that endanger others when they continue to engage in that pattern after they have developed the capacities and experience that allow them to recognize the risk they promote. Other offenders may promote similar dispositions in circumstances that do not support attributions of responsibility or that do not provide sufficient information to allow such attributions. I argue only that retributive punishment in a liberal state can legitimately reflect responsibility for developing such dispositions insofar as such evidence is available.

6 Conclusion

An offender might qualify as "so sick he deserves it" if that offender manifests pathological dispositions that endanger others, that he is responsible for promoting, and that he injects into the public domain by manifesting them in culpable criminal conduct. Insofar as a criminal offender is sick in this sense, his pattern of behavior that promotes these dispositions and manifests them in culpable criminal conduct justifies punishment in proportion to his culpability for committing the offense and for cultivating the disposition to commit such offenses. This interpretation of character retributivism is consistent with liberal political morality as represented by the harm principle, or by some variation of that principle, because it limits state punishment for character to those dispositions that the individual injects into the public domain through conduct that harms or endangers others.

Finally, this interpretation of character retributivism suggests one coherent interpretation of several Supreme Court opinions addressing capital sentencing under the Eighth Amendment. Consider first the opinions discussed in section 2 that apparently require punishment in proportion to culpability and accept dangerousness as a factor that can render offenders eligible for more severe punishment than they would receive if they were not dangerous. If these opinions are interpreted as authorizing more severe punishment for offenders who present risk to others by virtue of character dispositions that they are responsible for developing and for injecting into the public domain through culpable criminal conduct, then increased severity of punishment on the basis of determinations of dangerousness reflects the offenders' culpability for engaging in patterns of conduct that endanger others and that they have rendered subject to public evaluation and condemnation. Furthermore, by addressing responsibility for developing character dispositions as relevant to criminal sentencing, this interpretation provides one plausible approach to integrating these opinions with another series of opinions that require that the sentencer consider relevant mitigating evidence regarding the character and record of the offender (*Eddings v. Oklahoma* 1982, 110–112; *Lockett v. Ohio* 1978, 601–605; *Woodson v. North Carolina* 1976, 303–304 [plurality opinion]).

Acknowledgments

I am grateful for helpful comments and discussion from the participants
in presentations at the Inland Northwest Philosophy Conference and a
faculty colloquium at the University of Nebraska College of Law. I am
particularly grateful to Mike Austin, Barbara Sturgis, and an anonymous
reviewer who commented on earlier drafts.

Notes

1. The events and testimony reveal homicidal conduct that was vicious and callous,
but it remains unclear whether it was sexually motivated. Thus, I refer to this
example only as the "child murderer."

2. Both sources contrast responsibility for character with responsibility for choice
or conduct.

3. These authors distinguish moral and legal culpability, and they recognize motive
as relevant to moral culpability but beyond the scope of legal culpability. If one
understands liberal principles of political morality as defining a boundary between
public and nonpublic domains of morality, however, legal culpability is moral
culpability according to standards that fall within the public jurisdiction. By engaging in culpable criminal conduct, an offender injects his character dispositions that
endanger others into the public domain.

References

American Psychiatric Association. 2003. *Diagnostic and Statistical Manual of Mental Disorders*, 4th ed. Washington, D.C.: American Psychiatric Association.

Aristotle. 1985. *Nicomachean Ethics*. Trans. T. Irwin. Indianapolis, IN: Hackett.

Atkins v. Virginia, 536 U.S. 304 (2002).

Audi, R. 1997. *Moral Knowledge and Ethical Character*. New York: Oxford University Press.

Audi, R., ed. 1999. *The Cambridge Dictionary of Philosophy*, 2nd ed. New York: Cambridge University Press.

Black's Law Dictionary. 2004. 8th ed. Saint Paul, MN: West Group.

California v. Brown, 479 U.S. 538 (1987).

Dressler, J. 2001. *Understanding Criminal Law*, 3rd ed. New York: Matthew Bender.

Eddings v. Oklahoma, 455 U.S. 104 (1982).

Feinberg, J. 1970. *Doing and Deserving*. Princeton, NJ: Princeton University Press.

Feinberg, J. 1988. *Harmless Wrongdoing*. New York: Oxford University Press.

Garvey, S. P. 1998. Aggravation and Mitigation in Capital Cases: What Do Jurors Think? *Columbia Law Review* 98:1538–1576.

Gray, N. S., A. Watt, S. Hassan, and M. J. MacCulloch. 2003. Behavioral Indicators of Sadistic Sexual Murder Predict the Presence of Sadistic Sexual Fantasy in a Normative Sample. *Journal of Interpersonal Violence* 18:1018–1034.

Gregg v. Georgia, 428 U.S. 153 (1976).

Hurd, H. M., and M. S. Moore. 2004. Punishing Hatred and Prejudice. *Stanford Law Review* 56:1081–1146.

Idaho Code. 2004.

Johnson, B. R., and J. V. Becker. 1997. Natural Born Killers? *Journal of the American Academy of Psychiatry and the Law* 25:335–348.

LaFave, W. R. 2003. *Criminal Law*, 4th ed. St. Paul, MN: West Publishing.

Laws, D. R., and W. L. Marshall. 1990. A Conditioning Theory of the Etiology and Maintenance of Deviant Sexual Preference and Behavior. In *Handbook of Sexual Assault*, ed. W. L. Marshall, D. R. Laws, and H. E. Barbaree. New York: Plenum.

Lockett v. Ohio, 438 U.S. 586 (1978).

MacCulloch, M., N. Gray, and A. Watt. 2000. Britain's Sadistic Murder Syndrome Reconsidered: An Associative Account of the Aetiology of Sadistic Sexual Fantasy. *Journal of Forensic Psychiatry* 11:401–418.

MacCulloch, M. J., P. R. Snowden, P. J. Wood, and H. E. Mills. 1983. Sadistic Fantasy, Sadistic Behaviour, and Offending. *British Journal of Psychiatry* 143:20–29.

Model Penal Code. Official Draft, 1962.

Moore, M. S. 1997. *Placing Blame*. Oxford: Clarendon Press.

Morse, S. J. 2003. Bad or Mad? Sex Offenders and Social Control. In *Protecting Society From Sexually Dangerous Offenders*, ed. B. J. Winick and J. Q. LaFond. Washington, D.C.: American Psychological Association.

Murphy, J. G. 1995. Legal Moralism and Liberalism. *Arizona Law Review* 37: 71–104.

The New Shorter Oxford English Dictionary. 1993. Oxford: Clarendon Press.

Oklahoma Statutes Annotated. 2002.

Oregon Revised Statutes. 2003.

Penry v. Lynaugh, 492 U.S. 302 (1989).

People v. Decina, 138 N.E.2d 799 (N.Y. 1956).

Prentky, R. A., A. W. Burgess, F. Rokous, A. Lee, C. Hartman, R. Ressler, and J. Douglas. 1989. The Presumptive Role of Fantasy in Serial Sexual Homicide. *American Journal of Psychiatry* 146:887–891.

Resnek, L. 1997. *Evil or Ill*. New York: Routledge.

Ring v. Arizona, 436 U.S. 584 (2002).

Robinson, P. H. 1984. *Criminal Law Defenses*. St. Paul, MN: West Publishing.

Roper v. Simmons, 125 S.Ct. 1183 (2005).

Schopp, R. F. 2001. *Competence, Condemnation, and Commitment*. Washington, D.C.: American Psychological Association.

Schopp, R. F. 2003. Sexual Aggression: Mad, Bad, and Mad. In *Sexually Coercive Behavior*, ed. R. A. Prentky, E. S. Janus, and M. C. Slote. New York: New York Academy of Sciences.

Schopp, R. F. 2006. Two-edged Swords, Dangerousness, and Expert Testimony in Capital Sentencing. *Law and Psychology Review* 30:57–101.

State v. Joubert, 399 N.W.2d 237 (Neb. 1986).

Taylor, C. 1976. Responsibility for Self. In *The Identities of Persons*, ed. A. O. Rorty. Berkeley: University of California Press.

Texas Criminal Procedure Code Annotated. 2004–05 Supp. Pamphlet.

United States Code. 2000.

Woodson v. North Carolina, 428 U.S. 280 (1976).

Wyoming Statutes Annotated. 2003.

15 Types of Terror Bombing and Shifting Responsibility

Frances Kamm

When philosophers discuss intentional harm to noncombatants (NCs) in war or conflicts outside war, they tend to focus on terror bombing and its distinction from, for example, tactical bombing that can also cause harm and terror to NCs as collateral damage. In this essay, I shall consider some different ways in which deliberately causing harm and terror to NCs can occur. It seems that, at least through World War II, only some of these ways were considered by policymakers to be "terror bombing" that one had a moral obligation to avoid. (The latter has the characteristics typical of terror bombing as considered by philosophers.) I shall argue that non-standard forms of terror bombing are also wrong according to criteria that can be used to condemn standard terror bombing. However, different forms of terror bombing can distribute responsibility for outcomes in different ways and for different things. I shall consider the possible bearing of this on the morality of terror bombing.

1

The sort of terror bombing in war often discussed by philosophers involves intentionally bombing NCs in order to harm them with the further intention that this will cause terror among other NCs. The overall aim is to cause surrender or some other change in an opponent country's policies. This change is imagined to come about because the fearful NCs pressure their government into surrendering or because the government, in virtue of having a responsibility for the welfare of its fearful citizens, surrenders or changes its policy in order to protect them.[1] Call this the Standard Terror Bombing Case. Terrorism, defined as occurring outside war between states, can also involve such terror bombing.

Commonly, philosophers have argued that the intentions to harm and to produce terror to civilians are what make terror bombing impermissible, even if merely foreseen collateral harm and terror of the same sort do not make bombing of military facilities impermissible. Elsewhere, I have argued that it is not the difference in intention of the agent (or his leaders) who terror bombs versus the agent who causes collateral damage that could make the former act impermissible, even if the latter were permissible.[2] I have suggested an alternative account of the difference in permissibility that depends (roughly) on its being true of terror bombing but not of collateral damage that, given what an agent does, it is necessary that harm and terror are causal means to achieving his end when there are no other effects of what he does that could justify his act.[3] I shall here assume that something along these lines is correct. On this assumption, my concern now is to consider some nonstandard forms of causing terror and/or harm to NCs that also have this property but differ in other ways from standard terror bombing, and to compare them with standard forms.

2

I think that we should consider different ways in which terror and/or harm to a person might function. In order to make this clearer, consider the Human Tinder Case: An agent bombs NCs as a means to start a fire that will blow up a military target when there is no other way to start the required fire. In this case, no terror is produced or used for any further purpose. But NC deaths are causally required to achieve a military goal. Presumably, if one of the moral objections to standard terror bombing is that deaths of NCs are causally required to achieve an end, the Human Tinder Case should raise the same moral objection. But is this the strongest part of the objection to standard terror bombing, or is it the production of terror per se, as a required cause of some further end, that is most objectionable? To help us decide this, we could imagine a case in which there would be no physical harm to civilians but only terror to NCs brought about as a causal means to the destruction of the military facility. For example, suppose we project a three-dimensional video image of NCs being killed when no NCs are in fact killed, in order to create terror in other NCs that is necessary to get them to stampede and destroy a military facility. (Call this the Video Stampede Case.) Would this be as significant a wrong as killing NCs in the Human Tinder Case? I do not think so. If we had to choose whether to produce Human Tinder or Video Stampede to achieve our goal, I think we should do the latter. Indeed, I think that producing the terror via the video as a required means to the military end would be

morally preferable to killing NCs as collateral damage in achieving the
military end.

These results are consistent with there being a stronger objection to
(1) killing NCs as a required means to causing terror that is itself a required
means to achieving a goal than to (2) killing NCs as a required means
to achieving a goal whose production does not require terror. For an
example of (1), consider the following Stampede Case: An agent bombs
NCs to set them on fire as a means to create terror in other NCs so that
they will stampede and destroy a military facility. There are at least two
ways to account for the view that (1) is morally worse than (2), and so that
what is done in Stampede is worse than what is done in Human Tinder.
First, there are two bad things happening in (1), killing and terror, and
therefore there is a stronger moral objection to doing (1). Second, killing
is itself worse when it also serves as a means to terror rather than directly
producing a goal. The first account is correct, but the second is dubious,
I think. The second account is based, in part, on the sense that when
something as extreme as killing can by itself produce an end, independent
of other contributing causes, then the good due to it is, at least, great
and unshared with other causes. It is also based, in part, I think, on the
fact that in (2), killing's primary role is to produce something whose
existence alone is even less likely to justify the killing than the further
goal, and this thing has the most direct role in producing the further goal.
(This additional effect of killing could also be something trivial like
someone laughing, where the laughter causes the destruction of the military facility. The fact that something as extreme as killing NCs is needed
to produce laughter, and it is the laughter that directly accomplishes one's
goal, seems grotesque.)

Let us assume, therefore, that a very serious wrong is done to NCs in
the Human Tinder and Stampede Cases, and that Stampede is the more
seriously wrong of the two for reason (1), but not because terror is per se
worse than death. As I conceive of these cases, harm and terror are what
I shall call "mechanical" means to a goal. I say this because the destruction
of the military target in the Human Tinder Case is produced by treating
human beings as just any burnable substance, and the terror in the Stampede Case is like a fright-and-flight instinctive response and is in this sense
mechanical and not the result of any decision made by the stampeders.

By contrast, it is often true in standard terror bombing that the harm
and terror are meant to influence NCs' judgment and will, especially in
the political sphere. For example, fear as a result of the "mechanical"

deaths of some NCs is intended to give rise to a prudential or altruistic judgment (that one should save oneself or others) that is meant to provide one with a reason to alter one's behavior or get one's government to alter its policies. The fear is not a factor that causes one to bypass the exercise of judgment and reduces one to an instinctive fright-and-flight response. By contrast, in the Stampede Case, people act in a panic. This panic is somewhat like torture without the physical abuse, insofar as a torturer tries to undermine the victim's will rather than give him a reason (namely, to avoid pain) to change his willed behavior. This is what I mean by the mechanical–nonmechanical distinction.[4]

The Human Tinder and Stampede Cases differ from the Standard Terror Bombing Case not only in the purely mechanical way in which people are employed. In the Human Tinder and Stampede Cases, the attacker fights *with* the people harmed and terrorized in the sense that he uses them as tools in achieving a military goal in a military campaign. But in standard terror bombing, the agent could be seen as trying to terrorize people in order to bypass the need for a purely military victory that he may be incapable of achieving: In the Standard Terror Bombing Case, people are imagined nonmechanically to decide to get their government to change policies or petition for peace. It is also possible that the aim of producing nonmechanical terror is to get people to alter their social and economic behavior in ways that their government finds unacceptable. Then the government, without fear having led NCs to petition their government, surrenders or otherwise changes its policies without the other side having to win military victories.[5] So there may also be a distinction to be drawn between the military use of harm and terror and their political use.

Table 15.1 lays out the possible combinations of the distinctions I have been drawing. Notice that there could be a nonmechanical use of NCs to defeat the military, as when fear leads people, as a matter of prudence or altruism, to consider sabotaging their own country's military operations. And there could be mechanical uses that affect the political realm, as when NCs' terror leads them to stampede and interfere with an election, or

Table 15.1
Types of terror bombing

	Military	Political
Mechanical (harm and fear)	MM	MP
Nonmechanical (fear)	NM	NP

when people's daily panic stampedes lead the government to try to restore order by surrendering or otherwise changing its policies.

3

One of my purposes in considering cases involving mechanical and non-mechanical terror and/or harm to achieve military victory has been to show that they too involve wrongs to NCs. However, my further purpose is to bring to more prominent attention the fact—to me very surprising—that such cases may not have been considered "terror bombing" at all by the same governments who would have been concerned about standard terror bombing. That is, though philosophers typically focus on standard terror bombing, many of their criteria for condemning it could also lead them to condemn the Human Tinder and Stampede Cases. But many practitioners of war would not have followed them in this conclusion, it seems. I first became aware of this as a result of a PBS documentary on World War II.[6] It reported that the deliberate bombing by Allied forces of German civilians in order to stop them, and frighten away others, from rebuilding a road, because the repair would threaten a military aim, was not considered terror bombing. It might be said that, in this case, unlike my Human Tinder or Stampede Cases, the NCs who are harmed and terrorized are doing something that indirectly impedes a military aim, and for this reason, harm and terror to them to achieve a military goal does not raise the moral problem of terror bombing. However, subsequently I presented my Human Tinder and Stampede Cases to a historian of war.[7] His initial response was to deny that these would be considered terror bombing. I believe this is because they were directed at achieving a military goal in a declared war rather than simply being directed at undermining the will of the population in order to bring about a surrender without needing to achieve military victory. If this is so, then the fact that there is deliberate killing and terrorizing of NCs and that these are necessary to achieve a goal are not the characteristics that military leaders are focusing on in condemning standard terror bombing. Rather, the attempt to harm and terrorize people solely to bring about a surrender without military victory may be seen by them as crucial to terror bombing.[8]

I believe that philosophers should object to such a determinative role for the political versus military goal factor in demarcating morally problematic terror bombing. Instead, they should emphasize the required causal role of terror and/or harm in NCs in order to achieve a goal, political or military. If this is correct, it raises the possibility that from the point of view of moral philosophers, many acts in, for example, World War II that have not been classified as terror bombing, and therefore have not been thought to be morally problematic in the way that standard terror bombing is, were indeed morally problematic terror bombing. It is important to investigate this for historical accuracy. It is also important for purposes of future conduct in war that this issue be clarified, as there may well be disagreement about not only a conceptual matter (whether something is terror bombing) but about whether achieving a military goal can morally justify terror and/or harm to NCs as a necessary causal means.

4(a)

Now consider the case of mechanically produced harm used to produce nonmechanical terror for political purposes (NP) in more detail. In particular, consider cases where the aim is to create terror that will lead people to create political pressure on their government. This is the case of standard terror bombing (both in war and in terrorism outside war). The terror bomber is trying to change people's judgment and deliberately willed political behavior.[9] NCs, unlike soldiers, are often not prepared to die for a cause, both in the sense that they are not trained to fight to the death for it, and also possibly in that they would not be willing to fight to the death for it. The home front is often willing to commit to a policy only if it can rely on others who are soldiers doing the fighting and sustaining the losses for it. (So the bomber agent's attempt to pressure or harm people who are not prepared to die does not apply if those affected are soldiers who are not in combat.) This would help explain why bombing agents are often considered cowards even when they risk their lives. For they are bypassing fighting the military to win a war, relying instead on attacking NCs, who are not trained to sustain attacks. This idea—perhaps somewhat inaccurate—of a coward is of someone who does not fight someone else who is prepared to fight. He is concerned with easy victory in this sense, even if it costs him his life.

It might be argued that the terror bomber in the type of case we are considering is also trying to get people to behave in ways that exhibit a lack of the virtue of courage. When an agent harms combatants, she is trying to make them unable to fight. When she terrorizes NCs for non-mechanical purposes, she tries to make them unwilling to support a fight or otherwise stay the course, though they are not unable to do so. (The Stampede Case involves a mechanical form of terror that makes one psychologically unable to control oneself, so it differs from the unwillingness to stay a course that I am now considering.) It would be better if people did not give in to fear when doing so leads them to take factors on which they would not focus, except from fear, as reasons to change policy. They cannot be proud of their behavior when they change a policy merely because of fear and independent of merit. This is especially true when the fear is out of proportion to the real increase in the probability of death and destruction, for example, when there is a much higher probability of dying in a car accident than from a terror bombing. Hence, terror bombing of this type raises the specter of a war of cowards on both sides. (Suppose, though, that people mistakenly overestimate the probability of death, and the fear is proportional to the imagined probability. Overestimating may itself be a sign of fear. But if it is not, it may simply be a form of irrationality, which is also not admirable.)

Focusing on these factors in standard terror bombing (both in war and in terrorism) raises the larger issue of whether and when it is in fact cowardly to give in to fear as a reason for seeking a change in government policy. It seems reasonable, not cowardly, to surrender from fear when a criminal says, "Your money or your life." But pressuring one's government out of fear to get it to give in to the demands of agents of terror bombing is more like calling off the police from catching the criminal (to whom one gave in from fear) from fear. And this is wrong. It is also more like giving in to a criminal when what he asks for violates one's principles rather than just diminishes one's wealth. An analogy here might be petitioning to call off the police on criminals whose goal in killing and terrorizing is to stop racial integration from taking place.

In response to this last point, it may be argued that a nation's foreign policy or policy of going to war (if that is what the agent of terror bombing is trying to change) is a matter of national self-interest, not principles, and so if changing the policy to stop terror attacks were in a nation's interest overall, then there would be nothing morally objectionable (or cowardly) in doing so.[10] (Of course, in the long run, it might not be in the nation's interest to do this, but suppose it were.)

However, even if the substance of a nation's policy were only a matter of self-interest and not principle, giving in to the agents of standard terror bombing would not be like ordinary action from self-interest. In standard terror bombing (and in criminal threats), the agent takes or threatens to take something from NCs (e.g., their lives) that they have a right to not have taken in this way (or so it is being assumed in this essay). This threat is made in order to make it be in the NCs' or the government's interest to trade something else (e.g., foreign or war policy) in order to get back (or avoid losing) what the NCs have a right to have without such a trade. Contrast this with one nation saying to another, "We will not sell you our oil unless you change your foreign policy" (the Oil Threat Case). This, too, may be done in order to cause fear in people and lead them to pressure their government to change its foreign policy. Indeed, it may also be intended to lead to deaths. But such a threat does not involve taking the oil (or anything else) to which the second nation's citizens are entitled and then trying to trade it back to them for a change in national foreign policy. This is so even if failure to get the oil that is not theirs eventually leads to some NCs losing their lives. Indeed, if a threat of withholding oil were intended to produce terror, then it might be an instance of a morally permissible nonstandard way of producing terror, at least in conflict situations. (One might dislike such an attempt to alter one's policies, but this would not be enough to show that it is impermissible. It is like the embargo that the United States used to try to alter Saddam Hussein's policies.) The moral objection to the attempt to make something be in one's self-interest seems appropriately greater in the case of standard terror bombing than in the Oil Threat Case, even if we held constant the deaths that might result from each threat as required means to the end of a policy change.

I conclude, therefore, that if standard terror bombing is an attempt to give people a reason based on fear to give in to impermissible types of pressure and to change policies, especially principled ones, when the actual increase in probability of death or serious injury is perceived to be small, then standard terror bombing is an attempt to get people to behave in a cowardly manner. (If it is expected that people will unreasonably overestimate the increased probability of death for reasons besides fear, then there is at least an attempt by the agents of terror to get people to behave in an irrational way.)

4(b)

Giving in from fear is not the same as reconsidering the merits of a policy after terror bombing, when one sees how strongly some people object to the policy, for reasons besides fear. Suppose that one changed one's policy because on reconsidering it, one saw its inherent flaws. Will others believe that one changed the policy because of fear instead? That is, will they believe that one would have changed it even if it were not flawed? If so, this might encourage terror bombing as a tactic. Indeed, even if others believe that one changed the policy on grounds of merit only after terror bombing, then such terror bombing might seem to be a successful tactic for getting one to attend more closely to the merits of one's policy. This, too, could encourage terror bombing.

If these things might happen, then perhaps it is no longer a simple matter of changing one's policies on the policies' merits. The additional possible effects of encouraging terror bombing might have to be considered and weighed in the balance. Here lies the poignancy of the Spanish case in 2003. The majority of the Spanish people all along thought that the policy of supporting the U.S. war with Iraq was wrong (and not just on self-interested grounds). But they seemed to put real pressure on their government to disengage only after a terrorist act, and so some causal chain was suggested. But should they have gone on paying with their lives for what they always thought was wrong, just so as not to be thought to be giving in—or even being responsive in some other way—to terror bombing? This is a hard question.

5(a)

Suppose that an act of standard terror bombing attempts to make people act cowardly, to prey on their weakness or on their less-than-optimal rationality in calculating risks. Do these effects help make terror bombing at least prima facie wrong, in addition to other more serious factors that make it wrong? I believe so. This is because it is, prima facie, wrong to corrupt people's judgment and will. It is also because these effects are, given the agent's act, necessary to produce his further end (rather than only side effects). However, these factors are also present in the Oil Threat Case, and they do not make that threat overall impermissible. This suggests that these factors are more likely than the killing and terrorizing of NCs to be overridden or even have their negative weight canceled out in pursuit of a good cause in a conflict.

Nevertheless, the "nonmechanical" (by contrast to the mechanical) effect of terror bombing plays a special role, whether in NP or NM cases, even if not in determining impermissibility of the terror bomber's conduct. This is because it *shifts responsibility* for the change in policy or the failure of military action from the terror bomber to the civilians. Hence, relying on effects of nonmechanical fear is in some sense "uglier" because it may make terror bombing a morally worse event for its victims. After all, they may act in a morally wrong way (e.g., in a cowardly way). The responsibility for any wrong behavior by the victims will be theirs when they let their judgment be swayed by fear. They have the option of not doing this. To some degree, they even have the option of not feeling fear, as we have more control over this emotional response than over physical harms, at least when there is no panic attack (as in the Stampede Case). For this reason, the victims may prefer to be used mechanically, for then the responsibility for the outcome lies solely with the terror bombing agent.[11] (Notice that this sort of ugliness can be increased further by offering inducements rather than threats in order to achieve surrender or change of principled policies.)

However, I do not think that it is the responsibility of an agent involved in a conflict, when he decides whether to use harm and terror mechanically or nonmechanically to choose on the basis of sparing his opponents from their own bad decision making (if this will be bad only for his opponents). This is, I think, how the negative role of corrupting someone gets negated. (By contrast, in nonconflict situations, I think that we should act to promote and support each other's good reasoning and moral virtues.) Similarly, we need not correct the errors of our opponents, even when they consult us for advice. However, the victim's desire to avoid being placed in a situation where he may behave badly is an added incentive for *him* to try to extirpate terror bombing, even if his being placed in that situation is not what makes what the terror bomber does a more serious wrong.

Suppose that an agent did want to help the people he harms and terrorizes to avoid cowardly behavior or bad risk assessment, so that they would not later be ashamed of their conduct. He could make their behavior not exhibit these defects by increasing the harm he does, so that it could be truly reasonable for them to fear a high probability of further damage and not unreasonable for them to surrender. But this has several problems. First, it would do more harm to people, and that seems too great a price to pay in order to make one's opponent's conduct reasonable and noncowardly. Second, it seems unnecessarily solicitous toward someone in a conflict to want to cushion the blow of choices they are responsible for making, especially by taking it upon oneself to do more harm for which one will be completely morally responsible.

The first problem could be remedied[12] not by increasing the harm one actually does, but rather by realistically threatening to do much worse than one would actually do or by falsely magnifying the damage and frequency of attacks one has actually undertaken. Here, too, it could only be reasonable for others to be taken in and surrender. However, in these scenarios, the agent takes it upon himself to appear to be much worse than he actually is or possibly would be. From the agent's point of view, this can be too great a moral sacrifice to make just to spare his opponent shame.

5(b)

So far I have argued that, owing to the shift toward NC responsibility and the lack of a duty to be solicitous of one's opponent's behavior, achieving one's end via nonmechanical means does not make an agent's act a more serious wrong than achieving the end via mechanical means. Can we also argue that using the nonmechanical route—even though it will depend on eliciting poor judgment or cowardice on the part of one's opponent—is morally better than producing the same effects through mechanical means (holding the amount of harm and terror and their causal necessity in producing an outcome in both cases constant)?[13] That is, if it were a more serious wrong to use the mechanical, rationality-undermining means, then this, rather than merely the refusal to be solicitous of one's opponent, should lead one to use nonmechanical means.

In answering this question, recall the claim that mechanical terror is like torture without physical abuse of the one terrorized. (There is, of course, still physical abuse in all standard terror bombing of those whose deaths lead to terror.) Indeed, psychological torture is a bona fide category of torture that does not require physical abuse. So let us consider a certain aspect of interrogational torture.

Would it be morally worse to try to get a person to divulge information by breaking the person down to a nonrational, panicked state or by threatening him so that reasons of self-interest stemming from fear overcome his moral impulse to keep a secret? Even though the second course involves trying to corrupt someone, I think that it could be permissible to take it when reducing someone to a nonrational, panicked state is impermissible. This is so even if the corrupted person becomes less worthy of respect and the reduced person would be only an object of pity. This would explain why corrupting (by unpleasant or even pleasant prospects) is considered a morally permissible interrogation procedure, even if rationality-undermining terror is not.

It might be suggested that the fear leading to panic is greater than the fear that gives one a prudential reason to divulge information, and this is why the former could be prohibited when the latter is not. To deal with this possibility, I recommend that we imagine that the panic period is short and the lesser fear is extended in time. Alternatively, we could imagine options involving no fear at all. Suppose that we could for a brief duration give someone a truth serum that made it impossible for him to exercise self-control, so that he blurted out anything he knew. The alternative way to get information is to bribe the person with the prospect of rewards rather than punishments. Again, I suggest that it is no solution to the problem of corrupting someone to undermine his rational agency instead, even for a short while in the way described.

Why might it be true that it is preferable to avoid mechanical psychological means? This is a difficult question. I suspect that it may be better in some way for the person himself to lose control in a way that, in a sense, reduces him to a nonperson-level for a short while than for him to be corrupted. However, it is contrary to the *importance of being a person* to try to elicit responses from him by trying to bypass his rational control in this way. Furthermore, those who undermine a person's agency in this way bear full responsibility for his state and what he does in it. The alternative will involve encouraging him to make choices that reflect badly on his moral character. But the outcome, whatever it is, will be a function of his full humanity being exercised, not short-circuited, and more responsibility for his ultimate state will lie with him. We might say that although the short, tortured period could be (comparatively) better *for* him, it is more at odds with the importance *of him*. For similar reasons, it might be morally worse to create the mechanical panic response in a population rather than the fear that corrupts their judgment, even if we could equalize the fear involved. This is another reason to think that in conflict situations contributing to an opponent's moral corruption or poor judgment does not play a big role in accounting for the wrong of terror bombing.

Notes

This essay is a revised part of my presentation on April 1, 2006, as the keynote address of the Inland Northwest Philosophy Conference, "Action, Ethics, and Responsibility." It incorporates material in, but revises and adds to, section (E) of Kamm 2006.

1. I distinguished these two ways in which a country's change in policy could come about in Kamm 2006. At the time I wrote that article, I had not yet read Waldron 2004, in which he also draws this distinction.

2. Briefly, the argument for this is that it is the properties that an act has independently of the intention with which it is done that are the grounds for its being permissible or impermissible. So suppose that an act of bombing a military facility is justified, even when there is collateral death, when it is done for the sake of the properties that make it justified. Then it will also be justified if done by an agent who does not care about these properties but is only interested in bringing about the deaths of people who will die when the military facility is hit. For more detailed arguments to this effect, see Thomson 1991; Scanlon 2000; Kamm 2004, 2006, and 2007b.

3. This suggestion follows from my discussion of nonconsequentialist constraints in Kamm 2007a and is described in more detail in the articles referred to in note 2.

4. I drew this distinction and discussed Human Tinder and Stampede Cases in Kamm 2006. Waldron (2004) drew a similar distinction. What he referred to as "Arendtian" fear corresponds to what I called "mechanical," and what he referred to as "Jack Benny" fear corresponds to what I called "nonmechanical." In Arendtian fear, one is in an unreasoning panic; in Jack Benny fear, a threat leads one to weigh the costs and benefits of giving in. However, Waldron does not discuss the uses of either type of fear in the pursuit of achieving a purely military goal.

5. Waldron (2004) also emphasizes the latter possibility.

6. Unfortunately, I am so far unable to completely reference this program.

7. Professor John Lewis, Ashland University (in conversation, Bowling Green University, November 2007).

8. It was Professor Lewis's view that military operations also were meant to undermine the will to fight, but that was not their sole function.

9. As I noted in Kamm 2006, this is different from creating pressure on the government itself by killing and terrorizing its citizens, thus making the government incapable of fulfilling its duty to protect its citizens. Here the fate of the citizens would be used to alter the judgment and will of the government. And the government might be giving in not from fear but from a sense of duty to care for its citizens. (Waldron [2004] makes the same point.)

10. Elizabeth Harman and Joseph Raz suggested this.

11. In Kamm 1999, I discussed another example of shifting responsibility. In that case, it involved shifting responsibility from someone who kills to a person who makes his not doing something worse dependent on the killing.

12. This was pointed out to me by Alex Verhoove and Michael Otsuka.

13. One problem here is that we might not be able to equalize for terror. For the terror that will undermine judgment entirely and produce panic must, it seems, be more intense and hence greater than the terror that does not. (I owe this point to Jane Heale.) One response to this objection is to imagine that the less intense terror lasts for a longer time than the more intense terror. In this way, we equalize total terror. Let us assume that this is possible.

References

Kamm, F. 1999. Responsibility and Collaboration. *Philosophy & Public Affairs* 28: 169–204.

Kamm, F. 2004. Failures of Just War Theory. *Ethics* 114:650–692.

Kamm, F. 2006. Terrorism and Several Moral Distinctions. *Legal Theory* 12:16–69.

Kamm, F. 2007a. *Intricate Ethics*. New York: Oxford University Press.

Kamm, F. 2007b. *Terrorism and Intending Evil*. Oslo, Norway: The Oslo Lecture in Moral Philosophy.

Scanlon, T. 2000. Intention and Permissibility, I. *Proceedings of the Aristotelian Society* 74:301–317.

Thomson, J. J. 1991. Self-Defense. *Philosophy & Public Affairs* 20:283–310.

Waldron, J. 2004. Terrorism and the Uses of Terror. *Journal of Ethics* 8:5–35.

Contributors

Joseph Keim Campbell
Washington State University

David Chan
University of Wisconsin-Stevens
Point

Randolph Clarke
Florida State University

E. J. Coffman
University of Tennessee

John Martin Fischer
University of California, Riverside

Helen Frowe
University of Sheffield

Todd Jones
University of Nevada, Las Vegas

Frances Kamm
Harvard University

Antti Kauppinen
Trinity College Dublin

Alfred R. Mele
Florida State University

Michael O'Rourke
University of Idaho

Paul Russell
University of British Columbia

Robert F. Schopp
University of Nebraska

George Sher
Rice University

Harry S. Silverstein
Washington State University

Saul Smilansky
University of Haifa

Donald Smith
Virginia Commonwealth
University

Charles T. Wolfe
University of Sydney

Index